D1257336

THE UNIVERSITY SERIES IN PSYCHOLOGY

EDITOR: DAVID C. McCLELLAND, HARVARD UNIVERSITY

Fear of Failure

Robert C. Birney
Dean, School of Social Sciences, Hampshire College

Harvey Burdick
Professor of Psychology, Oakland University

Richard C. Teevan
Professor of Psychology, Bucknell University

VAN NOSTRAND—REINHOLD COMPANY

New York   Toronto   London   Melbourne

VAN NOSTRAND REGIONAL OFFICES: *New York, Chicago, San Francisco*

D. VAN NOSTRAND COMPANY, LTD., *London*

D. VAN NOSTRAND COMPANY (Canada), LTD., *Toronto*

D. VAN NOSTRAND AUSTRALIA PTY. LTD., *Melbourne*

BF
575
F14
.B5

PRINTED IN THE UNITED STATES OF AMERICA

This book is gratefully dedicated to the Office of Naval Research, Group Psychology Branch. Their support, both financial and psychological, made possible the research program that is the basis of this effort.

Reproduction of this work in part or whole is permitted for any purpose of the United States Government.

Preface

When *The Achievement Motive* by D. C. McClelland, J. W. Atkinson, R. A. Clark, and E. L. Lowell appeared in 1953, it signaled the beginning of a program of research that has not yet ended. McClelland had chosen to study a single motive system in hopes of contributing to motivation and personality theory in general. The motive chosen—need for achievement (n Ach)—was selected because it was central to our society, endorsed and taught to children, and thought to be important to actual accomplishment in various achievement situations. Judging from the appeal that such research has had to psychologists and sociologists beyond McClelland's original group, the assumption of centrality was correct. Today the list of references to research on n Ach as measured and defined by McClelland runs to several hundred, and there are several dimensions along which the research is proceeding (Birney, 1968). One such vector received hardly any mention in 1953. At that time only passing reference was made to the fact that some subjects seemed to have responded to the arousal treatments with a fear of failure (McClelland et al., 1953, pp. 327, 331). Since then concern with this avoidance motivation in the achievement situation has emerged as a program of research in its own right.

The emerging impression that avoidance motivation produces a more complex cognitive network for dealing with reality forced us to create a taxonomy of the achievement situation that goes far beyond that presented by McClelland or Atkinson (1954). This book opens with the presentation of this scheme in Chapter 1. Essentially it involves trying to isolate the particular role that motives play in behavior, and this has meant trying to measure and control other obviously important variables.

To this end we discuss the traditional definitions used in the literature on behavior in achievement situations, and we review the particular literature bearing on avoidance motivation. Our aim here is to give the reader the picture of the state of knowledge on this topic at the time we began our research.

Chapter 2 reports our efforts to learn more about the experience of failure. Some sort of operational definition of "failure" is required, and we wanted to settle on one that would at least satisfy us. In the course of doing this research we also evolved the set of research procedures now in use wherein we incorporate various self-report devices with the performance and motivation measures. It appears that the ancient distinctions among thought, action, and feeling remain operationally and functionally useful (Allport, 1937). Unfortunately, failure to measure the interaction between these variables does not eliminate their contribution to one's dependent variable.

Chapter 3 reports our experience in discovering the scoring system that seems to reflect fear-of-failure motivation in our subjects. As it turned out we took some detours before performing the arousal experiment we had thought to begin with. But we are satisfied that the findings reported in this book do support our contention that these scores reflect avoidance tendencies in achievement situations for our subjects and hence have a fair claim to reflect fear of failure. Work with scoring systems for stories written to TAT pictures has created a set of expectations about the properties such scores should have. These include stabilities across time, scorer agreement coefficients, and the score relationships to self-report measures that might be expected to tap the same domain of behavior. These latter studies raise the interesting possibility that unlike n Ach, which does not seem to relate to self-report measures, the fear of failure scores may, under certain conditions, show some relationship to reports of experience and behavior. This may mean that avoidance behaviors in general permit more congruity between fantasy and conscious experience of reality than do approach motivational systems. Such a lead seems worth following further.

In Chapter 4 we report the series of studies that convinced us that our scoring system would predict performance that implies avoidance motivation in achievement situations. The act of volunteering for achievement situations, defensive patterns of level of aspiration previously found in achievement tasks, and academic performance were all found to relate to our measure of fear of failure in a sensible way.

In Chapter 5 we present the work we have done relating fear of failure to level of aspiration. It is our conviction that aspiration behavior is important in the modulation of performance, but more especially in the nature of the achievement task experience of the subject. For this reason we have tried to learn more about the nature of aspiration itself as well as its relationship to motivation. Here we introduce a revision of the traditional level-of-aspiration questions that generates a new aspiration measure, the Confirming Interval. This shows promise as a sensitive measure of motivation brought to the situation by the subject.

A main source of variance in the achievement situation is the social relationship between the subject and the significant others in the situation. Chapter 6 reports studies conducted to learn more about the relationship between fear of failure and the social behaviors of acquiescence to others usually grouped under Social Conformity. Here for the first time we raise the possibility that fear of failure may generate certain behaviors that have adaptive significance in certain achievement situations.

In Chapter 7 we surround a suggestive set of findings, from a single study on reported child-rearing practices and the motive scores of the offspring, with some speculations about the possible origins of motivation in the patterns of reinforcement used by parents when their children are in achievement situations. At this writing we are just beginning to conduct a series of studies in this area; e.g. we report a relationship between college-student motive scores and parental discipline.

Chapter 8 is devoted to a discussion of the work of Atkinson, Heckhausen, and ourselves as it bears on the measurement of fear of failure. We face the issues raised by the failure of the measures of fear of failure used by different groups to agree. Here we are able to report the beginnings of some comparative research into the differences that currently exist, and to propose tentative hypotheses that may lead to resolution of these differences.

In Chapter 9 we discuss the theoretical positions that have guided the work of the three major programs on fear of failure. We emphasize their differences in order to clarify the bases for the different strategies of research being employed.

In Chapter 10 we present a tabular summary of research to date, current sense of the attributes of fear-of-failure motivation, their effect on behavior, and possible ways to test the validity of our proposals.

Here we make a frank bid for the interest of the young researcher who would like to begin work on human motivation.

Chapter 11 tries to relate the theory just described to the problems of fear-of-failure measurement. This effort also suggests research to be done, some of which is now in progress. Finally, we face the possibility that readers with applied interests might want to use some of the ideas presented in this work for the design of experimental programs to create positive achievement motivation in subjects dominated by a fear of failure. We consider this premature, really, but we offer our own ideas on the subject for those who feel they must begin.

The book also contains a set of scored stories so that the student who wishes to learn our scoring practices for himself may do so. We try to maintain throughout the sense of a progress report. This work is in progress, and hopefully will continue so for a long time to come.

Many people have had a part in the preparation of this manuscript. Most of them are mentioned in the book because they had a hand in the research we have reported. We would like to single out for special mention four graduate students at Bucknell who have acted as graduate "supervisors" of research over the last several years. They are Barry Smith, Paul McGhee, William Poffenberger, and Robert Fischer. Our dedication points out the debt we owe to the Office of Naval Research. Luigi Petrullo and his colleagues Abe Cohen, Bert King, and Leonard Green made it possible for us to spend the time on research which was necessary to get the job done. Most of the work reported in this book was done under a contract between the ONR and Bucknell University (Richard C. Teevan, Principal Investigator). In the final translation of ideas to manuscript, we must acknowledge our debt and gratitude to the secretaries who made this part of the job possible and as pleasant as it can ever be, Mrs. Ann Steinbach at Bucknell and Mrs. Mary Kuzmeski at Amherst.

In a task of this kind it is impossible to tell where an idea came from and who was responsible for its fruition. Having no logical way to determine whose name should come first, we fell back on the arbitrary method of setting our names in alphabetical order. This order of names has no other significance.

R.C.B.
H.B.
R.C.T.

Contents

jecting the Performance of a Measure of the Skill • Preferring Vague
Achievement Standards • Preference for "Practice" and "Games" •
Rejecting Responsibility • Reducing the Importance of the Attribute •
Not Trying • Seeking Social Support

MISJUDGING PERFORMANCE
DISTORTION OF PROBABILITIES
FORGETTING NONATTAINMENTS
SENSITIVITY OF POTENTIAL

The Defense Again Punishment: FF²

Defense Against a Loss in Social Value: FF³

INFORMING OTHERS OF ATTAINMENT
MAKING EXCUSES
LEVEL-OF-ASPIRATION STATEMENTS
SUMMARY

CHAPTER 1

Avoidance Motivation in Achievement Situations: Definition of the Problem

FOR THE PAST CENTURY THE VALUES OF WESTERN SOCIETY HAVE been changing from prerogatives of birth to those of merit (Young, 1958). High society has become a society of high achievers, and the values of these leaders have filtered down to the masses. Personal success rather than family status has become the measure of a man's worth, and the Great Society in the United States is reaching out to help those who will help themselves. Pre-school and in-school programs such as Head Start and Upward Bound are supported by the national government and are designed not only to increase technical skills but to increase achievement motivation as well. But the problem in bringing about achievement striving in a society is that striving does not always pay off with success. In fact, achievement striving is somewhat perilous since it exposes the individual to the possibilities of failure.

An unfortunate paradox develops when a society presses for achievement if the rewards and situations that are presented as being worth the struggle can only be attained by a fraction of those who are striving. Aside from things whose main value resides in their function of contributing to the maintenance of life (food, water, shelter, etc.), we desire some things precisely because they are not attainable by all who may strive for them. The measure of success is essentially determined by who and how many others have accomplished the same thing. The successful person needs those who have failed, and those who have failed need hope that some day the tables will be reversed. There is no total escape from the achievement race, although an alarming number are trying. It is our suspicion that the popularity of psychedelic drugs rests partly on the way they allow the user to believe he is accomplishing much without the dangers inherent in actual striving. Communities of expatriates, where painters don't paint and writers don't write, smugly maintain the belief (at least among their members) that they are centers of advanced cultural accomplishment. Lotus eating is one way out of the race for success, but one must have both the carfare and the willingness to leave behind family and friends. Most people are not so fortunate and must remain where people evaluate one another on the quality of their successes. It is not surprising that there are large segments of our society that avoid achievement situations whenever they can and, when they cannot, do not try to succeed. We are becoming increasingly sensitive to the prevalence of such dispositions not only among the downtrodden, where they have always been endemic in character, but among those who "should know better" because they are the children of the hard-working and ever-striving middle class.

Fear of Failure and Level of Aspiration

No doubt deficiencies in achievement motivation and the search for a cozy nonfailure situation have been characteristic of many members of all societies now and in the past. But the history of research into "failure" motivation is a brief one. The conception of fear of failure as a stable personality trait has its historical roots in such clinical problems as anxiety, guilt, shame, and feelings of inferiority. But it came to be the target of empirical research during the early studies of level of aspiration, when it appeared to offer a convenient explanation of some of the individual differences in the patterns of aspirational levels. Dembo (1931) suggested that the individual's level of aspiration affected his satisfaction with his performance. Hoppe (1930) had conducted a study and concluded that feelings of success and failure were contingent on attainment or nonattainment of the level of aspiration. The next step was taken by Hausmann (1933), who attempted to establish a connection between personality and the differences between performance and aspirational levels. He used only six subjects, five of them psychiatric patients; thus his conclusions, at best, can be considered only tentative. However, his methodology became the model for the aspirational studies that followed, and he was the first researcher to describe the goal-setting behaviors of persons we now conceive of as "fear of failure." If, as was assumed, feelings of failure were aroused by nonattainment of one's level of aspiration, then it was logical to infer that anyone who set his level of aspiration (LA) consistently below his actual performances was doing this to avoid the failure experience. It was just such a conclusion that Frank (1935) came to, following the lead of Hausmann. His observation of one subject who followed this seemingly cautious strategy led him to conclude that he was fearful of failure. That the conclusion was more analytic than empirical did not detract from its apparent validity, and it has remained as a basic tenet in LA studies.

Some weak support for the argument that people who were fearful of failure engaged in cautious goal-setting came in a study by Gardner (1940). Subjects were rated by the E on the dimension of fear of failure (FF) and it was noted that those who were rated high on FF predicted that they would surpass a smaller percentage of their peers than those rated low. Unfortunately, it is difficult to know what was meant by fear of failure, since the basis of the ratings was not made clear. Furthermore, it is impossible to compare the nature of the goal-setting in this study with the goal-setting in typical LA studies.

In LA studies a goal-discrepancy score is obtained by subtracting the performance score from the aspirational score. Clearly cautious goal-discrepancy scores are negative. Positive discrepancy scores are somewhat more difficult to interpret. In the Gardner study there is no way of determining whether the goal-settings of the high FF would have been negative or positive goal discrepancies. In a study by Gould (1939) goal-discrepancy scores were obtained for six different tasks. The author found low correlations among the tasks for goal-discrepancy scores. This finding, replicated in other studies, throws doubt on the use of LA patterns on any one task as diagnostic of stable personality traits. But relevant as this problem is to LA studies, it is not relevant to defining fear of failure. The importance of the Gould study is that the author claimed that the subjects with low discrepancy scores appeared to be fearful of failure. Such subjects anticipated that their performance level would decrease and considered performance increases as flukes. However, the author argued that high discrepancy scores could also be an expression of failure fears. She believed that the desire to avoid failure could produce high or low estimates and that these were merely different ways of coping with the problem. Since there was no independent measure of fear of failure, the conclusion regarding the relationship of failure fears to goal-setting is more intuitive than objective. However, the suggestion that a fear-of-failure attitude could characterize those with a low and a high discrepancy score received some support in a study by Sears (1940). Sears found that subjects with high discrepancy scores appeared to be unresponsive and inflexible and reacted to failure by becoming apathetic and escaping from the field. In a second report on the same group of *S*s, Sears (1941) set up three goal discrepancy groups; low positive, high positive, and negative. The low-positive group was described as self-confident and desiring to do well for reasons of self-esteem. Members of the high-positive group were rated as low in self-confidence, tending to discount success but having a strong desire for success. The negative discrepancy group were described as self-conscious and fearful of failing in the eyes of others.

The studies by Gould and Sears suggest that goal-setting patterns function as interpersonal strategies more clearly than as achievement strategies. The individual who sets his aspirations below his performance may not be doing it to avoid failure, as was assumed, but to present himself as a modest and acceptable person. On the other hand, the individual who sets his goals considerably above his performance may want to impress the observer with his self-confidence. In the study by Gould this is how the high-discrepancy group was described.

We are making much of this point because of our growing conviction that the experiences of success and failure can be best understood *only in an interpersonal context*. The person who is described as "fearful of failure" may well be a person who is simply fearful of losing value in the eyes of others. In an achieving society, success is highly instrumental in gathering esteem and respect, while failure is a standard way of losing esteem. But there are other ways of maintaining good relations and respect; modesty is one and self-confidence is another. An amusing description of how we go about presenting ourselves to others trying to create the impression of confidence can be found in William Sansom's novel *A Contest of Ladies* (London: Hogarth Press, 1956).

It is not our intention to review the literature of LA even though it was the quarry from which the fear-of-failure concept was cut. During the decades of the forties and fifties LA studies occurred with high incidence in the journals, but since the beginning of the sixties their number has dwindled. Where once they were thought to permit direct access to goal-setting behavior, we now know that the subject's response depends on a number of factors, one being the type of question asked. The subject may be asked what he expects to do, what he intends to do, what he hopes to do, or simply what he aspires to do. Goal-discrepancy scores vary with the question, and the inter-correlations among the answers (when more than one question is asked), is far from perfect (Festinger, 1942b; Preston and Bayton, *J. soc. Psychol.*, 1961).

Another problem with the use of LA studies for getting at orientation to failure lies in the difficulty of interpreting the goal-discrepancy scores. What is observed when such scores are obtained from a normal population (typically a college group), is that the scores range in a normal distribution from low negative to high positive with the peak in the low-positive range. Since it is a continuous distribution, it becomes somewhat arbitrary to cut it into discrete groupings characterized by different attitudes toward success and failure. Nevertheless, Rotter (1954), in a series of studies summarized in his book, attempts to do just that. He recommends that distinctions be made among patterns of high-negative, low-negative, very slightly positive, low-positive, and high-positive goal-discrepancy scores. He claims that the high-negative pattern is characteristic of Ss who desire to avoid failure at any cost, and that the low-negative–low-positive patterns are normal but cautious. The high-positive pattern he describes as an unrealistic solution to frustration, suggesting that it might be an alternative method of handling failure. "This lack of contact with reality is often emphasized by a larger number of shifts up after failure, and by the 'repression' of failures" (1954, p. 321). The picture one gets from Rotter's description of LA patterns is that there is a curvilinear relationship between goal-discrepancy scores and the magnitude of the desire to avoid failure. The difference between the Ss with the two patterns is merely a difference in the technique chosen for handling the possibility of failure.

We see two major problems in using LA patterns for gaining insight into orientations toward success and failure. The first is that goal-discrepancy scores are relative to the task, the question, and the particular group. Until the tasks and the questions are standardized and norms are established on large samples, the interpretation of the discrepancy score is going to remain intuitive and closely tied to the way a particular researcher decides to fractionate the distribution. The second problem is the lack of an independent measure of failure and success orientation. Using goal-setting as an indication of failure and success attitudes and then turning around and using the attitudes to explain the goal-setting patterns is patently circular.

Nevertheless, low goal-setting seems to be a cautious act having as its purpose the avoidance of failure. It therefore made sense to assume that low goal setters were fearful of failure. It may well be true that such is the case, but it is merely an assumption based upon the intuition that the low goal-setting was in fact a way a person *could* avoid failure. The observations of Sears strongly question such an assumption and the conclusions of Gould, in particular, and even those of Rotter suggest that the fear-of-failure motivation can be seen expressed in more than one goal-setting pattern. What is needed is a measure of the fear-of-failure motive, and the major part of this book is dedicated to its description. Once such a measure was designed, we would be in a position to determine the relationship of fear of failure to LA patterns. Of course, this can be done with a modicum of precision only when the tasks, questions, and groups are well defined.

Fear of Failure (FF) and need for Achievement (n Ach)

Interest in the fear-of-failure motive was given a new impetus by a group of psychologists concerned with investigating the intricacies of achievement motivation. Under the leadership of McClelland, a projective measure was devised on the paradigm that when the stimulus field is sufficiently ambiguous we tend to perceive things that satisfy our wants (McClelland, Atkinson, Clark, and Lowell, 1953). From the results of their earliest studies it was apparent to McClelland and his associates that an adequate understanding of achievement behavior would have to include failure motivation as well as achievement motivation. Gould had made a similar suggestion when she pointed out that individuals with strong needs to achieve may also have an intense fear of failure. In a study by McClelland and Liberman (1949) it was noted that subjects who had n Ach scores in the middle third of the distribution were slower to recognize tachistoscopically presented negative-achievement words than those who scored high and low on n Ach. They interpreted their findings to indicate that "middle" n Ach Ss were security-minded and concerned with avoiding failure. On the other hand, it was noted that high n Ach Ss were quicker to recognize the positive achievement words and this was interpreted as indicating that these Ss were concerned with achieving success. A study by Atkinson (1953) showed that Ss in the middle third of the n Ach distribution tended to forget tasks they were unable to complete, while *S*s in the upper third remembered the incompleted tasks. He interpreted his findings as indicating that the moderate n-achievers were defensive and regarded their inability to complete a task as a failure. Subjects with high n Ach, he felt, tended to regard their incompleted tasks as a challenge. McClelland (1951) interprets the results of these two studies as indicating two kinds of achievement motivation. One he sees as oriented towards the avoidance of failure and the other as directed towards the attainment of success.

The suggestion that there are two achievement orientations supports the contention of the early workers with level of aspiration. The suggestion, however, comes as a post hoc explanation of the unexpected behavior of the *S*s in the middle third of an n achievement distribution. Furthermore, it is questionable whether a test designed to measure one achievement attitude will adequately measure another—unless, of course, it can be assumed that the desire to avoid failure was the true counterpart of the need to achieve. But this assumption was never made, and in the literature it is generally assumed that the two orientations need have no correlation with one another. Addressing himself to the problem, Atkinson (1954) pointed out that the categories scores for n Ach included both negative and positive indices. Thus, a person could be scored high for n Ach by writing about unsuccessful instrumental activities, anticipation of frustration, and obstacles to success, none of which suggest a positive approach to achievement. As Atkinson argues, we need to define the avoidance motive as clearly as the approach motive has been defined.

The recommendation of Atkinson that the negative be separated from the positive criteria in scoring for n Ach was taken up by Moulton (1958) but with little success. In lieu of a satisfactory fractionating of the n Ach categories for measuring success and failure motives, Atkinson chose to combine the n Ach measure with the Mandler-Sarson Test Anxiety Questionnaire (TAQ) to get at the motive to approach success and the motive to avoid failure. What began as two possibly independent motives was now combined into a single dimension. Although the use of the two measures permits the researcher to divide his subjects into four subgroupings. Atkinson has argued that the combination of high n Ach and low TAQ defines hope of success, while low n Ach and high TAQ defines fear of failure. One advantage in using these two measures was their very low correlation (Raphelson and Moulton, 1958). But the implication of the combination of the tests is that Fear of Failure persons are not high on n Ach.

Patterns of the two measures have been used to test various deductions from Atkinson's theory of risk taking (1957). The choice of the nonprojective measure for fear of failure was based on its ability to correlate with the behaviors predicted from the theory. This was not the basis for using the n Ach measure, which had been validated through experimental arousal techniques. Whereas the n Ach measure stands on its own and is independent of a particular theory, the TAQ as a measure of fear of failure is wholly dependent on the theory. If the theory is wrong, the n Ach measure maintains its status, but the TAQ will have to revert to being a test-anxiety measure. This sounds more ominous than we intend: we merely wish to point out that the two measures do not have the same status. And since it is our intention to describe a measure of fear of failure that is not dependent on any one theory, but would be capable of being used with any theory where fear of failure plays a role, we feel we must make the point.

Projective Measures of Fear of Failure

From the very outset those working with the development of the n-achievement measure were alert to the possibility of an avoidance dimension in the stories. "It is quite possible that our present scoring criteria do not discriminate between (1) affective responses which allow the inference that the character in the story is really concerned about his inability to get ahead, and (2) affective responses which suggest annoyance, hostility, and other diffuse emotional reactions that appear achievement-related but may be the result of the author's characteristic emotional reaction in competitive situations. In the latter case, the categories would be more representative of fear of failure than the desire to succeed" (McClelland et al, 1953, p. 216). The effects of prior induced failure experience on the scoring categories were analyzed both in terms of absolute frequencies and of relative comparisons which permit an estimate of dominance or preoccupation of one category over another. A failure experience was shown to increase the incidence of personal and environmental obstacles to goal achievement, and there was a hint of an increase in negative goal effect and nurturant press. Relative comparisons suggested that failure caused a preoccupation in the stories with negative goal affect and positive anticipation of goal attainment, while the success condition produced just the opposite. Here the argument ran that it is our common experience that success follows failure and may not follow itself. Hence an increase in achievement motivation caused by task failure could be expected to produce stories whose figures struggled with obstacles and failure while anticipating eventual success, while an increase in fear of failure might produce stories whose figures' efforts go smoothly while anticipating eventual failure.

The next attempt to pursue the possibility of two-factor scoring of stories for Hope of Success and Fear of Failure was that of Moulton (1958), who used the criterion group technique to identify his fear-of-failure group (those who recalled completed tasks in a Zeigarnik situation). Contrasting the stories of this group with those who recalled uncompleted tasks (Atkinson, 1953), he created a new system whose Imagery category was scored when the central figure in the story expressed various efforts to withdraw or escape from the task situation. Adding negative affect categories from the n Ach system gave a more or less thematic scoring system. A cross validation of the system on the majority of the data collected in the Atkinson study showed a negative relationship between fear of failure scores and recall of incompleted tasks. Moulton used this system in a study with Raphelson (1958) which found that increased task anxiety interacted with reported test anxiety (TAQ) to produce a positive relationship between reported anxiety and the projective measure of Fear of Failure under low arousal. Essentially this work established that certain negative categories of the n Ach scoring system were sensitive to task-arousal conditions as McClelland et al. (1953) had initially shown.

One limitation on Moulton's system experienced by the authors has been the low level of Imagery provided by most of the pictures used in measuring n Ach. The original picture H, the boy in the checked shirt, provides the majority of the stories. Perhaps similar pictures which also provide n Ach stories would increase the range of scores.

Anderson (1962) continued this line of research, once more studying the effect of degree of anxiety arousal on projective scores of n Ach and fear of failure. He modified Moulton's scoring system.

The chief revision was the adding of the "negative" affect categories (1-, GA-, Bp, Bw, G-), which apeared in stories otherwise manifesting positive achievement motivation, to the f Failure score (Anderson, 1962, p. 294).

In other words, he did not limit the negative scoring to stories displaying Moulton's Imagery criterion. Instead he expanded the definition:

Failure imagery is scored when there is (a) any indication of poor performance in customary achievement situations, (b) any doubt of ability to reach achievement goal, (c) any anticipation of failure, (d) any indication of discouragement or negative affect at the possibilty of achievement evaluation, (e) an expressed preference to leave an achievement situation or situation in which achievement might take place, (f) daydreaming in an achievement situation unless the subject of the daydream is of successful achievement (p. 294).

This definition of Imagery says, in effect, that the story will be scored if either Moulton's conditions or any negative n Ach categories appear. Anderson also used four new pictures and three levels of arousal achieved by using the forced-failure technique. The Ss were eighth-graders who were first told they had failed an "intelligence" test (digit-symbol task), then given the TAT (non-"test" instructions for low arousal, "test" instructions for medium arousal), or given a second failure on the digit-symbol prior to the TAT (high arousal).

The fear of failure scores show a curvilinear relationship to arousal, mid-arousal group being highest, and n Ach scores show a positive relationship to arousal. Again it is argued that "the high arousal group displayed less f Failure than the medium-arousal group, and only slightly more than the low-arousal group, because of a defensive reaction to an anxiety-provoking situation" (p. 297).

In summary, these researches establish that failure experience prior to story writing can affect the type and frequencies of categories which appear. In general, these categories are negative in tone and meaning, and yield relationships to performance which differ from those of the total n Ach score.

The most recent study using essentially the same approach of extracting the fear-of-failure score from the n Ach system a priori is that of DeCharms and Davé (1965). In this study

each story containing achievement imagery was further categorized either as indicating Hope of Success or as indicating Fear of Failure depending on the *outcome of the story* [italics ours]. The scores attempted to distinguish between general approach and avoidance reactions (optimism-pessimism) which were *specifically related to achievement goals* and *not* a generalized anxiety or hostile press. Thus if the achievement goals in the story were not achieved, it was scored fear of failure. If the outcome was questionable, the story was arbitrarily scored fear of failure (p. 560).

Thus the n Ach score was the sum of the Hope of Success and Fear of Failure totals. This procedure was followed on the assumption that

Achievement goals should be important for Fear of Failure subject. Thus we have tried to separate Hope versus Fear-oriented subjects *from among those who show strong achievement motivation* (p. 559).

This method produces high positive correlations between each sub-score and the total n Ach score (Hope of Success vs. total n Ach is .84, and Fear of Failure vs. n Ach is .72, Hope of Success vs. Fear of Failure is .38). The *S*s with high n Ach (high Hope and high Fear) proved most successful at the performance task, and the interaction of low Hope of Success and high Fear of Failure showed a significant tendency to avoid the modal risk preference of the total group (around .30 to .40 success), in preference for greater risks. This study stands alone as one showing some success with factorial scoring of the n Ach system to generate fear of failure scores which identify those *S*s (here 4th-, 5th-, and 6th-grade boys) adopting defensive risk-taking strategies. Interestingly enough, the combined n-Ach-TAQ patterns did not confirm Atkinson's findings with college age groups.

In counterpoint to these efforts to produce a projective measure of fear of failure, we turn to the work of Heckhausen, published in 1963 as *Hoffnung und Furcht in der Leistungsmotivation*. Heckhausen had undertaken a program of research designed to provide both hope of success and fear of failure measures taken from Mc-Clelland-type TAT's. He, too, had begun with a priori definitions of Imagery based upon approach-avoidance assumptions. However, his table of intercorrelations suggests greater independence of measures from the McClelland n Ach score (Hope of Success vs. n Ach is +.60, Fear of Failure vs. n Ach is +.21, and their sum vs. n Ach is +.62). These relationships were achieved by using an individual difference measure of Level of Aspiration strategy as the criterion to be predicted. Then progressive changes were made in the scoring definitions to maximize relationships between hope of success (HS) and positive LA, and between fear of failure (FF) and negative LA. This led to using statements of need to avoid failure as the basic "imagery" plus instrumental activity to avoid failure, appearance of praise and blame, negative affect, and failure outcomes. Thus, the Heckhausen system uses the most direct expression of failure in projective stories. Much later a "shift" study was done (Heckhausen, 1964) to show that arousal of achievement involvement using the forced-failure method does produce reliable increases in the FF scores. The other major changes Heckhausen made were in the pictures which were developed to fit German work settings.

Heckhausen's book and subsequent publications are devoted to the use of the HS and FF systems with a wide variety of populations and dependent variables. In general his findings parallel those being obtained by the American researchers using other ways of identifying the fear-of-failure Ss. These will be discussed in greater detail later in this book. The major point to make here is that our own strategy described in Chapter 4 was similar to Heckhausen's. After evolving a scoring system quite different from his, we became aware of his work. Initial efforts to use his scoring on our stories yielded almost none of the Imagery he scores. Overt, fully detailed stories of persons afraid of failure were not common with our American college samples. Therefore, we have continued to pursue the development of our system while at the same time looking forward to eventual collaborative work with Heckhausen to learn more of the source of the difference. Some of this work will be discussed subsequently in Chapter 8.

Fear of Failure Motivation

The problem with instructional techniques that use punishment as a motive source is that the individual's chief concern is with the avoidance of the punishment and only secondarily with the escape route that the punisher might have in mind. If there are a number of options available, the best-educated guess we have is that he will choose the most dependable alternative, the one that has worked best for him in the past. In a similar vein, the individual motivated by a fear of failure is going to select the strategy that gets him away from a failure experience. But in this situation, as in the former, it gets pretty tricky trying to predict what strategy will be selected without knowing the individual's history in achievement situations.

There are many ways a person can avoid failure and we shall be referring to them throughout the book, but at this juncture we simply want to point out that the most clear-cut technique of avoiding failure is by succeeding. However, it is generally assumed in the literature that striving for success is one of the options least likely to be chosen by someone motivated by a fear of failure. Although we are inclined to agree with our colleagues, we cannot dismiss success striving as a possible strategy for the FF. We can think of many people who appear to be "running scared" and knocking down one success after another with the prime motive of avoiding those terrifying moments of failure. But we would guess that these are the exceptions, since success tends to be a very undependable strategy. In fact, it is the nature of success to be undependable. For if the attainment of a goal were presented as a certainty, its character of success would be denied. Success involves risk and it is the thorn of risk that keeps the FF from the sweet smell of success.

Task Difficulty vs. Subjective Probability. What is the value of a performance when the individual doing the performance is completely convinced of his ability to do it? Festinger (1942), Lewin et al (1944) and Atkinson (1957) say that it is zero. Their argument is eminently reasonable, difficult to refute, and probably right, but possibly for the wrong reason. The reasoning goes as follows. If a normally intelligent adult were given the task of writing his name, adding two and two, or naming the President, the valence of success at these painfully simple tasks would be zero; there would be no sense of success. This is certainly a reasonable argument, for we can all think of silly tasks we can do without trying that would produce no sense of success in the doing. But it is also true that these simple tasks are those that everyone else can do as well. Is the lack of a success experience when the goal is attained due to the individual's certainty of attainment or due to the high proportion of others who could do the job equally well? If the value of success increases as the probability of that success decreases, which probability is being referred to? Is it the personal or subjective probability, the one generally used to calculate the valence of success? Or is it the probability across people (the proportion of people capable of attainment), the probability that defines the difficulty of the task? Although in many instances the two probabilities go hand in hand, in a given instance they can be quite divergent. A task may be difficult, i.e., few people can do it, but a given person may feel completely confident in his ability to accomplish it. Task difficulty is not equivalent to subjective probability and we suspect that their effects upon the success and failure experiences are quite different. Whereas the attainment of a difficult task will have implications for social esteem, attainment of a goal characterized by a low subjective probability will have implications for self-esteem.

Subjective Probability and Information. Personal expectancies of success or failure are a function of experience with the task or related tasks. Subjective probability is essentially an expression of a self-evaluation regarding the ability that the task demands. Whether or not we are capable of converting self-evaluation into precise probability statements is questionable, but this is a methodological problem. When a person predicts his performance and then performs precisely in line with the prediction, the value of the performance is purely instrumental, having no intrinsic worth. This is what happens when the individual does something that he knows he can do. Our daily lives are filled with activities whose sole value is getting them over with, getting paid for doing them, and getting home to spend the money. But every so often we savor the sense of success that goes with doing something we didn't think we could. For the moment we were poor predictors. Since the prediction was based on our self-evaluation, one implication of the predicting error is that the self-evaluation was wrong. It is our guess that it is the information regarding the self-evaluation implied by the predicting error that generates the sense of success or failure. If the information suggests raising the self-evaluation, we feel successful; if the information suggests lowering the self-evaluation, we sense failure.

The first meaning, therefore, of success and failure is the raising or lowering of the self-estimate because a performance did not follow a prediction made on the basis of the self-evaluation. No one questions the assumption that we all desire to raise our self-evaluations and try to avoid lowering them. If there is a difference between people who can be characterized as hope-of-success as opposed to those described as fear-of-failure, it would seem to be that the latter group is simply less concerned about raising the self-evaluation, and more concerned about its being lowered. These would be the achievement-conservatives striving to maintain the status quo. The best way to protect what one believes is not to have it tested, and the fear of failure (FF) person is often described as achievement avoidant.

One way of avoiding a test of one's opinion regarding a skill is not to participate in the achievement situation. Another way, when nonparticipation is not feasible, is to engage the task in such a manner as to receive the least amount of information possible. The most obvious way of doing this is not to try. The only time a performance carries any information regarding the relevant skill is when the individual is putting out maximum effort. Anything less than maximum effort prevents the evaluation of the skill.

Another way of reducing information from the performance is to choose to do the task so that effort is irrelevant to the performance. When the task allows the participant to engage it at different levels of difficulty, the choice of the completely impossible level insures nonattainment regardless of effort. In such a situation, the skill cannot be evaluated and thus the reigning self-evaluation is maintained. Similarly, the FF individual may choose a difficulty level so low that attainment is assured and once again performance is not informative. It is just such a prediction that Atkinson makes from his theory concerning the behavior of the FF in a task that can be engaged at different levels of difficulty.

Task Difficulty (Group Probability) and Social Concerns. At the beginning of this chapter we pointed to the well-known fact that the value of an accomplishment increases with scarcity. If everyone could do the job, then the accomplishment itself carries little glory. We don't admire and respect others for doing things that we too can do. When a skill performance can be managed by only a few, then those few are considered successful and are paid off in esteem and other rewards more tangible in nature. Since we rear our children in this reinforcement context, it is not surprising that they develop our preferences for accomplishments on difficult tasks. When we succeed on tasks few others can perform, we expect to be highly evaluated by others. On the other hand, failure on tasks that most others master recommends a low evaluation.

Individual or personal expectancies of accomplishment are irrelevant to the level of evaluation, which is solely a function of the actual performance. If the individual is concerned about the evaluation by others, he may avoid exposing himself in an achievement situation when he suspects his performance will not meet the standard demanded. If he is confident in a good performance, however, he may well go out of his way to expose himself to the observation of others. What such a person is afraid of is not the lowering of evaluation in his own eyes, but his de-evaluation in the eyes of others. It is a person of just such a kind that Sears described in her study. The subjects described by Sears as fearful of failing in the eyes of others set their aspirations below their actual performance.

There are consequences of achievement performances other than the possible change in self-evaluation and/or the possible change in the evaluation by others, and these will be discussed in the next chapter. We merely want to point out that a fear-of-failure attitude is not monolithic but can involve two kinds of fears: (1) a lowered self-estimate and (2) a lowered evaluation by others.

Correlates of the Fear of Failure Motive

In *A Theory of Achievement Motivation,* Atkinson and Feather (1966, pp. 369-70) provide an "image" of the "fellow who is dominated by a dread of failure, a failure threatened personality":

In contrast, we have the individual in whom the motive to avoid failure greatly exceeds the motive to achieve. He is dominated by the threat of failure, and so resists activities in which his competence might be evaluated against a standard or the competence of others. Were he not surrounded by social constraints (i.e., spurred by a need to be approved for doing what is generally expected by his peers) he would never voluntarily undertake an activity requiring skill when there is any uncertainty about the outcome. When forced into achievement-oriented activities, he is most threatened by what the other fellow considers the greatest challenge. Constrained, but given a choice, he will defend himself by undertaking activities in which success is virtually assured or activities which offer so little real chance of success that the appearance of trying to do a very difficult thing (which society usually applauds) more than compensates for repeated and minimally embarrassing failures. Given an opportunity to quit an activity that entails evaluation of his performance for some other kind of activity, he is quick to take it. Often constrained by social pressures and minimally involved, not really achievement-oriented at all, he will display what might be taken for dogged determination in the pursuit of the highly improbable goal. But he will be quickly frightened away by failure at some activity that seemed to him to guarantee success at the outset. The dogged persistence is really rigid, apathetic compliance, as is his tolerance for continual routine success at tasks offering virtually no possibility of failure. This fellow's general resistance to achievement-oriented activity opposes any and all sources of positive motivation to undertake the customary competitive activities of life. Thus he suffers a chronic decrement in achievement tests. His long history of relative failure means he will view his chances in new ventures more pessimistically than others unless there is specific information to contradict a simple generalization from past experience. Most startling, perhaps, are the erratic changes in his level of aspiration, which take place when the least likely outcome occurs. Should this fellow fail at a task he undertook as a reasonably safe venture, he might respond with a startling increase in his level of aspiration instead of persistence at the initial activity. Should he begin to succeed at a task initially conceived as very difficult, he might then exhibit a dramatic decrease in his level of aspiration, a retreat to the safest of ventures. These apparently irrational moves—like his inability to move away from continual failure when the probability of success is remote—are to be understood as aspects of a defensive strategy, the avoidance of an intermediate degree of risk, the peak of competitive activity, where his anxiety reaches an intolerable level.

The level of anxiety is symptomatic of the degree of resistance to an activity. When it is strong we know that the individual has been constrained to overcome great resistance. When it is weak the resistance to that activity must be weak. Because the level of experienced anxiety is symptomatic of the strength of resistance (i.e., the tendency to avoid failure) we are able to assess the strength of this man's motive to avoid failure from self-report questionnaires concerning the great amount of anxiety he has experienced in the nonvoluntary achievement tests endured in schooling. In the strange pattern of defensive behavior expressed by the person who is dominated by dread of failure, we confront pathology in the domain of achievement-oriented activity.

In the remainder of this chapter we wish to discuss the data base from which the above portrait was projected as we used it to guide the research reported in this book. The reader will recall that our project began six years ago, and our own research was being pursued and developed even as the above portrait was emerging from the Michigan group. If fear of failure is a motivational condition that may affect anyone, given the proper conditions, then a study of these conditions permits us to learn about this important human motive without assuming we are trying to identify some particular personality type. Essentially this has been the attitude of most researchers. The reader should bear this in mind when he finds us referring to the FF person. We mean a person motivated by fear of failure, rather than a particular type of "personality." It need not be the same person from one study to the next. Our interest is in the motive, not in the personality.

Difficulty in predicting what an FF person will do has not deterred anyone interested in the problem from making such predictions. Beginning with LA studies, FF persons were said to set goals below their performance (Frank, 1938; Sears, 1940) or goals above their performance (Schroeder & Hunt, 1957) and/or set their goals with great variability (Rotter, 1954). The problem in comparing these predictions is that the aspirational question varied among the studies, and the tasks were different. Nevertheless, there appears to be a strong conviction in the literature that any kind of goal-setting that veers from the norm (aspirations moderately higher than performance) can be indicative of FF.

In a study investigating the behavioral correlates of the achievement motive, McClelland and Liberman (1949) suggested that one characteristic of the FF person is that he is slow to recognize negative achievement or failure words. The assumption underlying the suggestion is that FF persons will tend to deny failure and thus become insensitive to failure cues. Some support for this argument was presented in a study by Atkinson (1953) when he noted that FF subjects (those located in the middle of the n-Ach distribution) tended to recall fewer uncompleted tasks as the conditions for recall changed from relaxed to achievement-oriented. The argument in Atkinson's study is similar to that of McClelland in that the FF person is viewed as one who in denying failure cues will tend to repress (forget) failure experiences. The argument has a great deal of apparent validity in that a person who is fearful of failure should strive to avoid failure, and one way of doing this is not to notice failure cues or remember failure experiences. But reasonable as this assumption is, there is another position just as reasonable, namely, that an FF person would be oversensitive to failure cues. In a study by Postman and Brown (1952) it was found that *S*s who failed in a level-of-aspiration experiment were more sensitive to failure words than either the success group or the control group. They interpret their findings as supporting their hypothesis-confirming theory which argues that people tend to report what they expect. If we assume that FF persons anticipate failure (McClelland et al., 1953; Atkinson and Feather, 1966), it would follow that they would be more sensitive to failure cues. Whether a person who is fearful of some experience will tend to be more or less sensitive to signs of that experience will depend in part on the intensity of the motive. Until we have a test that can measure differences in intensity, mere use of decreased or increased sensitivity to failure cues makes a poor criterion for the FF motive.

Another factor affecting whether an FF person will engage in defensive or vigilant behavior is his ability to avoid the failure experience. If there is no way of avoiding it then the defensive or denying attitude would be the most useful. Past failure experiences cannot be avoided, since they have already taken place, and we would expect that the FF person would tend to forget them. This tendency to repress failure was noted in a study by Schroder and Hunt (1957) when it was observed that *S*s who gave failure-avoidant interpretations to a paper-and-pencil test also ignored criticism and avoided interpreting their own performance as a failure.

The primary characteristic of the FF person is that he strives to avoid failure experiences. But the avoidance of failure can take many forms. The most obvious strategy is to avoid achievement situations, where failure always exists as a possibility. It was on the basis of this assumption that Clark, Teevan, and Ricciuti (1956) argued that *S*s who would settle for a score considerably below what they expected to get and could be bought off cheaply by offering them the opportunity to be excused from an achievement situation (taking a final exam), were FF *S*s.

But the opportunity to avoid an achievement situation is not always available, and the next question is, What will the FF person do when constrained in an achievement situation? He may then become very wary of signs that indicate failure. At this early stage he is vigilant because even though he has been constrained by some threat, he can still essentially avoid failure by not trying. The choice of trying or not-trying must be decided, and in this pre-decision conflict we expect the FF person to be quite accurate in judging signs. Festinger (1964) in clarifying the difference between decision making and dissonance reduction (a post-decision problem) showed that before the decision is made the subject is highly sensitive to information. It is consistent with Festinger's position, therefore, to suggest that for a person motivated by fear and a desire to avoid, there will be more failure cues noticed than by someone less concerned. Whether he sees failure cues when they are objectively absent has not been established, although some researchers claim that this is one expression of an FF person. Such a claim is consistent with the finding that people who are anti-Semitic tend to classify more people as Jewish than are actually Jewish (Allport, 1958).

After commitment to the task is made (perhaps based on the expectation that he will succeed) vigilance turns into defense, the decision-making process turns into the dissonance-reducing process and the FF person begins to deny the failure signs. In an extended study of failure avoidance, Schroder and Hunt (1952) found that *S*s who used failure-avoidant behavior tended not to interpret their performance as failure while the non-avoidant *S*s did so interpret theirs. This finding fits with Atkinson's (1953) results, where FF persons tended to forget their uncompleted (failed) tasks.

One consequence of failure that we pointed out earlier involved the lowering of one's self-evaluation. Schroder and Hunt also noted that failure-avoidant *S*s did not decrease their self-evaluations after criticism while the non-avoidant *S*s did. Further findings indicated that *S*s who tend to avoid interpreting their behavior as failure also tend to overevaluate their performance. Overevaluation is certainly one way of denying failure possibilities and explains in part why some FF persons place their aspirations considerably above their actual performance. Gould and Sears describe these *S*s as trying to prop up their self-estimates (in their own and others' eyes) by high-level aspiration implying that they are really much better than they seem to be.

In a level of aspiration situation the FF person apparently has two strategies to choose from: (1) to set his goal considerably above his performance or (2) to set his goal below his performance. The first strategy opens him to the risk of not performing at the level of his aspiration and thereby incurring the opinion that he is immodest and possibly unrealistic. However, the high LA can serve the purpose of implying that the person is better than his actual performance and that the actual performance should be ignored in evaluating him. The second strategy avoids the judgment that he is a braggart and hopefully maintains the opinion of his skill in line with the performance. Since the performance will be the major data for forming the opinion of his ability, the cautious goal setter is essentially avoiding a poor character opinion. Unfortunately, by not laying claims to the performance by predicting it the cautious LA will remove some of the implication of the performance for the underlying skill. The risks involved appear to be primarily interpersonal. The high-LA person has opted for a good evaluation on the basis of his skill (claiming a high skill level by his great expectation) while the low-LA person has opted for a good evaluation on the basis of his modesty. It would be premature to claim that the two strategies are expressions of the same motive. Eysenck and Himmelweit (1946), Himmelweit (1947), and Miller (1951) found that hysterics tend to predict scores below their performance while neurasthenics maintain high positive goal-discrepancy scores.

Determining whether or not FF persons distort failure signs by exaggerating their cue value is difficult unless there is some objective measure of the number and strength of the signs. In a typical achievement situation there is no accurate way of measuring the failure and success cues. However, in a risk-taking situation it is possible to establish what the probabilities are for attainment and nonattainment. In a simple gambling situation the odds can be established with great precision, and distortions up or down can be easily determined.

Will the FF person, when confronted with an objective probability of failing, misjudge the probability by increasing it? If we begin with the assumption that an FF person anticipates failure, then we might guess that he will distort the probability against himself winning. But if we begin with the assumption that the FF person will deny failure cues, we would predict that he will distort the probability in favor of his winning. The data from Schroder and Hunt (1952) describe the failure-avoidant person as overestimating his chances. But then Pottharst (1955) described high n Ach as setting higher aspirations than low n Ach. We mention this study because in many studies now n Ach has been one of the measures of FF. It was the assumption that FF persons would tend to lower their probabilities of winning from the actual probability, while Hope-of-Success (S) persons (high n Ach) would have a higher subjective probability than the actual, that permitted Atkinson to account for the observation that when objective probabilities were 50 : 50, low n Ach subjects worked harder than the high n Ach subjects, who worked harder when the objective probabilities were 1 out of three.

We know of only two studies where the relationship between expectations of success and FF and motivation to achieve was investigated directly. Both studies done by Feather point up the difficulty of assuming any simple monotonic relationship. In the first study (1965) the task (an anagrams test) was presented to half the Ss as easy and to the other half as moderately difficult. The Ss were also given the Mandler-Sarason Test Anxiety Questionnaire and the n Ach measure. It has become standard procedure among those who have worked with Atkinson to use high scores on n Ach and low scores on the TAQ to locate the motive to achieve success, and a low score on n Ach together with a high score on the TAQ to locate the FF. Feather found that the high-n-Ach–low-TAQ subjects had a significantly higher initial probability estimate than the low-n-Ach–high-TAQ subjects, but only for the moderately difficult task. Feather's argument is that the effect upon probabilities of success will take place only when the motive to achieve and the motive to avoid achievement are highly aroused, and this he claims takes place when the initial probabilities are around 50 : 50. If Feather is correct in his assumption, then the hypothesis that FF persons will underestimate their chances of success will be correct only for a small part of the probability range. But Feather's assumption is somewhat questionable, since there is no way of determining what probability level his instructions triggered off. The average estimated probability of all subjects for the easy condition was .59 and for the difficult condition, .41. It would seem that both conditions were in the moderate probability range. In any case, there is no way of determining if there was in fact a distortion of the objective probabilities, since the objective probabilities were not available. In a follow-up study, Feather (1966) created a high expectation of success condition by telling his Ss that some 70 percent of people like them were able to do the task, and a low expectation of success condition by telling the Ss that only about 30 percent of like people could do the task. The results show that initial estimates of the probability of success for the success and failure oriented Ss are almost indistinguishable from one another. Whatever distortion is taking place appears to be a regression to a middling probability: the high-expectation group reduces the .70 probability to .64 and the low-expectation group raises the .30 probability to .54. But certainly there is no evidence that failure-avoidant people distort any differently from success-oriented people.

We must confess some disappointment in Feather's findings; it makes a lot of intuitive sense that failure-avoidant people would have *different* expectations of success and failure than success-oriented people. Of course, it is always possible that the measures Feather used to locate the failure and the success groups did not do the job. Using low scores on the n Ach measure as half the indicator of FF denies (1) that low n Ach scores are merely indicative of an indifference to achievement and (2) that high n Ach people can be FF. Using the TAQ as the other half of the FF indicator suggests that anxiety is generated only by a fear of failure and not by a concern about not succeeding.

The argument for the n Ach and TAQ measures as indicators of FF and hope-of-success motivations is so deeply embedded in the studies emanating from Atkinson's theory of risk taking that it is difficult to know where to begin the disentanglement. One problem with the theory is that although it seems to make precise predictions, the confirming data always seem to need methodological medication. But one prediction that appears to have accumulated considerable empirical support is that FF people prefer either low risk or high risk. One study designed to test this prediction of the theory was conducted by Atkinson and Litwin (1960). The Ss were allowed to toss rings over a peg from any distance they wanted. They found that Ss, regardless of their classification as FF or success-oriented, preferred to toss rings from an intermediate range. Although the success-motivated Ss spent more time throwing from the middle distance than the FF's, the two distributions followed the same pattern. The authors explain the "unexpected" pattern of throws of the FF's by suggesting that even those classified as FF were in fact more motivated by an interest in success than a "true" fear-of-failure person. Their argument is that "most persons in whom the avoidance motive is actually stronger in an absolute sense are eliminated long before they reach college (p. 61). Since so many studies dealing with avoidant motivation, including Atkinson's, have been conducted using college students as subjects, we quail at the implication of this ad hoc explanation.

Aside from the fact that Ss classified as FF generally preferred the intermediate range, the design of the study prevents us from determining just what the intermediate range means in terms of probabilities. The middle range preferred by both groups of subjects centered around 10 feet. But did the subjects see this distance as having a probability of 50 : 50? It is doubtful, certainly, to anyone who has played the ringtoss game.

One of the problems in bringing evidence to bear on correlates of FF involves the establishment of failure- and success-motivated groups. In studies using the n Ach and TAQ measures the Ss are classified in comparison to one another. It may well be, as Atkinson has suggested, that the subjects being used are generally more motivated to succeed than they are failure avoidant. It might be preferable not to use college students where there has already been considerable selection in achievement motivation. Perhaps with this in mind, Moulton (1965) chose subjects from the junior and senior classes in high school. The Ss were allowed to choose one of three tasks that varied only in difficulty. He found a significant difference in preference between the success-oriented and the failure-oriented group. But although the success group showed a greater preference for the task of intermediate difficulty, the failure group did not show a decided preference for the easy or difficult tasks. Another prediction from the Atkinson theory, tested by this study, was that the FF's would show a preference for the easy task after success on the intermediate task, and a preference for the difficult task after failure on the immediate task. The data clearly show that the FF's show a greater preference for these atypical shifts than the success group. But if we consider the FF group alone, only one third of the Ss engage in atypical shifts. It seems that it has not yet been established whether FF-motivated people prefer to avoid moderate risks, or whether their preference for moderate risks is merely *less* than that of those motivated to succeed.

Recapitulation

There have been many claims about the cognitive, perceptual, and behavioral outcomes of the motivational state generated by a fear of failure. Although the claims have not always been consistent with one another, there seems to be emerging some clustering of agreement weakly supported by empirical research. One major hitch in this area is that there is no agreed-upon measure of the fear-of-failure motive. It may well be that the motive has many dimensions and that no one person is fearful of failure in all situations. Nevertheless, if there is a factor of failure fear that permeates achievement situations, the common assumption is that it should express itself in avoidance behavior. But there are many paths leading away from a failure threat, and the activity of locating the escape routes lends itself to the temptation of projecting one's own idiosyncratic techniques. We have played the game of characterizing the FF and have often found ourselves in painful contradictions. We have given up the game as fruitless and turned to the job of spinning out empirical relationships with our projective measure of fear of failure.

But the covert tendency to judge certain kinds of behavior as manifestations of fear of failure persists and so it would be useful, if not cathartic, to describe what these behaviors are claimed to be.

Goal Setting. Three claims have been made about the goal-setting behavior of the FF. One claim is that he sets his goals lower than he should, considering his ability. This might take the form of a negative goal-discrepancy score in LA studies (Frank, 1935; Gould, 1939; Sears, 1940) or simply a low estimate of ability in comparison to others. A second claim is that the FF sets his goals much higher than his actual ability indicates.

These two claims, although apparently contradictory, are easily subsumed under the more general category of "unrealistic aspirations." The third claim accepts this as the critical feature of the goal-setting behavior and "allows" the FF to set his goals either considerably above or below his ability level. This claim does not distinguish between two types of FF, but assumes that a given FF person will engage in both low and high goal setting (Rotter, 1954; Mahone, 1960).

Risk Taking. Risk taking and goal setting are not unrelated behaviors and so we find that claims about the FF in risk taking are similar to the claims about levels of aspiration. The FF, it is claimed, prefers either small risks with small payoffs or high risks with high payoffs. A great deal has been made of this point by McClelland in his book *The Achieving Society* (1961). His argument is that in a properly functioning achieving society, people who prefer moderate risks are essential.

At one period in the investigation of the risk-taking propensities of FF it was assumed that it made little difference whether the gamble involved skill or pure chance (Atkinson, Bastian, Earl, and Litwin, 1960). But data from the studies of Meyer, Walker, and Litwin (1961) and Littig (1959) indicate that claims about risk-taking are only appropriate for achievement settings.

A question still remains in the minds of some researchers about the degree of consistency of risk-taking across situations. In an attempt to explore the construct validity of the risk-taking concept, Slovic (1962) correlated risk-taking propensities in tasks, gambling situations, occupational preferences, and self-ratings. Only 5 out of 28 correlations reached significance. Slovic concludes that risk-taking measures do not demonstrate convergent validity and is in agreement with Wallach and Kogan (1961) that conceptualization in the area is still inadequate.*

Recognition Thresholds. Will an FF be sensitive to failure cues or will he deny them and look the other way? In this area we have what appear to be contradictory claims. One claim is that the FF person will be on his guard and be particularly sensitive to signs of failure (Postman, 1953). The other claim is that the FF, because of his anxiety about failure, will protect himself by not noticing failure-related cues (Schroder and Hunt, 1957; McClelland and Liberman, 1949).

Both arguments are reasonable and there are research data to support both points of view. It may well be that both behaviors are characteristic of the FF. Vigilance and sensitivity to signs of failure are most useful to someone fearful of failure when escape routes are actually available and there is still time to make use of them. But when the commitment is irreversible and there is no escape, defensive denial might be the most useful approach for someone who gets anxious about failure.

The Recall of Failure and Success. Past failure is irreversible and it would make functional sense for someone anxious about failure to forget the experience. But then it would be just as reasonable to expect that a failure-anxious person would have a better memory for past failures than past success because a failure would have been a more intense experience. Or it might be as Alper (1957) suggests: the failure-anxious people, because of an inadequate defense against failures, will tend to mull over them and remember them.

The evidence in support of more or of less recall for failure by

* In 1967 Kogan and Wallach surveyed the literature dealing with the effect of individual difference variables on risk-taking. Their own work (1964) with personality self-descriptive scales had yielded a "pattern of results [that] was not especially encouraging" (p. 192). Recognizing that "no other personality variable has received the massive attention vis-à-vis risk-taking behavior that has characterized the need-achievement and fear-of-failure dimensions" (p. 190), they are nevertheless forced to the conclusion that questions of incentive definition, social context, and task history have not been sufficiently controlled to permit a clear understanding of motivational effects on risk-taking. Oddly, they condemn the development of new motive measures as contributing to proliferation and confusion rather than "consolidation," without considering that the path to coherent findings may require a resolution of the puzzling relationships between motive measures, through the development of new measures which in theoretical and empirical status are superior to those now extant.

FF is equivocal. Using the n Ach measure as an indirect indication of FF, Atkinson (1953) and Reitman (1961) have taken the position that FF's tend to repress their past failures. But in the Atkinson study, the FF group was located by having the lowest scores on n Arch, while in the Reitman study, the FF's were designated as those in the middle range of the n Ach distribution.

Some indirect evidence in support of the position that failure-anxious people would be inclined to forget past failures is suggested in a study by Rosenzweig (1943). He found that more completed tasks were recalled when the tasks were ego-involving and incompletion could be interpreted as failure. The implication of the findings is that when failure anxiety is aroused, the individual tends to repress failure experience. But it is somewhat dangerous to equate momentarily aroused failure anxiety with chronic FF. The facts as they have been established do not allow us to say how the FF will remember his failures.

Performance. If an FF becomes anxious in an achievement setting one would expect that he would have difficulty performing up to his ability. This appears to be a reasonable claim and there are some data showing that the FF performs poorly under achievement stress and after experiencing failure (Atkinson, 1954; Mandler-Sarason, 1952; Schroder and Hunt, 1957). A possible reason, other than sheer anxiety, for the poor performance is that the FF tends to be rigid in his problem-solving (Schroder and Hunt, 1957).

One qualification has to be made to the general thesis that anxious persons perform more poorly than nonanxious persons in an achievement task: a study by Sarason (1961) showed that the poor performance of anxious subjects took place only when the task was presented as a threat. When the Ss were informed that failure on the task was normal and expected, the high anxious Ss actually did better than the low anxious subjects. The findings of the study suggest that the FF motive can serve the positive function of moving a person towards success when the implications of failure have been softened. In any case, good or poor performances seem to be affected by the degree of failure threat in the achievement setting, in combination with the degree of failure concerns of the person.

Expectations of Failure. Judging achievement cues as indicating chances of failure or success is closely related to the recognition and memory of failure and success cues. But like the data in recog-

nition and recall, the evidence in regard to failure anticipation by
FF persons is somewhat equivocal. The argument that an FF would
be more inclined to anticipate failure than the success-oriented person nevertheless makes a lot of common and theoretical sense. If
an individual is fearful of some particular experience, then it becomes a good strategy to be particularly sensitive to any and all
signs of that situation arising. The error of engaging in an achievement task and failing is more aversive than avoiding an achievement task at which one might have succeeded. To make sure that
the first kind of error is minimized, signs of impending failure should
be exaggerated. But such a strategy makes sense only when the
individual still has the opportunity of avoiding the task. When the
person has engaged in the task and there is no backing out, he may
well distort the objective probabilities of failure downward.

One further point should be made before leaving this topic. If
there is distortion of actual probabilities as a function of the failure
fear, the chances are that the degree of distortion is not equivalent
or even proportional throughout the probability range. If Atkinson
is correct in his suggestion that tasks of intermediate difficulty are
most likely to arouse failure anxiety, then it might be that the
magnitude of distortion would be greatest at the intermediate probabilities. But even if the theory is incorrect, the suggestion that the
intermediate probability range would produce the greatest amount
of distortion can still hold. If the avoidance of the error of assuming
success and then failing is what is paramount for an FF, then the
decision to engage or not to engage is most difficult at the intermediate probabilities. In order to minimize the critical error and
help make the decision, we might expect considerable distortion
when the actual probabilities are in the 50 : 50 range.

Miscellaneous Correlates. We have discussed some of the behavioral correlates of the FF motive which have been directly researched. There have, of course, been many more claims than we
mentioned, but these are generally assumed to be "obviously" true.
We have become extremely wary of any claims in this area that are
not carefully established empirical relationships. We have also been
somewhat disappointed in the lack of empirical support for the
many claims that have been put forward. A major stumbling block
has been the inadequacy of measures. But then this is characteristic
of the field of personality research as a whole.

As an example of how easy it is to get embroiled in confusion,
consider the claim that the FF does not trust his own ability and

therefore sets himself cautious goals. In order to avoid negative self-evaluation, he engages in the protective strategy of setting his aspirations so low that he is assured of attaining them. Furthermore, it has been claimed that the FF will make small of his failures either by not noticing failure cues or simply forgetting failure experiences. But if an FF denies his failure experiences and latches onto his success, it would follow that such a person would have an inflated self-esteem. If he has an inflated self-esteem it becomes difficult to understand why he sets his goals below those of others with comparable ability. The fact of the matter is that we do not know whether the FF has a low or a high self-esteem, although it is tempting to guess that it would be low. Certainly speculations about the origins of failure fear always involve the assumption that persons so motivated have had more than their share of failure experiences. With a background of failure one would suppose that such people would generally have a lower self-estimate than the average person.

But according to Cohen (1959), people with high self-esteem show a preference for avoidance defenses in response to experiences which threaten the self-esteem. Some support for the argument was presented by Silverman (1964), when he showed that high-self-esteem persons had the poorest improvement scores in acquiring information in the failure condition. Then Dittes (1959) suggests that persons with low self-esteem engage in defensive behavior, one form of which he describes as impulsive closure. But in the same article he also suggests that "persons who attach strong value to achievement show more impulsive closure than persons weak in achievement valuation."

It seems that there are many facets that high self-esteem and low self-esteem have in common with the FF. At the present time we cannot say whether the FF tends more towards high or towards low self-esteem, or whether the two dimensions are at all related. Furthermore, it has not been adequately established whether the FF is high or is low on achievement concerns, or even if achievement motivation is related to fear of failure. It is our suspicion— and we shall consider this position in more detail in later chapters —that the fear-of-failure dimension is independent of achievement motivation.

If failure is to have any meaning for an individual, it must be assumed that the individual who is afraid of failing is taking some responsibility for his nonattainment. If attainment or nonattainment is completely due to some factor not under the control of the person, nonattainment cannot be construed to mean failure. For this reason one would expect that an FF would be more inclined to blame himself for nonattainment rather than some external factor. Some support for this tendency was developed in a study by Doris (1959). Further support of the possibility that FF's see themselves as responsible for achievement outcomes is available in a study by Rotter (1966), where a person who sees reinforcement contingencies as under his control is generally more concerned with his ability, particularly his failures.

Suggesting that an FF person is more inclined to see his destiny as under his own control would raise many eyebrows. In fact, we are very much disinclined to make such a suggestion. Characteristics of the internally controlled person, as described by Rotter, have a number of points in common with the high n-achiever as described by McClelland et al. (1953). Thus the person who views himself as in control (1) takes steps to improve his environmental condition, (2) places high value on skill and achievement reinforcements, and (3) makes proper use of failure and success information in setting his aspirations.

Equating FF's with those who see themselves as controlling success and failure outcomes is premature and probably a mistake. As we shall argue later when we discuss the Hostile Press System, viewing achievement outcomes as being strongly affected by *external* controls is possibly one dimension of the FF outlook. It is just such people who engage in atypical goal-setting shifts, i.e., raising expectations after failure and lowering them after success—a trait often ascribed to the FF.

By now the reader can appreciate the complexities faced by researchers of fear-of-failure motivation. It became clear to us that an effective program of research would require (1) a careful definition of the variables known to operate in the achievement situation, (2) a study of motive-arousal techniques, (3) a measure of fear-of-failure motivation, (4) and the use of the measure in as wide a variety of achievement settings as possible to develop the mosaic of its construct validity. The remainder of this book is devoted to these efforts. Our work is presented as a beginning, not a conclusion, and much of what we have "found" may not stand as valid. It has been possible to do only a fraction of the work needed, and this has meant striving to make each study illuminate a different part of the theoretical network bearing on fear-of-failure motivation. We close this chapter with a presentation of the schema of variables we have considered in designing our studies.

The Achievement Situation

In previous treatments of the taxonomy of variables in achievement situations the emphasis has been on "process" variables (McClelland, et al., 1963; Atkinson, 1954). The S is described as experiencing motive arousal in the face of achievement cues, anticipating positive or negative gratification, performing successful or unsuccessful instrumentalities, and finally experiencing positive or negative goal affects. We have chosen to expand our characterization of the situation using "content" terms which guide the researcher in this choice of operations for engaging fear-of-failure motivation.

The categories we use are presented in Table 1.1. Following a time sequence from left to right under Outputs, we first encounter the behavior of *engagement* in the achievement situation. We list as contributing variables to this dependent variable approach-avoidance motivational tendencies—i.e., hope of success and fear of failure—objective source of self-esteem for the attribute required for success, cognition of probable performance in this situation, and anticipation of affect generated by three classes of incentives—self-evaluation, social evaluation, and nonego consequences (by which we mean all nonsocial rewards or punishments).

Next we consider *choice* of tasks when these are open to the S. Given engagement, the S may be able to choose from among various tasks to pursue the incentives. Although one might conceive of all of the above factors being operative here as well, we emphasize the role of probability of success, motivation, and source of self-evaluation.

Given engagement and choice the S must then *perform* the task. Here we expect to find important interaction between motivation, aptitude, ability, and experience, as well as the obvious effects of knowledge of results. In fact, we are most interested in the situations where knowledge of results is delayed, as is often the case in important achievement situations, since this seems to be the circumstance where motivation plays the greatest role in producing variability in performance between persons.

TABLE 1.1. A TAXONOMY OF THE ACHIEVEMENT SITUATION

INPUTS	OUTPUTS				
	Engagement	Choice	Performance-Aspiration	Experience	Reaction
Objective					
Task requirements					
Ability		x	x		
Experience		x	x		
Effort				x	x
Probability of outcome					
Skill vs. chance	x	x			
Outcome					
Social evaluation	x			x	
Nonego consequences	x			x	
Subjective					
Motive tendencies					
Approach-avoidance	x	x	x	x	x
Cognitive structures					
Probability estimates	x	x		x	
Evaluation of task	x			x	x
Source of self-evaluation	x	x		x	x

While performing, the *S*s continue to cognize the situation and construct a sense of meaning and experience about it. That is, they *experience* the task as well as perform. Reports of this experience have not been vigorously researched in the past. We feel that the *S*s will be most shaped by the standards used to judge performance and by the evaluations being made of self by others and by the self. Thus we suspect that the motive pattern may again interact with these evaluation conditions to produce widely varying experience with similar kinds of performance.

The performance and the report of outcome do not end the sequence. Rather, we know that one must now incorporate into one's experience what has happened, and one must entertain the prospect of facing the situation again. Thus the *reaction to outcome* is very much a part of the achievement situation. The chief contributing factor here is thought to be the revised level of self-esteem as it interacts with motivation. Finally, we ask how the total experience with the achievement situation will effect the *S*'s next encounter with a similar situation, i.e., his *subsequent achievement-task behavior*. This implies studies of performance seriatim, or more longitudinal studies. Motivation must interact with aspiration, probability of success, and self-esteem as the major determinants here.

This has been the taxonomy of variables which has guided our choice of problem and style of operation. It has not always been possible to incorporate each variable into a study as this scheme dictates. But at the end of the book we will return to our scheme and ask what we have learned about fear of failure as it operates throughout the achievement situation.

CHAPTER 2

Studies of the Failure Experience

THE INITIAL STUDIES OF NEED ACHIEVEMENT FOUND THAT THE motive was engaged by telling subjects that the tasks provided good estimates of intelligence, potential for further training, leadership, and the like. If the experimenter was convincing and the tests plausible, the Ss showed increased fantasy of achievement strivings, better task performance, and post-task comments indicating hope of success. This was especially true if the Ss were given a test but had no knowledge of the results before taking the fantasy measure. We have already said that some of the fantasy contents included suggestions that the Ss were more concerned with failure than with success, but basically the situation was not one in which the possibility of failure was emphasized. In the original series of validation studies of n Ach the false-norm technique was used, and there was no doubt that Ss who were told that they had outperformed another group seemed to feel successful, while those told they had performed less well than the competition took the fact seriously. That is, it was an engaging situation for most of the Ss, which increased the frequency of negative affect categories in their stories (McClelland et al., 1953). However, no other information was collected from the Ss to supplement the fantasy material with estimates of cognitive reactions.

Since our concern was with fear of failure, we were faced with the necessity of creating conditions which would engage such motivation. The false-norm techniques used by McClelland had not seemed to create enough fear of failure effects on fantasy to suggest a high degree of arousal, and we felt we should explore the conditions required to produce a *subjective* sense of failure. Obviously this meant turning away from fantasy toward conscious estimates of the situation by a series of cognitive studies.

At the end of this chapter we will see that the trail led back to the use of the false-norm technique as a method of arousing fear of failure. However, this research on subjective report of failure experience strengthened our conviction that fantasy measures were necessary for the measurement of fear of failure motivation. Despite the finding that self-reported n Ach bears no relationship to the TAT measure, we could not be sure that the same would hold true for avoidance motivation. Conceivably one is more aware of negative affect than positive, and a set of well-phrased questions might have proved useful. Ineed, this is one of the arguments for the use of the Test Anxiety Questionnaire (Sarason, 1960). So, too, the social desirability of confessing fear of failure to psychologists might be positive rather than negative. At the outset none of the answers to these questions were known, and since our initial efforts at devising a TAT scoring system for fear of failure had been unsuccessful, we initiated this series of studies while working on the problem of picture construction and selection for new TAT studies.

In these studies the reader will be quick to note that our sample sizes are sometimes quite small. This reflects our belief that the type of effect we were seeking would be quite great, and that our pilot studies gave it ample opportunity to appear. Where an effect was obtained, it was studied with a much larger sample permitting more precise analysis. The effect of the work in this chapter is to raise a question about the role of self-esteem as a variable interacting with motivational states in achievement situations. Subsequently we will return to this problem (Chapter 8). Now let us describe our efforts to obtain self-report measures of the effects of objective failure.

The Effect of Failure on a Simple Motor Task: Reaction Time

Our initial effort to explore some of the cognitive dimensions surrounding an achievement task experience used nineteen college sophomore males who were having their first experience with a simple reaction-time apparatus. Prior to the experiment they were given Experiment Reaction Sheet (I) to fill out.

Following the collection of the data, the obtained reaction-time rank in class of each subject was computed, and two weeks later

---

EXPERIMENT REACTION SHEET (I)

Regarding reaction time as described for this experiment, I consider myself:

SLOW   1 2 3 4 5 6 7 8 9 10   FAST

Personally, I consider reaction time as:

OF NO   VERY
IMPORTANCE   1 2 3 4 5 6 7 8 9 10   IMPORTANT

Assuming the normal operation of chance factors in my performance, and in the light of my past experience, I expect to rank _____ out of 22.

The task, used in this experiment, strikes me as:

A POOR   AN EXCELLENT
MEASURE   1 2 3 4 5 6 7 8 9 10   MEASURE

---

subjects were given the post-task reaction sheet, Experiment Reaction Sheet (II).

Understandably the subjects were not accurate in their predictions

---

EXPERIMENT REACTION SHEET (II)

Name _____ Expected _____ /22 Actual _____ /22
                                                   Rank   Rank

The task used to measure reaction time strikes me as:

A POOR   AN EXCELLENT
MEASURE   1 2 3 4 5 6 7 8 9 10   MEASURE

Regarding reaction time as described for this experiment, I consider myself:

SLOW   1 2 3 4 5 6 7 8 9 10   FAST

Personally, I consider reaction time as:

OF NO   VERY
IMPORTANCE   1 2 3 4 5 6 7 8 9 10   IMPORTANT

Comment:

of rank standings. Nine subjects underestimated their ranks; one was accurate; and nine overestimated them. Table 2.1 shows that the pattern of averages which emerged was stable across conditions.

TABLE 2.1. THE EFFECT OF REACTION TIME TASK
EXPERIENCE ON SUBJECTS' RATINGS OF SELF-
RANK, IMPORTANCE OF THE REACTION TIME,
AND ADEQUACY OF THE TASK

(ten-point scale; 10 is high)

$N = 19$	Self-Evaluation	Importance of Reaction Time	Task Adequacy
Pre-task	6.4	8.2	6.7
Post-task	5.7	7.6	5.9
Change	−0.7	−0.6	−0.8

The rather small movements in the data implied clearly that despite the small number of subjects, we would have to contrast those given positive reinforcement with those experiencing negative reinforcement to permit the possibility of differential response. When this was done the data of Tables 2.2 and 2.3 appeared.

An interesting feature of these data is that not only did the self-evaluations move in a manner consistent with the experience,

TABLE 2.2. THE EFFECT OF POSITIVE TASK
EXPERIENCE ON SUBJECTS' RATINGS OF SELF-
RANK, IMPORTANCE OF THE REACTION TIME,
AND ADEQUACY OF THE TASK

(ten-point scale; 10 is high)

$N = 10$	Self-Evaluation	Importance of Reaction Time	Task Adequacy
Pre-task	5.7	7.7	6.9
Post-task	6.5	7.2	5.8
Change	+0.8	−0.5	−1.1[a]

[a]test of sig. n.s.

TABLE 2.3. THE EFFECT OF NEGATIVE TASK
EXPERIENCE ON SUBJECTS' RATINGS OF SELF-
RANK, IMPORTANCE OF THE REACTION TIME,
AND ADEQUACY OF THE TASK

(ten-point scale; 10 is high)

$N = 9$	Self-Evaluation	Importance of Reaction Time	Task Adequacy
Pre-task	7.3	8.7	6.6
Post-task	5.0	8.0	6.0
Change	-2.3[a]	-0.7	-0.6

[a] $t = 4.05$, $p < .01$.

but both groups lowered their judgments of the adequacy of the task
as measure and of the importance of reaction time; or to put it
more precisely, these two measures did not respond to the effects
of reinforcement. The lowering of the adequacy rating by the success group was particularly intriguing, since one might have thought
it would bolster their standing to raise the ratings. Actually, only
one of the ten subjects did so. Another surprising aspect of these
data was the use of such high positions for the Importance dimension. Perhaps this reflects an implicit suggestion by the experimenters, i.e., "It is important or we would not be measuring it." Another
feature of this experiment was that the subjects spoke in terms of
"chance," suggesting they had still another dimension for changing
their views of their performance we had not tapped.

Taking all these results together it seemed wise to repeat the
basic experiment with larger numbers of subjects and more adequate
controls. Thus we were led to the Steadiness Experiment.

The Effect of Failure on a Simple Motor Task: Steadiness

The subjects were 68 college sophomores taking the laboratory
of the Introductory Psychology course. Their instructions for the
task are shown in the General Instructions for the Steadiness Test.

The experimental manipulation used was the reporting of the
S's score at the end of the 7th and 14th (last) trials. The E reported
the same percentile standing on both occasions to the S, providing

GENERAL INSTRUCTIONS FOR THE STEADINESS TEST

Practice will be with the current *off.*

Face the apparatus from such a distance that the arm can be extended and the elbow locked. You are free to move the hand at the wrist but best scores are obtained when both wrist and elbow are stiff.

Trial procedure:

1. Trials will last 15 seconds with a 45-second rest between trials.

2. Each trial will be preceded by a short countdown from the control room to permit you to place the stylus in position.

3. All trials will use the second hole from the bottom, the second smallest.

4. The 15-second trial will begin with the word "Zero" from the control room and the panel light above S's head will come on and stay on for the 15-second period.

5. E will record the clock time in 100ths of a second. *Do not reset the clock. Do not report the time to S.* The clock records the time of stylus-aperture contact. A click will be heard each time the clock is activated and the hand will continue to sweep as long as the stylus touches the sides of the aperture.

6. Reporting scores:

   CONDITION I.   Control will first ask each room to report the trial 7 score. Each room will next receive the percentile standing of the score from Control.

   CONDITION II.   After *each trial E* will set the selector switch, reporting in units of 100.

                        S will see his position in the group on the TOTE board.

                        Each switch position signifies "equal to or greater than".

positive reinforcement for half the Ss, and negative reinforcement for the other half. Under Control conditions an uninterrupted series of 14 trials was used with no norm comparisons. The percentiles reported to the Ss were determined by the level the S had estimated he could attain as reported on the pre-task questionnaire. Since Ss

Fear of Failure

could not compare performance scores they had no basis for judging the accuracy of the percentile statements.

In the interest of creating extreme conditions the *E* made comments on four occasions throughout the series which were congruent with the percentile standings to be given the *S*. Thus if the *S* was
given a norm in excess of his pre-task estimate of what he would
do, the comments were supportive of the task as a measure of
steadiness; e.g., "This is a real challenge." If the norm received was
below that of the pre-task estimate the comments were derogatory

---

POST-TASK REACTION SHEET

1. What proportion of your score do you think was due to chance or
   extraneous factors?

   > 0 10 20 30 40 50 60 70 80 90 100   percent

2. After this experience with the task how adequate a measure of eye-
   hand coordination do you feel it to be?

   >   HIGHLY
   >
   > INADEQUATE   1 2 3 4 5 6 7 8 9 10   ADEQUATE

3. What percentile standing was reported for your first block score? _____
   total score? _____

4. What was your reaction to your standing report:
   (a) after the first block?
   (b) after your total score?

5. In what percentile of an Amherst College sample of students do you
   think you stand on this general ability?

   > 10 20 30 40 50 60 70 80 90 100   percentile

6. In general, how important do you feel eye-hand coordination to be?
   > OF NO   GREAT
   > IMPORTANCE   1 2 3 4 5 6 7 8 9 10   IMPORTANCE

7. Write out verbatim any remarks *E* made during the experiment which
   might have provided a form of social facilitation.

8. Describe your reactions to these remarks at the time.

Items 1, 5, and 6 composed the pre-task questionnaire.

of the task; e.g., "I don't think these scores will mean a thing." The purpose of these suggestions was to strengthen the tendencies to accept or reject the adequacy of task under the respective conditions of success or failure.

Prior to the task the subjects were asked a series of questions about their steadiness ability, its importance to them, and the extent to which chance would play a part in any score. Following the task a more extended series of items was asked (Post-Task Reaction Sheet).

Results. Ideally one would wish to control the discrepancy between estimated percentile standing and that returned to the subject, but in view of the wide range of estimates received, it was felt that subjects given low estimates, i.e. 30th percentile, should be given larger increases than those who thought they would be in the 80th percentile. The range of positive reinforcement given the subjects was 10 to 30 percentile points with a range of 10 to 50 points used under negative reinforcement conditions.

By giving the subjects questions about the role of chance, the adequacy of the task as a measure of steadiness, and their steadiness ability we wished to see what sort of pattern of change would result following the experimental treatment. Table 2.4 shows the results for the Control Group.

We find that with practice on the task the group raises its self-

TABLE 2.4. THE EFFECT OF STEADINESS TASK EX-
PERIENCE ON SUBJECTS' RATINGS OF PERCENTILE
STANDING, IMPORTANCE OF HAND STEADINESS,
ADEQUACY OF THE TASK, AND PERCENT OF SCORE
DUE TO CHANCE FACTORS

	Ability Percentile	Importance of Task	Adequacy of Task	Chance % Score
Control Group (N = 18): Knowledge of Standing by Trial				
Pre-task	55	7.3	6.3	32.2
Post-task	58.9	6.0	5.5	36.9
Change	+3.9	−1.3	−0.8	+4.5[a]

[a]Test of sig., n.s.

estimate of ability, though not to a significant degree, while the same downward trend for importance of the ability and task adequacy appears, though not to a reliable degree, that occurred in the pilot study using reaction time. Chance as a factor goes up though not significantly. Thus the basic effect of task acquaintance seems to be confidence and contempt.

For the Experimental Groups we use the comparison of differences, since the positive and negative reinforecement, as we are calling the false norms given them, must be compared for effect (see Table 2.5).

Using the test for difference of differences for the self-estimate data, we find a highly reliable movement in the predicted directions, but

TABLE 2.5. THE EFFECT OF POSITIVE VS. NEGATIVE
REINFORCEMENT ON SUBJECTS' RATINGS OF PER-
CENTILE STANDING, IMPORTANCE OF HAND STEADINESS
ADEQUACY OF THE TASK, AND PERCENT OF SCORE
DUE TO CHANCE FACTORS

	Ability Percentile	*Importance of Task*	*Adequacy of Task*	*Chance % Score*
Experimental Group (N = 18): Positive Reinforcement				
Pre-task	56.6	8.3	6.7	24.4
Reinforcement	75			
Post-task	66.6	7.8	5.4	32.7
Change	+10[a]	−0.5	−1.3	+8.3[b]
Experimental Group (N = 17): Negative Reinforcement				
Pre-task	54.1	7.1	6.4	28.4
Reinforcement	33.5			
Post-task	42.4	6.8	5.3	37.4
Change	−11.7[a]	−0.3	−1.1	+9.0[c]

[a]Difference of differences $p < .01$.
[b]$p < .10$, $t = 2.08$, 17 df.
[c]$p < .10$, $t = 1.83$, 16 df.

for the remaining task estimates both groups move in the same downward directions. Single group tests for the "chance" estimates show that both groups moved these estimates up, the significance level being $<.10$ for both the positive and negative reinforcement groups.

The Controls knew their comparative standing in their group at the end of each trial, thus balancing off those above and below the norm just as was true of the Reaction Time Group. At the outset each group gave a range of ability estimates which averaged to slightly above the 50th percentile. Changes in the self-evaluation then follow the pattern of reinforcements to a significant degree. However, with acquaintanceship with the task, we again find both experimental groups lowering the importance of the task and the adequacy of the task as a measure, and increasing their estimates of chance in determining the score. Interestingly, the movement of the subjects' ability estimates was approximately one-half of the distance suggested. The increase in chance estimates is congruent with the decrease in task adequacy, and overall the pattern appears to show changes in self-evaluation with concomitant cognitive shifts whose total impact is to lower the importance of this particular test of skill. Apparently this strange and novel task, which none of the subjects had seen before, permitted shifts in self-evaluation to occur, in part because it was new to the subjects and in part because it was not considered an adequate measurement.

Taken together we found these results both encouraging and disturbing. On the one hand it appeared that failure on a simple laboratory test of psychomotor skill was viewed by the subject as cause for lowering his self-estimate; but experience with the tasks seemed to lead to a general lowering of respect, if you will, for the task itself. Thus it appeared we could produce a subjective sense of failure all right, but it might not have much threat to it.

The Effect of Public Failure: The Quiz Contest

About the time we were mulling these findings over, an opportunity appeared to study reactions to success and failure under extreme conditions of involvement. One of the authors (Birney) was appointed "coach" of a group of four undergraduates who would appear on a nationally televised quiz show. Certainly this situation was the extreme opposite of those just discussed, and when the students agreed to fill out brief questionnaires prior to and follow-ing their contest, our attention turned to the intensive study of four subjects over a period of some weeks. The first issue to overcome was the absence of agreement on the dimensions of ability and skill required for success in quiz contests. Accordingly it was decided to let each man state which attributes he felt were most critical, and to use those for his self-judgments throughout the period. These attributes then became the basis for "self-evaluation." The data were gathered three times prior to the contest, as indicated in Table 2.6, and once immediately after the contest. A summary of findings ap-pears in the table.

Two of the men began with patterns of inferior Self-evaluation to the opponents, low Importance, and high Chance estimates. Such conditions imply objective failure—which they predicted. When it occurred they changed none of these elements, but there did emerge from their interview reports of rewarding experience along lines peripheral to the contest itself, which rendered their participation sensible and accounted for the absence of failure feelings. Two other men felt the contest to be of moderate Importance, evaluated them-selves as equal to their opponents, and felt that Chance played a less critical role. Under these conditions they predicted a victory, but the one who shifted to a greater Chance estimate also shifted to predicted defeat on the day of the contest. When defeat came, one man expressed less confidence in his Self-evaluation and in the team as a whole in anticipation of the defeat, restoring the team ratings after the contest but leaving his own ratings depressed. The second man, JGo, increased his Chance estimate greatly but did not change his evaluation. He also expressed negative affect over losing, as did JeG.

Two men emerged from an objectively important contest, having experienced defeat, saying that they had had a good time and they considered the affair a success. Knowledge of certain cognitive ele-ments preceding this event suggests that they are not being defensive about failure, but rather they expected to fail and had resolved the problem of dealing with the extrinsic consequences. A third man apparently began to anticipate failure and, since he had expected success and considered the event important, began to resolve his "anticipated" dissonance (Festinger, 1957) by increasing his esti-mates of Chance and devaluing his teammates. When defeat came he held to the Chance estimate but permitted the teammate evalu-

TABLE 2.6. SUMMARY OF QUIZ-CONTEST CONTESTANTS' REPORTS TAKEN TWELVE DAYS, EIGHT DAYS, AND ONE HOUR PRIOR TO THE CONTEST, AND IMMEDIATELY AFTER LOSING THE CONTEST

CONTESTANTS

	DR			LC			JeG			JGo		
	12 days	8 days	1 hr.	12 days	8 days	1 hr.	12 days	8 days	1 hr.	12 days	8 days	1 hr.
Pre-Game												
Importance (−10 to +10)	−5	−3	−2	5	5	4	3	4	4	3	5	4
Self-evaluation	5.0	5.6	5.3	6.5	6.3	6.5	7.0	7.0	2.5	7.0	7.8	7.2
Percent of Chance role in Outcome	60	50	55	75	75	85	35	75	75	40	40	40
Expected score outcome	200	150	150	180	160	120	200	200	150	160	170	170
Post-Loss												
Importance (−10 to +10)			−4			4			7			4
Self-evaluation			5.3			5.5			6.0			6.8
Percent of Chance role in Outcome			50			85			75			60
Feelings			"Relieved; better than winning"			"Good experience"			"Angry"			"Good fun, might have won, sad to lose"

ation to rise, questioning himself instead. He also markedly increased the Importance report, thus moving several of the elements in a joint fashion which permits him to react to the feeling of failure he expressed. The fourth man expected to win, and lost. He increased his Self-evaluation and revised his estimate of Chance and Ability. He reported feelings of failure and regret. Apparently the Chance attribute alone carries the burden of his resolution of the dissonance generated by the outcome.

Thus we see two men failed, and two did not—subjectively speaking. And their behaviors are consistent with these subjective definitions of failure in *all* cases, while the objective definition of failure would produce two cases described as defensive.

This study emphasizes more than ever the importance of getting pre-task estimates (though a contrast group uncontaminated by these questions may be needed for some studies). Here, under a high degree of objective involvement, we find the role of Chance suddenly coming to the fore as the attribute most susceptible to change in the situation. It was as if under a condition of high stakes, one suddenly noticed every undetermined event which contributed to the defeat despite the even distribution of these for both sides. Here, too, there was a distinct sense that one should *not* change his Self-evaluation in the face of a single defeat. No one changed his estimates of his abilities, and only one man indicated he had less confidence following defeat.

This study suggested that we needed to learn more about reactions to personally important failures before trying to bring the situation under laboratory control. Obviously we could study reactions to academic failures. Here the best possibility seemed to be reactions to grades received after six weeks of the freshman year.

The Effects of Academic Failure in the Freshman Year

There is little doubt but most freshmen in college are highly motivated to receive at least passing grades during the first six-weeks' marking period. Since these are rather capricious grades, based on a small sample of the student's work and not highly predictive of the semester's grade, we knew that a larger number of failures would be given than would stand at the semester's end. Hence it seemed an excellent opportunity to continue our effort to learn more about the nature of the reactions to important failures in the life of the student.

Immediately following the receipt of the six-weeks' grades by the students, approximately every third person on the class list was asked by a student interviewer to fill out a questionnaire composed of items taken from the Sussman study at M.I.T. (1960) designed to measure both personal morale and esprit toward the school, plus items dealing with the importance of obtaining each grade level on the average, the estimated accuracy of the grade as a measure of academic accomplishment, the proportion of the grade due to Chance, and the highest, most probable, and lowest expected grade average for the semester. These items again probed the Self-estimate, Adequacy of the measure, role of Chance, and Importance of the task.

Dividing the group into the lowest Grade Point Average quartile, middle two quartiles, and highest quartile, we obtained the averages shown in Table 2.7.

Here we see that expressed loyalty to the school increases as the academic record decreases, while those doing well feel that their grades are a bit inflated, just as those doing poorly feel the grades are underestimates of their true value. Interestingly enough, the lowest quartile group seem to be using this "true" value as the base line for their aspirations for the semester, rather than their obtained grades, which serve as the Expected scores for the other two groups. The pattern becomes even more intriguing when we learn that the High group attributes 27 percent of their grade determination to Chance, the Mid group 24 percent, and the Low group only 16 percent. Thus we now find the role of Chance *positively* related to performance. This capacity for distinguishing between obtained grades and "true" grades seems to be reflected in Table 2.8, which gives the frequencies of response to the items asking for expressed satisfaction with "the way grades are going," and "the amount you are learning."

Apparently these failing students seized this opportunity to claim satisfaction in the face of public failure, while those doing well actually express the most dissatisfaction with their learning, although they profess satisfaction with their grade standing. Successful students also attach the most importance to averaging middle B grades over the four years, and this may be an important fact. The general effect of these ratings of each grade average is to say that they will settle for nothing less than honors grades, while the Low group will settle for "average" grades.

TABLE 2.7

Group Averages	Morale[a] Score	Esprit[b] Score	"True" Average	Semester Average		
				Highest Possible	Expected	Lowest Possible
High GPA (84.0) N = 23	16.0	17.5	83.1	86.5	83.5	78.5
Middle (77.2) N = 37	14.8	18.5	79.2	82.6	78.7	73.5
Low GPA (70.1) N = 18	15.1	19.3	73.6	78.2	74.2	69.6

[a]$F = 3.65$, $p < .05$.
[b]$F = 3.46$, $p < .05$.

TABLE 2.8

	Honors High	Pass Mid	Pass-fail Low
"...the way grades are going"			
Satisfied	19	15	3
Dissatisfied	4	22	15
$X^2 = 18.96, < .001$			
"...the amount you are learning"			
Satisfied	12	23	14
Dissatisfied	11	14	4
$X^2 = 2.82,$ n.s.			

In summary, it appears that those experiencing early academic failure in the freshman year reacted to it by asserting that they do not have long-range expectations of honors-level work, that grades underestimate their learning (about which they feel satisfied), and that they do not think chance factors produced the low grades. On the other hand, the successful students do profess an interest in an honors-level performance, but think their grades may be on the high side, are due more to chance than the Lows assert, and are not entirely satisfied with the amount they are learning. This latter pattern almost suggests an unwillingness to test fate by taking full credit for an excellent initial academic record. In effect, those failing have distinguished between grades, about which they feel dissatisfaction, and learning, about which they feel fine. This splitting of the incentive properties of the situation is predicted by current attitude change models for stress conditions (see Brown, 1962).

These findings seem to fit into our work at the intermediate level of ego-involvement with failure. The students who are failing refuse to devalue themselves to the point of agreeing that their grades are accurate measures but, unlike the failing quiz team, are not ready to attribute the burden of the outcome to Chance. Partly, of course, this reflects the realities of the classroom situation where several opportunities to perform contributed to the grades, and some classmates were doing well.

The second surprising finding came with the most successful

students, who did tend to devalue their performance in the face of success and who were most prone to attribute grade success to Chance factors (27 percent). If standing in the upper third of one's class constitutes a positively reinforcing condition, this hardly seems an appropriate reaction. Here it appears we may have happened upon a condition of success surrounded by anxieties of loss, uncertainty, or temporariness which are alleviated through these responses. Again, we are impressed with the multifaced pattern of reaction to achievement failure and success.

This study also reveals the importance of having pre-experience measures, since one of its serious limitations comes from the absence of base-line measures gathered at the start of the semester. It is always possible to argue that the group differences we found were present before academic success or failure occurred. When we have asked academic aspiration items at the outset of the semester we have not encountered students who predict they will fail or even perform in the lower third of the class. They expect to do at least average work. Yet there is no question but that pre-task measures are most valuable. With these considerations in mind the Public Speaking Study was designed.

The Effect of Failure in a Test of Public Speaking

In searching for an achievement situation of moderate importance which would provide some estimate of experience, value of the outcome, and a credible task we turned to the test of public speaking held by the Department of Speech to award exemption from the one-semester requirement in the sophomore year. The format, by which students nominated themselves to give the test speech, were tested individually before an audience of testees, and received the judge's verdict at the end of the hour, was ideal for the purpose. We were able to require that they fill out question booklets when they first signed up for the test, when they arrived at the test room, immediately following their individual speeches, and following the verdict. Thus we were able to get a running account of self-estimates, performance estimates, and key variables surrounding the situation.

The Ss were 124 second-semester freshmen, with control data gathered from 84 of the 150 members of the class who chose not to try for exemption. The Ns reported in Tables 2.9 to 2.12 vary with the completeness of the data return. The Control data gathered on a random basis consisted of the same personal-history sheet initially filled out by the testees, with the item concerning passing the test taken as a hypothetical case. The questions used and their time of administration was as follows.

At the time of registration (Q1):

1. I intend to take the public speaking test. _____
2. Approximately how many hours of preparation do you *intend* to spend on your speech? _____
3. State in a few words the most important consequences for you, personally, of passing this test.

Immediately prior to the speech (2):

1. In a few words describe your primary reasons for taking this test, and how you prepared for it.
2. Describe your background of public speaking experience. (courses, debate, dramatics, addresses, etc.)
3. Circle the number on the Importance Scale below which indicates how important you feel public speaking ability is to *you*.
   LOW   1 2 3 4 5 6 7 8 9 10 HIGH
   IMPORTANCE   AVERAGE   IMPORTANCE
4. Approximately how many hours have you spent in preparing your speech?
5. What kind of performance do you expect to give?

(Q2-2)

5. In general terms would you describe your public speaking ability as compared to other members of your class as:
   _____ superior to most
   _____ better than average
   _____ average
   _____ worse than average
   _____ inferior to most
6. Success on this test has at least three consequences. Using the ten-point scales indicate your feeling about each of these consequences, where 1 represents Low importance and 10 represents High importance.
   a. Relief from taking the public speaking course, per se.
      LOW   1 2 3 4 5 6 7 8 9 10 HIGH
   b. Opportunity for lighter course load or elective.
      LOW   1 2 3 4 5 6 7 8 9 10 HIGH
   c. Receive an expert's judgment of your speaking ability.
      LOW   1 2 3 4 5 6 7 8 9 10 HIGH
   d. Indicate the degree of importance that you personally attach to public speaking ability.
      LOW   1 2 3 4 5 6 7 8 9 10 HIGH

Just prior to the speech (Q3):

Answer this question before giving your speech.

1. Your speech will be judged by Mr. Allen using the four categories given below. Check off the judgment you expect to receive.

    FAIL   BARELY FAIL   BARELY PASS   PASS

    _____   _____   _____   _____

After speech and before the verdict (Q3a):

2. How do you feel about your performance?
3. Check the outcome you expect.

    FAIL   BARELY FAIL   BARELY PASS   PASS

    _____   _____   _____   _____

Following the speech, post-verdict (Q4):

Your speech is judged to be:

    FAIL   BARELY FAILING   BARELY PASSING   PASS

    _____   _____   _____   _____

Please answer the questions on the following pages.
1. How do you feel about this verdict?
2. In general terms would you describe your public speaking ability as compared to other members of your class as:
    - _____ superior to most
    - _____ better than average
    - _____ average
    - _____ worse than average
    - _____ inferior to most
3. Indicate your feeling about the three consequences below using the ten-point scales as before.
    a. Relief from taking the public speaking course, per se.
        LOW 1 2 3 4 5 6 7 8 9 10 HIGH IMPORTANCE
    b. Opportunity for lighter course load or elective.
        LOW 1 2 3 4 5 6 7 8 9 10 HIGH IMPORTANCE
    c. Receive an expert's judgment of your speaking ability.
        LOW 1 2 3 4 5 6 7 8 9 10 HIGH IMPORTANCE
4. Indicate the degree of importance that you personally attach to public speaking ability.
        LOW   1 2 3 4 5 6 7 8 9 10 HIGH IMPORTANCE

Non-testees—Controls (Q5):

1. Describe in a few words your reasons for choosing *not* to take the proficiency test.
2. Describe your background of public speaking experience. (courses, debate, dramatics, addresses, etc.).
3. Had you chosen to take the test what kind of performance do you think you would have given?
4. In general terms would you describe your public speaking ability as compared to other members of your class as:
    - _____ superior to most
    - _____ better than average
    - _____ average

—————— worse than average

—————— inferior to most

5. Success on this test has at least three consequences. Using the ten-point scales indicate your feeling about each of these consequences where 1 represents Low importance and 10 represents High importance.

 a. Relief from taking the public speaking course, per se.

      LOW   1   2   3   4   5   6   7   8   9   10   HIGH IMPORTANCE

 b. Opportunity for lighter course load or elective.

      LOW   1   2   3   4   5   6   7   8   9   10   HIGH IMPORTANCE

 c. Receive an expert's judgment of your speaking ability.

      LOW   1   2   3   4   5   6   7   8   9   10   HIGH IMPORTANCE

6. How many hours of preparation for this test do you feel are necessary? —————

7. What verdict would you have gotten?

 FAIL   BARELY FAIL   BARELY PASS   PASS

 ———————   ———————   ———————

8. Indicate the degree of importance that you presonally attach to public speaking ability.

      LOW   1   2   3   4   5   6   7   8   9   10   HIGH IMPORTANCE

In general public speaking is rated a skill of moderate Importance, the exemption from the Public Speaking course was an outcome of at least moderate value to these subjects, and the test by a single five-minute address was accepted as a reliable measure as a matter of necessity if nothing else. The students understood that no other technique could be used. It seemed to us we had a situation where we could carefully follow the course of the subjects' reactions to the experience of success or failure in this situation.

Results. Our initial comparison of Speakers and Controls shows the generally greater self-estimated degree of competence and involvement with public speaking of the Speakers.

There seems to be a fair tendency for the Speakers to rate themselves as average or above in speaking ability and to report secondary school backgrounds consistent with such ratings. The Speakers also asserted that relief from the Public Speaking requirements was more important to them, as was getting an expert's opinion of their ability, than did the Controls. The next table gives the average ratings on a ten-point scale for Relief from coursework; opportunity to take an Elective; Expert's Opinion; and Importance of Public Speaking Ability.

As expected, the Speakers had a higher proportion who expected to pass the test (80 percent) than the hypothetical estimate of the Controls (50 percent). In summary, those nominating themselves

TABLE 2.9. SELF-RATED SPEAKING ABILITY

	Superior	Above Average	Average	Below Average	Inferior
Speakers ($N = 119$)	16	46	41	5	1
Controls ($N = 82$)	2	20	39	20	1

$X^2 = 38.99$, $p < .001$

	H.S. Course, Prizes, etc.	H.S. Course, Extra-Curric.	Drama, Addresses	Little Experience	No Experience
Speakers ($N = 124$)	6	39	40	33	6
Controls ($N = 84$)	1	19	21	30	13

$X^2 = 11.74$, $p < .02$

TABLE 2.10

	Relief[a]	Elective	Expert's Opinion	Importance (1st)
Speakers (N = 119)	7.0	7.7	5.1	8.2
Controls (N = 82)	5.9	7.5	4.4	8.0
		Z = 6.29		

[a]$p < .001.$

for the test do seem to be more confident, express more involvement, and possess greater experience with the task than do those not volunteering.

When the Speakers arrived at the test room they immediately filled out the second questionnaire. The above items from that booklet were accompanied by a follow-up item concerning the number of hours actually spent in preparation compared with those originally estimated at sign-up time. Although the average estimated preparation time was 2.6 hours, the reported actual time was 3.2 hours. The stability coefficient for the time estimate was + .74 (prod. moment). This rather high stability suggested that the preparation measure might also have some other relationships, and we were interested to find subsequently that it had none. The Importance scale was given twice in this booklet to provide some estimate of immediate test-retest stability following a series of items asking the subject to anticipate his performance. Although there is fair stability (prod. moment, r. = + .64), many of the subjects who initially used high Importance values of eight, nine, or ten lowered these on the second rating. As a result the average rating shifts from 8.2 downward to 7.6 merely as a result of filling out the intervening questions—prior to the task itself. The first rating of Importance had a significantly positive relationship to the initial estimates of one's ability as a speaker (r. = + .29). Finally a classification of the adjectives used in response to the question of what kind of a performance they "expect to give" shows that 45 percent use positive terms, e.g., "good," "better than average," "interesting;" 36 percent used neutral terms, e.g., "fair," "average," or "OK"; and

19 percent used negative terms, e.g., "poor," "mediocre," "terrible."

It appears that a small group of subjects had decided to take the test despite a willingness to say they did not feel they had even average ability, did not expect to do well, and attached little importance to speaking ability. In other words, the incentive of released time had attracted them, but just as we found in the quiz team data, it is not likely that failure to pass the test would produce a sense of subjective failure on the tested attribute. In general the group of Speakers appear committed to doing well on the test and there was reason to hope that failure will be personally experienced as an unpleasant surprise.

At the appointed time the subjects appeared in groups of ten to have their speeches judged.* As each student became the next speaker, he was given the four categories to be used by the judge and asked to estimate what he would receive. The remaining presentation of data will incorporate all of the information gathered in the remaining questionnaires. Table 2.11 shows the manner in which the group became progressively divided by their answers and the verdict, with the dependent variable of Self-evaluation as a Speaker on the bottom line.

We first see that only 22 percent of the subjects predicted failure immediately prior to speaking, but in fact 51 percent did fail. Some hint that this may not have come as a surprise appears in the finding that 41 percent of the optimists stated they had done poorly upon completing the speech, 74 percent of them now expected to fail, and 62 percent of this latter group did, in fact, fail. Approximately the same level of accuracy was achieved by those thinking they had done well and stating they expected to pass. Of these, 57 percent did in fact pass. But these proportions leave us with sizable groups whose expectations were thwarted by the verdict. If we follow each of these groups to the dependent variable we quickly see that it was so stable following the verdict, that the most we can say is that the majority of those changing came from the group who originally expected to pass, while those expecting to fail show practically no movement whatsoever. However, the pattern of movement among the expected-pass group divides across both pass and fail verdicts, and gives little hint of a major effect. It was our expectation that Self-evaluation might show little change, but of

* We wish to acknowledge with thanks the cooperation of Professor Ronald Allen, under whose supervision the work was done.

TABLE 2.11. EXPECTATIONS, FEELINGS, AND REACTIONS IN A TEST OF PUBLIC SPEAKING ABILITY ($N = 122$)

Before the speech: of subjects who expect to

	Pass 95				Fail 27				
After the speech: of subjects who feel they did	Well 56		Poorly 39		Well 23		Poorly 4		
and now expect to	Pass	Fail	Pass	Fail	Pass	Fail	Pass	Fail	Total
Received a verdict of:									
Pass	30	0	6	11	3	9	0	1	60
Fail	23	3	4	18	3	8	0	3	62
Change self-evaluation on public speaking									
Up	3 0	0 0	1 0	1 1	1 0	1 0	0 0	1 0	9
Down	2 4	0 0	2 1	1 3	1 0	1 0	0 0	1 0	13
No change	25 19	0 3	3 3	9 14	2 3	8 8	0 0	0 3	100

course predicting absence of change is an awkward thing. Perhaps it is best to observe that the test-retest coefficient for the Self-evaluation scale is + .79, which seems quite high.

Would there be a change on the other attributes of the situation? We had not offered the subjects an opportunity to attribute the outcome to Chance, and we are left with the three incentives—to be relieved from the requirement, to make room for an Elective course, to get an Expert's opinion, and finally the estimate of Importance of public-speaking ability. Neither the Importance scale nor the Elective scale shows changes following the speech and the verdict. However, those who expected to pass and passed show a considerable increase in value placed on receiving an Expert's opinion, 51 percent moving up, 44 percent remaining the same, and 5 percent moving down; while the group that expected to fail and passed showed increases on Course Relief with 52 percent moving up, 38 percent remaining the same, and 10 percent moving down. The test-retest coefficients for all five scales appear in Table 2.12.

TABLE 2.12. CORRELATIONS FOR RATINGS
TAKEN BEFORE AND AFTER
PUBLIC SPEAKING PERFORMANCE VERDICT (N = 120)

	Prod. Moment
Self-evaluation	+.79
Relief from public speaking course	+.815
Reduced course load	+.84
Receive expert's opinion	+.85
Importance of public speaking	+.77

We saw earlier that the average Importance scale value had dropped from 8.2 to 7.6 prior to the speech, but the average value following the verdict was 8.0, indicating that no pattern of change is reflected in response to this scale.

Summary. This study had been designed in the hope that it would involve a high level of motivation on the part of the students, and because it seemed likely a sizable group would suffer an unexpected defeat in a genuine test of an important ability, hence giving us an opportunity to observe their reactions to such failure. The data support our hopes. The students who volunteered for this test had a good opinion of themselves for the attribute being tested, and a sizable group did suffer an unexpected defeat. However, it appears that following the performance itself a majority of these correctly anticipated that their performance would bring failure, and said so on our reaction sheets. *None of the failing groups show shifts on any of the scales provided.* The only significant shifts found came for those who passed. Those who had expected to pass increased the value of receiving the Expert's opinion, i.e., the value of independent confirmation of their own estimates of their ability; and those who had expected to fail increased the value of the chief incentive itself, relief from the public-speaking-course requirement.

Once again, as with the quiz show situation and the freshman six-week grades, it appears that the degree of involvement with the situation was sufficiently great to block the possibility of change in conception of the self and of the situation for those who failed. The effect of positive reinforcement for those passing was to heighten the value of the incentives originally preferred. On the basis of these findings it appears that the laboratory studies reporting changes in self-evaluation involve very low levels of motivational engagement vis-à-vis the task itself. We had not collected fantasy materials with our field groups, but the stability of the self-report material suggests that changes in fantasy could be expected. A tentative hypothesis is also suggested, i.e. *that the effects of achievement task failure on self-evaluation vary inversely with the degree of self-involvement.* The more one's self-image is involved, the less likely one is to concede or accept as personally relevant a failure outcome. This suggests that in those achievement situations having the greatest value, only a successive string of failures will finally produce a shift in structuring of the self-situation matrix. One thinks immediately of the aging professional athlete who cannot accept personal responsibility for failures in the field.

These studies made it clear to us that the antecedent conditions for engaging subjects would have to carry the burden of proof that a negative outcome implied subjective failure. That is, only under low motivation can we demonstrate the effects of failure on subjective report indices. The chief exception to this statement in the data is the role played by the Chance scale. Apparently failure in important tasks may be accompanied by an increased estimate of the role played by Chance in the outcome, but as we saw, the direction of movement may vary.

A second important finding of these studies is that fear of failure, when based on a realistic judgment that failure is highly probable because one is not competent for the task, does not seem to create a subjective sense of failure. Thus the distinction between fear of failure consequences, which are themselves valuable to the subject, and fear of the experience of failing becomes an important one. It is the latter that should have a generalized effect on fantasy and should be most important as a motivational component of the personality.

Finally, the very fact that neither failure nor success did have noticeable effects on self-estimates suggested the need for a program of research covering motivation, performance, and cognition in the achievement situation. Thus, further study of the motivation-cognition relationships would require experimental manipulation of performance itself, while studies of the effects of either area on performance requires "control" of the other. Assuming that fear of failure is not socially endorsed and overtly taught by society, and given the forces of self-preservation from failure acknowledgment, we concluded the effects would be best measured at the fantasy level. Since this requires laboratory control techniques we set out to produce such situations. We had to do this without having established the usefulness of operations beyond those of objective failure. Such objective failure conditions can be produced by reporting false norms, rigging the apparatus score counter under control by the *E* or selectively sampling those whose failure is bona fide. We have used all of these techniques in our subsequent research. However, it seemed wise to continue our efforts at devising self-report measures following objective failure in the hope that some type of inquiry might prove sensitive to failure effects. The studies reported in the next chapter reflect these considerations.

CHAPTER 3

Measuring Fear of Failure

THE DEFINITION OF MOTIVE DISCUSSED EARLIER IS TOO BROAD TO specify the type of operation best suited to the measurement of motives. The reintegration of an expected change in affect by a situational cue does not suggest which method might be best suited to testing for its presence. It might be that the expected change in affect is fully conscious and hence quite reportable by the S if he is so inclined. However, he may have little or no awareness of the suggestion, so that only an indirect device, such as a projective test similar to the Thematic Apperception Test, provides material indicative of such expectations. Trying to frame self-descriptive questions bearing on a particular motive area so that the S can report his motivation has not proved successful with n Ach according to McClelland (1958). The trouble seems to be that if a motive is socially desirable it attracts endorsement from those not having it, while if it is socially undesirable confession is avoided. Edwards (1954) has tried to avoid this issue by producing a forced choice questionnaire. Forcing the S to choose between descriptions of equal desirability is thought to heighten the probability of learning what the S thinks of himself. However, this may merely produce a more refined measure of what the S thinks he ought to think. Not that such a measure may not have motivational implications. After all, what we think we ought to do is in fact what we do most of the time. For instance, it is our impression that students low on the n Endurance, n Achievement, and n Autonomy scales are less likely to display sustained and productive engagement in academic studies. But it is also a fact that n Ach as measured by Edwards had shown

61

no correlation with n Ach as measured by McClelland's system (1958) nor do they seem to correlate with the same behavioral variables, i.e., the fantasy n Ach material does not predict general academic involvement at the college level.

Assuming that this relationship between the direct and fantasy measures of n Ach represents a general condition, we did not feel the need to conduct studies of both approaches to fear of failure simultaneously. We were interested in studying the effects of fear of failure as displayed in fantasy, and the construct validity of such a measure. It was for this reason that we set out to search for a fantasy measure of fear of failure that would extend the assump- tions and practices used for the study of n Ach.

Our studies of the failure experience had left us feeling that we would have to depend on arousal operations alone for the assertion that failure expectations would be suggested to some Ss. The task we chose was a test of reading speed using the Controlled Speed Reader. This is a device that presents a line at a time through a scanning window which can be increased in speed. The task is novel and involving, and clearly involves an important ability. The design of the speed reading failure experiment followed the lead of Raphelson and Moulton (1958). We used three groups: a Con- trol group which wrote stories under neutral conditions, an Experi- mental (I) group which wrote stories prior to the failure experience induced by the task, and an Experimental (II) group which wrote following the failure experience. To further define the amount of experienced failure, a questionnaire was given at the end of the experiment which was designed to permit self-report of attitudes and feelings toward the task experience. Finally, the task itself per- mitted calculation of the actual amount of success and failure. Thus we could designate Ss by their performance, self-report about the performance, and experimental condition.

Hypotheses. On the basis of previous work we expected that the amount of n Arch in the stories would be

> greatest in the control group;
>
> next greatest in the expected failure group;
>
> least in the failure group

This follows from the assumption that increasing fear of failure would interfere with expression of n Arch. We also hoped that the failure group would report feeling most badly about their perform- ance, and that Ss in that group who were doing most poorly on the task would report feeling worst.* Finally, we wished to search the contents of the stories for categories of failure imagery which might distinguish between the conditions.

Procedure. The Ss for the experiment were male college students enrolled in the introductory course in psychology. The control and failure groups were run in four laboratory sections in the same week by the same E (Birney). Subsequently another group was run under Expected Failure conditions.† This group consisted of 23 male students taken at random (every fourth name from the directory) from the sophomore class.

The test session consisted of three tasks. For the control group, (N = 19), the order of tasks was TAT, speed-reading task, and reaction questionnaire. For the three experimental groups (total N = 65), the order of tasks was speed-reading, reaction questionnaire, and TAT.

Description of Tasks. For the Failure groups the purpose of the speed-reading task was to induce a feeling of failure. This was accomplished by using a Controlled Reader.‡ This device exposes one line of an article at a time with an illumination area approximately one-third of a line wide which scans from left to right. It is possible to adjust the speed of exposures to provide reading speed requirements from 200 to 1000 words per minute. By beginning at a low speed and progressively increasing the speeds it is possible to run beyond the reading speed of all Ss. The task tends to "involve" Ss immediately and produces a high sense of frustration as the speed increases.

The TAT was administered using the standard instructions of McClelland et al. (1953) and an especially selected group of pictures described as office headache (man with head in hands bending over his desk in a barren office), nepotism (man at file looks through door at two men smiling and shaking hands with a third), baseball (the ball is between pitcher and batter), man at mirror (man with hand on tie before mirror), football (loose ball with two

---

* We had found that expressions of feeling about performance in the public-speaking experiment had shown some validity when compared to judged performance. Therefore we shifted our self-report to the affective dimension.

† We are indebted to René Steuer, who ran this group.

‡ Educational Development Laboratories, Inc., 75 Prospect St., Huntington, N.Y. The figures mentioned in the instructions represent the machine setting which, multiplied by the words per line—from five to seven—determines the speed rate.

players diving for it), and commencement exercises (rows of men in gowns with a corner of the speaker's platform).

The reaction questionnaire consisted of four questions asking how the *S* felt he did compared to others, his feelings about his performance, his estimate of his general reading speed relative to others, and whether he felt this task was a good estimate of reading speed.

Administration of Instructions.

Task 1. "The first task today will be a measure of the speed with which you read. I have here a controlled speed projector. With this projector I can vary the speed with which the sentences are displayed. We will start with slow speeds and move to progressively faster ones until your thresholds have been reached." (Demonstrate with the clutch disengaged to show the nature of the stimulus.) "Any questions?"

"Take the answer sheet marked Reading Speed. Notice there are three columns. We will start with column 1, which will be a series of ten practice trials. Now here is what I want you to do. You will be shown five lines per trial. Your task is to put down *one complete line out of the five*. As soon as you think you have one complete line begin to write. At the end of the five lines I will shut off the projector and give you time to attempt a line, since we will score both word elements and sentences. Any questions?

"All right; here is trial 1 of the practice period." (Run off ten trials of five lines each with speed settings of 50, 55, and 60. Three trials per setting.)

"You will notice that in this practice run the speeds were increasing slowly. Now we begin test trial 1. Here the speeds will be progressively increased through the fifteen trials." (Run off fifteen trials of five lines each at speed settings of 65, 70, 75, 80, 85, three trials per speed.)

The Effects of Conditions on n Ach

Following the paradigm used in past research with these motive measures, we might have expected that arousal of failure feelings would be accompanied by an increase in n Achievement. McClelland et al. (1953) report a higher mean n Ach score under Failure arousal conditions. However, Atkinson (1960) has argued that the presence of increased amounts of failure imagery (however defined) should produce less n Ach, unless of course the failure indices are varieties of the n Ach categories. In this experiment we used the usual n Ach scoring system (C), and Table 3.2 shows the effects of our conditions on n Ach.

There is a progressive drop as the failure experience moves from expected to experienced. However, this drop is reversed within the

TABLE 3.1. THE EFFECTS OF TASK EXPERIENCE
ON EXPRESSED FEELINGS ABOUT TASK PERFORMANCE

QUESTION	N	RESPONSE CATEGORIES		p
1. *How did you feel about your* *performance?*		*Very badly;* *badly*	*O.K.; good;* *very good*	
Control group	19	4	15	
Expected failure				
slow	11	5	6	
fast	12	1	11	<.002
Failure				
slow	33	21	12	
fast	31	6	25	<.001
2. *How well do you think you* *did relative to the others?*		*Much below Avg.;* *below Avg.*	*Average;* *above; much* *above Avg.*	
Control group	19	4	15	
Expected failure				
slow	11	5	6	
fast	12	2	10	<.003
Failure				
slow	33	16	17	
fast	31	5	26	< .05
3. *Do you feel this is an ade-* *quate measure of your* *reading speed?*		*No*	*Yes*	
Control group	19	9	10	
Expected failure				
slow	11	5	6	
fast	11	10	1	<.003
Failure				
slow	25	14	11	
fast	31	23	8	< .20

Failure condition when we contrast the *S*s by the actual success experienced on the task. Both sets of differences are reliable for the extreme groups. McClelland has made the distinction between arousal techniques which say to the *S*, "This is an achievement situation," and those which say "This is an achievement situation in

Fear of Failure

TABLE 3.2. THE EFFECTS OF
FAILURE AND EXPECTED FAILURE ON n ACH

Condition	N	Mean n Ach	Sigma	Diff.	t	p
Control	19	4.83	7.73			
Expected Failure	22	2.36	5.12	2.47	1.18	n.s.
Failure	63	1.70	5.08	3.13	2.01	.05
slow	33	2.96	5.12			
medium	16	.50	4.65	2.46	1.59	n.s.
fast	14	.07	4.63	2.89	1.78	.10

which you have (succeeded, failed, both succeeded and failed)."
It has been the former which produced increases in n Ach while
the latter showed a high level of n Ach with internal shifts of
categories emphasizing blocks to success under the failure condition. At any rate, our drop in n Ach would imply that the failure
in this experiment has produced a withdrawal from achievement
fantasy and something else has taken its place.

The Relationship Between Reported Feelings and Motive Score

Within the Failure group three Ss reported feeling good when
in fact they had done poorly, and four reported feeling badly when
in fact they had done well. The remaining 56 Ss gave reports consistent with their actual performance though no scores were available to them. If we assume that the expressed feeling reflects degree
of arousal, the expected relationship between n Ach and feelings
with the task is not obvious, since feelings of success might be
associated with either high or low n Ach. Table 3.3 gives the
answer frequencies to these questions. For n Ach we find the
middle group of "feel O.K." or "don't care" is low with both the
"badly" and "good" groups higher. The difference between the
middle group and the negative-feeling group is reliable.

Thus we find the n Ach is associated with aroused feeling (positive or negative) on the task. This suggests that the characterization
of n Ach as a socially acceptable motive may be correct.

Extensive analysis of the stories was performed on a variety of
imagery categories and subcategories of the n Ach system. *None of
these led to a coherent system for scoring fear of failure which*

TABLE 3.3. COMPARISON OF THREE GROUPS
DIFFERING IN EXPRESSED FEELING ON n ACH

Motive Scores	Groups by Expressed Feeling		
	"Badly" (N = 25)	"O.K." (N = 29)	"Good" (N = 9)
Mean n Ach	3.08	.45	1.88
Sigma	5.44	3.96	6.11
Diff. "badly" – "O.K."	2.63		
t	2.01		
p	.05		

showed any differences between the conditions under which the stories were written. Still it was the feeling of those reading the stories that differences did exist which for some reason we could not conceptualize. At this point the experiment had to be judged a failure as an effort to produce an arousal of failure effects sufficient to influence the fantasy materials, despite the supportive evidence of observation and subject report that the experience of failure or impending failure had been present.*

Although we felt that these conditions had "worked" we decided that the criterion group method might give greater assurance that we were dealing with a fear of failure motivation. We turned to a level-of-aspiration task. There is an extensive literature to show that unrealistic and exaggerated patterns of aspiration are given by some Ss when faced with the demand to produce aspirations for a laboratory task, and the usual interpretation of these patterns has been that they reflect avoidance motivation on the part of he Ss. We set out to contrast stories written by Ss using realistic aspiration strategies with those written by Ss of unrealistic aspirations. That is, findings from these studies suggested that Ss who placed their goal expectation below their actual performance were cautious and defensive, and were even sometimes characterized as "fear of failure." In a study by Sears (1940), the author characterized the negative-discrepancy group (goal expectation below performance) as having

* Recalling that in the Reaction Time and Steadiness experiments we had encountered changes in Self and derogation of the task, these results suggested that the arousal level in the earlier situations may have been too low to effect fantasy.

a depressed desire for achievement and a fear of failing in the eyes of others. As far as we can tell, there has been no further investigation of this "social reactivity" characteristic of fear-of-failure people. On the other hand, Atkinson and Litwin (1960) have suggested that low n Ach should be related to fear of failure. In a series of experiments designed to test this theory it was found that a low-n-Ach–high-TAQ pattern did behave more or less as the theory suggested that fear-of-failure Ss should.

Schachter (1959) in a recent study of affiliative behavior noted that fear (in his case, fear of pain) was positively related to the desire to affiliate with others. His findings appear to support the clinical and qualitative characterizations of Sears; people who are afraid seem to be concerned about their relationships with others. Taking a step further, we might expect that people who are fearful of failing in an achievement situation would score high on a measure of affiliation.

To summarize, we hypothesize: if Ss having negative discrepancy scores in a level of aspiration situation are, in fact, "fear of failure" motivated, they should have low n Ach and high n Aff. If we found this pattern, as well as the unrealistic LA's, we could place confidence in the group as a fear of failure group.

One last statement should be made before describing the study and the results we obtained. Level-of-aspiration measures have not in the past been successfully related to independent motivation or personality variables. Trends have been noted, but few statistically significant differences have been found (Ricciutti, 1954).

The Darts Study

Subjects. The Ss were 53 male undergraduates who were required to participate in an experiment as part of their regular course load.

Procedure. The task was a slight modification of a simple dart game. Instead of the usual concentric circles, there was only a six-inch target mounted two feet in front of a blackboard. The effect of such a target was to accentuate the distinction between hitting and any kind of miss, near or far.

The Ss came at different times, as they were to engage in the task individually. They were given five trials. For each trial the S threw 20 darts from a distance (chosen by the S) ranging from 4 feet to 30 feet from the target. After each trial he was asked a number of questions. The two which will concern us here are the following:

1. How many darts do you think you would get into the target if you were to throw 20 more darts from that line right now?
2. If you were to throw 20 darts from that line, how many hits would you have to get in order for you to feel pleased with your performance?

Answers to the first question permitted us to calculate the classic discrepancy score. We use the term "classic" because it has been the one generally used in level-of-aspiration studies. It is the difference between actual performance and what the S expects to get on the next trial. In the following tables it will be referred to as D_1.

Answers to the second question permitted us to calculate a discrepancy score which has not been used in previous published research. It is the difference between what the S expects to get and what he would have to get in order to be pleased. We felt that the "pleased-expected" distinction might prove valuable because it was getting at a relationship between objective estimate and wish goal. In a sense, then, we were getting a fantasy response in a level of aspiration situation which might stand a better chance of relating to the fantasy measures of achievement and affiliation. In the following tables this discrepancy score will be referred to as D_2.

The McClelland modification of the Thematic Apperception Test was given to the Ss prior to the level of aspiration task. The Ss met in four groups of approximately twenty each. The TAT was administered under standard instructions. Six pictures were used: the four usually used for n Ach, plus a picture of a man in a barren office and one of a man looking into a mirror fixing his tie. The TAT was scored for n Ach using McClelland's scoring system (1953) and for n Aff using Shipley and Veroff's scoring system (1952).

Thus, for the purpose of this report, we obtained four indices on each S. Two were motivation measures, and two were LA discrepancy scores. It is important to state at this time that the relationship between the two motivaion measures, n Ach and n Aff, was — .03; in other words, there was no relation. Furthermore, there was no relation between the two discrepancy scores, correlation being + .08. Apparently Ss who defended themselves one one dimension did not do so on the other. We will return to this point after the results are presented.

Results. The distributions of both discrepancy scores were fairly normal. Our first step was to divide each distribution into three groups—zeros and negatives, low positives, and high positives—and to see if they distinguished themselves on the motivation measure. Table 3.4 presents the results for the breakdown on the classic D (actual score from expected score). There are three points to note in this table.

1. The Neg group is lowest on n Ach and highest on n Aff.
2. The LPos group is the highest on n Ach.
3. The HPos group is midway on n Ach and the same as the LPos group on n Aff.

The largest difference occurs between the Neg and LPos groups on n Ach but this difference is significant only at the 10 percent level. These results are in line with previous findings and are in the expected direction. The fact that we did not obtain significant differences is also in line with previous results.

Table 3.5 represents the results for the breakdown on the fantasy-discrepancy score (expected from pleased). Although this score is not correlated with the classic D score, we note similar results on the n Ach and n Aff measures.

Although the differences are not as great as we would wish, they are improved. The difference between the Neg and LPos groups on n Ach is significant at the .08 level, and on n Aff at the .10 level. The difference between the Neg and HPos groups on n Aff is significant at the .04 level.

It was at this time that we became interested in the patterning of n Ach and n Aff for the three strategy groups on each of the two dimensions of level of aspiration. It struck us that we had unintentionally offered the Ss two different ways of defending themselves if they were so inclined, and that having made use of one strategy of defense it was not necessary to use the other as well. In short, once having decided on one method of defending themselves against failure, they permitted themselves to act normally on the other dimension. Thus, if they said they expected to get a score lower than the one they actually got, they could, without trepidation, say they would have to get a score higher than they expected in order to feel pleased. On the other hand, if they placed their pleased score below their expected score, they could, without fear, place their expected score above their actual score. This line of thought seemed consistent with the notions about defense mechanisms in

TABLE 3.4. N ACH AND n AFF FOR THREE STRATEGIES BASED ON D_1 (EXPECTED SCORE MINUS ACTUAL SCORE)

	n Achievement			D_1 p value	n Affiliation			D_1 p value
	Neg and Zero	Low Pos	High Pos		Neg and Zero	Low Pos	High Pos	
N	11	29	13	Neg vs. LP .10	11	29	13	n.s.
Mean	.64	2.90	1.38		4.45	2.86	3.00	
S.D.	2.82	5.36	3.13		2.88	3.13	2.90	

TABLE 3.5. N ACH AND n AFF FOR THREE STRATEGIES BASED ON D_2 (PLEASED SCORE MINUS EXPECTED SCORE)

	n Achievement			D_2 p value	n Affiliation			D_2 p value
	Neg and Zero	Low Pos	High Pos		Neg and Zero	Low Pos	High Pos	
N	13	29	11	Neg vs. LP .08	13	29	11	Neg vs. LP .10
Mean	.31	2.76	2.27		4.77	2.97	2.09	
S.D.	3.36	4.80	4.55		3.36	3.00	2.20	

general. That is, people have favorite defense mechanisms and do not defend all across the board. At least this reasoning permitted us to believe we understood why there was no positive correlation between the two D scores.

The next step was clear, and Table 3.6 shows what happens to n Ach and n Aff when the six groups are combined in a three-by-three table.

TABLE 3.6. MEANS ON n ACH AND n AFF
FOR THE SIX STRATEGY GROUPS COMBINED
(CELL *N*s SHOWN IN PARENTHESES)

D_2 (Pleased Score Minus Expected Score)	D_1 (Expected Score Minus Actual Score)					
	n Achievement			n Affiliation		
	Neg and Zero	Low Pos	High Pos	Neg and Zero	Low Pos	High Pos
Neg and Zero	—	0.0	.17	—	5.0	4.5
	(1)	(6)	(6)	(1)	(6)	(6)
Low Pos	.11	4.38	2.25	4.67	2.25	1.5
	(11)	(16)	(4)	(11)	(16)	(4)
High Pos	—	2.0	2.67	—	2.14	2.0
	(1)	(7)	(3)	(1)	(7)	(3)

The first thing that strikes one as one looks at this table is that so long as an *S* scores Neg on one dimension, regardless of what he does on the other, he is low on n Ach and high on n Aff. Apparently what was suggested has indeed occurred. If an *S* has expressed his fear of failure by engaging in a defensive strategy on one dimension, he scored low n Ach and high n Aff, even though he might be low positive and, therefore "normal" on the other.

However, direct your attention to the means of the groups that are either LPos on the classic D score or LPos on the fantasy D score. By considering the LPos group on one dimension and then looking at the three strategies on the other dimension, regardless of whether we start with the classic D score or the fantasy D score, we note the same patterns of n Ach and n Aff. Thus, if we take the LPos group on the classic D score and distribute them on the fantasy D score, we note that the Negatives are low on n Ach and high on n Aff, and that the LPos are high on n Ach. We can now understand why the differences on n Ach and n Aff, using only one D score, were not very significant. The differences between the Neg and LPos groups, both on n Ach and n Aff, were depressed because the LPos group included Neg and HPos people on another dimension. If fear of failure is expressed by cautious strategies in a level-of-aspiration task, then the so-called normals, as defined by their LPos scores on one dimension, actually included fear-of-failures as defined by their Neg and HPos scores on another D score dimension. Table 3.7 represents the final analysis.

TABLE 3.7. n ACH AND n AFF FOR SUBJECTS
WHO ARE LPOS ON ONE DIMENSION AND
NEG, LPOS, OR HPOS ON THE OTHER.

	n Achievement			p value	n Affiliation			p value
	Neg LPos	LPos LPos	HPos LPos		Neg LPos	LPos LPos	HPos LPos	
N	15	16	11		15	16	11	
Mean	.07	4.38	2.09	.05	4.8	2.38	1.91	.05
S D	3.04	5.37	4.72		3.37	2.76	2.35	

Each category refers to *S*s who are LPos on one D score but who are also Neg, LPos, or HPos on the other. The differences between the Neg-LPos and the LPos-LPos groups on both n Ach and n Aff are now significant beyond the .05 level. We must admit to some difficulty in understanding the HPos group. On n Ach they lie midway between the Neg and LPos groups and do not differ significantly from either. On n Aff, although the HPos are lower than the LPos, the difference between them is of no consequence. If the HPos, like the Neg, are fear-of-failures, but are using a different strategy of defense—"no one could really expect me to achieve what I said I expected to achieve"—they do not distinguish themselves from the LPos on n Ach and n Aff. The fact that they are the lowest on n Aff, however, does agree with the findings of Sears (1940) who described the HPos as being least concerned about the bad opinions of others. However, let us ignore the HPos at this time and return to the Neg, who were our reason for doing this study in the first place.

The pattern that seems to be clear, and that we believe has been established, is the low-n-Ach–high-n-Aff for those who cautiously engage in a level-of-aspiration task. Whether fear-of-failure people avoid writing achievement stories because they are not achievement-oriented, or avoid thinking about achievement because of the anxiety generated by the possibility of failure, could not be determined at this time. This group first had to be identified by a measure that gets at fear of failure; then we would be able to see just how achievement-directed they were, and whether or not their achievement scores had been depressed by the fear of failure.

The Hostile Press Scoring System

We have said nothing to indicate how tentative we felt such data must be considered. Our analyses had carried us beyond the hypotheses, which were not sustained, the N's shrunk accordingly, and we could not be sure that the pattern made sense merely because we had evolved one sensible explanation in a post hoc fashion. Still there was another way to test whether the groups so isolated were motivated by a fear of failure. Again we set to work searching the stories of the contrasting groups for differences in imagery and content categories. This time the sense of difference was much stronger. In contrast with those using realistic patterns of LA the overwhelming impression the reader got was one of threat and despair. One of us (Birney), in reading the literature on content analysis, had discovered Innocentia's (1959) report that teachers rated as good or bad by students had distinguished themselves from each other on the TAT by writing stories whose themes concentrated either on active working heroes, as written by the "good" teachers, or heroes passively withdrawing or giving up, as written by the "bad" teachers. These seemed to be the qualities of our groups as well. At this point it was recognized that the fear-of-failure Ss were writing stories with what Murray (1938) had called Press, and threatening Press at that. Furthermore, the Press filled the story. That is, the central figures were not persons whose needs had been frustrated or blocked but people whose needs were in the service of adjustment to some threat which had appeared of its own accord. Turning back to the original development of the

Need scoring system, it now seemed that our treatment of the Press concept had been incomplete. If we follow Miller's (1944) conflict analysis, which postulates a sharply increasing fear gradient as one approaches a fearful situation, it seems reasonable to argue that an *S* whose fear is paramount would write a story of someone experiencing or avoiding some fearful situation.

Murray's Press concept may be either positive or negative. (Positive Press themes do not concern us at the moment though they may in the future also prove useful.) Our concern was negative or threatening Press, and here we encountered our second difficulty. Murray conceived of Press as being as specifically thematic as Need. But would we find it so—that is, would our *S*s tell Press achievement-failure stories? Every story in the experiment was scored for the nature of the Press where the Press was thematic, that is, where the action of the story dealt with someone trying to deal with a situation not created by his own needs but by someone or something else. (Nonthematic Press were rare.)

About twenty-five varieties of Press were found. They seemed to group themselves conveniently into three major groups. Abstractly we may label these "legitimate demands," "exercise of judicial power," and "catastrophe." The first refers to exhortations for success, avoidance of failure, efforts to teach, admonish, warn, or exhort. The second included arrest, trial, arbitrary use of power, reprimands for actual or alleged acts, and simple exercise of authority over the central figure in the story. The third category covered physical conditions, destruction of beliefs, vague, hostile situations described only as tragedy, loneliness, deprivation of loved ones, various forms of nonphysical attack such as personality analysis by psychologists, and any major assault on one's well being.

Since we had assumed that *S*s with low n Ach would show the greatest proportion of fear of failure, the next step was to contrast the low n Ach group to the high n Ach groups for these Press categories. The findings, presented in Table 3.8, are clear-cut. The first category, "legitimate demands," is evenly divided between the two groups. This is not surprising if we consider that stories in which the central figures react to the Press with achievement need and striving will get high n Ach scores. The second category, "exercise of judicial power," did not discriminate, nor did Press aggression (defined as a story begun by a hostile physical act against the central figure). But the low n Ach *S* group showed twice the

TABLE 3.8. A COMPARISON OF HIGH AND LOW
n ACHIEVEMENT GROUPS FOR INCIDENCE OF PRESS
THEMES CATEGORIZED AS LEGITIMATE DEMANDS,
JUDICIAL POWER, AND CATASTROPHE

High n Achievement $N = 120$ (24 Ss = 5 stories)		Low n Achievement $N = 145$ (29 Ss = 5 stories)
	Legitimate Demands	
7	P Achievement	4
0	P Failure	2
4	P Guidance	2
1	P Information	1
	Judicial Power	
6	P Authority	4
7	P Aggression	7
2	P Justice	4
5	P Reprimand	11
0	P Arrest	1
0	P Power	2
	Catastrophe	
2	Vague hostile environment	3
0	Negative interpersonal affect	3
1	Hostile personality analysis	2
1	Rejection	3
0	Shock	1
0	Undefined tragedy	1
0	Hunger	2
0	Belief destruction	2
0	Impending death	1
0	Vague loneliness	1

number of the remaining "power" Presses as the highs. The third category, "catastrophe," discriminated even more.

How, then, to put all of these various Presses into a scoring system? It appears that we are dealing, first of all, with stories of threat rather than need, and that the threats are expressed as retaliation or catastrophe. By using the other categories for scoring need themes, such as Instrumental acts, Goal anticipations, and Goal affects, in combination with Press Imagery, we get an estimate of the total preoccupation of the story writer with his Press theme.

At this point it seems wise to digress briefly for the benefit of the reader who is not familiar with the type of content analysis we are using. The model used in scoring n Ach reflects a sequence of need, action, affect, anticipation, and outcome. The story must have a narrative quality reflecting instrumental action. No use is made of inferences about identification of writer and story figures, symbolism, or, following Murray, the incidence of a priori codes or markers. To sustain the narrative the *S* is given a worksheet divided into four sections headed by the questions

    (a) What is happening? Who are the persons?
    (b) What has led up to the situation?
    (c) What is being thought? What is wanted?
    (d) What will happen? What will be done?

The first task facing the scorer is to read the story for the presence of Imagery. If this category cannot be scored no other scoring is done. Once Imagery is scored the story is reread for the presence of the additional categories. These categories are scored following careful definitions which must be stated. Ambiguous statements requiring inference or deduction by the scorer are *not* scored. Since it is impossible to catalogue all the ways that a particular theme may be expressed, the judgment of the scorer is important and acts as a source of unreliability. For this reason scoring is best learned where consultation with an expert scorer is possible.

In Appendix I we provide sets of stories with scores so the interested reader may practice scoring according to the categories which follow shortly. Finally, before describing the scoring system for Hostile Press, let us review the category terminology. Table 3.9 lists the full name, abbreviation, and a brief description of the categories used.

The use of + and — for I, Ga, and G reflects quality of expressed emotion and outcome of instrumental actions. This system

TABLE 3.9. DESCRIPTION OF
THE STORY SCORING CATEGORIES

Imagery	Im	Content validated as sensitive to arousal operations and showing thematic quality around which a narrative can be organized.
Need	N	Statements of need, want, wish, or in some contexts, hope for need attainment or press removal.
Instrumental Activity	I +, −	Action (successful or unsuccessful) by someone in the story toward the thematic goal.
Goal anticipation	Ga +, −	Anticipation of goal attainment or loss.
Goal affect	G +, −	Statements of emotional involvement, positive or negative, with the goal or action leading to it.
Blocks		Obstacles to goal related action of a personal or environmental nature.
Personal	Bp	
Impersonal	Bw	
Thema	Th	A point is scored if the story is free from achievement Imagery.

gives us a total of eleven scorable attributes. Each is scored no more than once, regardless of the number of times it appears in the story. This places the emphasis on the thematic completeness of the story.

The reader is now acquainted with the type of scoring system for which we were searching in our study of fear of failure. By adapting it to use with Press Imagery we are, in effect, adopting an instrumental avoidance model. The fantasied story deals with circumstances similar to those of an organism which suddenly finds itself standing on a shocked grid. It wants to escape, avoid, or seek relief. It takes action to do so with or without success. And it experiences affect appropriate to its condition.

With these statements of introduction to this type of content analysis let us now turn to the Hostile Press scoring system.

Hostile Press Imagery. The basic question in determining if Hostile Press Imagery is present is whether the story is about people *reacting* rather than energizing. However, to be scorable, the story must specifically fit one of the following criteria.

(a) *Reprimands for personal actions.*

This guy is in school and was drawing dirty pictures in his notebook. *Unexpectedly the teacher came up behind him and started looking over his shoulder.* He had been caught doing things like this before. Once he was taken up before the class and made to show his pictures. Obviously, aside from being embarrassed, he is worried because the next time that he was caught it was threatened that he would be sent to the principal. He will be sent to the principal and he will be sent to a private school which will help rid him of his dirty mind.

We are scoring the fact that being caught in this type of situation implies reprimand unless otherwise stated. The next story contains an explicit statement of the punishment:

Little Johnny is returning home from school. He is coming home in the middle of the day. He was sent home for talking back to the teacher. The principal has given him a note to give to his mother requesting a conference. Johnny is thinking he will be punished, but that his parents will never hear his side. That teacher is so strict. It isn't fair. *Johnny will be punished.* His mother will be chagrined when visiting the principal. His parents will never hear Johnny's side.

Notice that as yet we score all such references regardless of their placement in time—past, present, or future. Also, reprimands are scored only when they come from a superior. This may include a wife if she is clearly superior in the story. Self-reprimands are not scored."

Note especially that

(1) The superior must *clearly* be a superior in the story.
(2) Simple daydreaming is not a reprimandable situation.
(3) Pointing out to an inferior that he has made a mistake isn't necessarily a reprimand—it is often more of a correction. Instead we define reprimand as condemnation or reproachment. Specifically, in a case in which a boy does poorly on a test and is "made to do extra homework," there is no reprimand implied.

(b) *Legal or judicial retaliation for action or alleged action.* In general these stories are written to the Father-Son picture and deal with the central figure as defendant:

The young man is an Amherst College student sitting in a courtroom waiting for his case to come up. The bailiff is sitting in the background. *He had been arrested* for disturbing the peace, drunkenness, and assault. The man is wanting to get out of there as soon as possible without having any punishment. He is worried about his parents and if he will remain in school or not. He will sit there until the bailiff calls him. Then he will go up before the judge, be convicted and all his fears will come true. He will feel that his life has been ruined and proceed to ruin it.

The fact that some person's action is *against* the law or would be punishable by law is not enough for scoring; the legal or judicial action must actually be occurring in the story. It often involves police, arrests, judges, lawyers, or clients.

(c) *Deprivation of affiliative relationships.* The deprivation may occur through rejection by others, death, or simply "circumstances." A special case of this category is divorce, which is always scored *unless* both parties specifically deny that this caused an affiliative deprivation.

Man overcome by loneliness of life—looking out at its barrenness. The man has come to this city in search of independence. His loneliness has crept in on him. He's lost him family, his friends, the old life. He's thinking of how he stands. He needs very personal love—a girl—not a whore—a new life, inspiration, a feeling of going somewhere. I don't know.

Now the student (me) will use this picture to diagnose some of his problems. He is very lonely. *His mother has deprived him* of normal love. He can't talk to anyone. He is completely ostracized by his classmates. They have branded him. He can't understand why people are mean. He was always honest—until he found out that people weren't. He wants to describe specific instances but he has to go into the house soon. He will be very lonely for a long time. He is afraid to try because that is why people ostracize him. He doesn't want to be really noticed. He won't really try to become outstanding in any field.

This story is almost a perfect example of the web of associations which our present theory of fear of failure demands. Early rejection and deprivation of love lead to a perception of the entire world as one of hostility which in turn leads to adjustment through withdrawal and deliberate "failure" in achievement situations so as to avoid social contact.

Note that

(1) Usually family arguments cannot be scored.

(2) The threat of divorce is not enough for scoring. An actual divorce must occur, and only those statements which occur after the time of the divorce can be scored for further categories. E.g., if a man has had an argument with his wife and feels bad about it, and a divorce results, the G-category cannot be scored for "feels bad" because the Press of divorce has not yet been inflicted.

(3) The basis of this category is a *feeling* of *rejection*. Therefore if no divorce results but a husband "feels rejected by his wife," the story is scorable. However, the statements "is rejected by his wife" or "feels neglected by his wife" are not scorable because "is rejected" is not a statement of affect, and "neglected" does not necessarily show rejection.

(4) The "deprived" person need not have *had* an affiliative relationship which has been broken for deprivation of affiliation to exist, e.g., "a lonely bachelor" would be scored.

(5) Deprivation of affiliation must be between persons, e.g., a little boy who has lost his best friend, his dog, would not be scored; nor would break-offs in relations between countries be scored.

(d) *Hostile, vague environmental forces or physical conditions, violation of privacy, inducement to crime, destruction of beliefs, or any major assault on their well-being.* The story below was scored for its vague sense of environmental threat.

Oh God this is tough. I am sailing to hell on a popsicle stick. They won't let me in. Actually this is from writing this I mean but oh this *but the sky can't fall.* The world began and the floods came and then there was Noah smart bastard Noah was, but it really is worth it to be saved. Who wants to live in a zoo. Everything is being wanted by people who don't know what they want run, run, run, run, run, but he's tired. You lose. *St. Peter said No.* I laughed. I didn't want to anyway. Unreal, unreal, unreal, unreal, and stupid, fat St. Peter said no. What will happen. Bang, bang, bang, oh hell who cares.

In scoring the category "hostile, vague environmental forces" it is important to remember that *vagueness* or a large *number* of forces are criteria for scoring.

(1) Often the vague press has almost a paranoid quality. If the character makes any statement *against the world* (e.g., with "he's bitter about the world" we can assume a vague and scorable press). Note that the statement "he feels trapped" is not enough in itself to be scorable. A specific hostile environmental force, as a boy with a father who will not let him go to college, is not scorable because it fits neither the vagueness nor number criterion.

(2) If however, there are *many* specific hostile environmental presses present in the story, the category may be scored. An example of this is

> Everything has gone wrong at the office today. The man has a headache, can't work anymore, but doesn't want to go home to his complaining wife and screaming children. He's recently gone heavily in debt because of failure in a business venture.

(3) Hostile vague environment must be more than a temporary (afternoon, day, or week) downheartedness.

Violation of privacy is a seldom used category. It must involve a fairly powerful authority figure forcing an answer about something private. A statement that "people keep bothering him" is not enough. It is conceivable that a woman being forced to tell her age would be scorable.

The story below was scored for inducement to crime.

An older and younger man on the street. Not father and son. The older man is a casual and interesting acquaintance of the younger— *he is being introduced by him to heroin.* The younger man has been a typical sucker for slick talk and interesting products. He has done some borderline jobs—borderline between law and not—he is wondering how much he can trust the older man. The older man knows he'll be victorious. A client and a producer is wanted by the two. He will become an addict. He, the older man, will live comfortably on his many gains while the younger will die crossing a street.

The inducement-to-crime category can be scored if another person or persons are willfully trying to get the character to break a law. (Note that for every crime committed, something—perhaps hunger, adventure, bankruptcy, "circumstances"—has induced the character to crime, but we score only for deliberate inducement by people.) For the time being "crime" is being defined objectively as going against a government law—not church laws or individual moral standards. The character need not *submit* to the inducement for this category to be scored.

Finally here is a story of belief destruction.

This is a father telling his son that there is no Santa Claus for the first time in his life. This problem has been bothering the boy since last winter (it is now summer) when he waited up all nite, but never heard Santa's reindeer land on the roof. The father who has finally had to tell the boy, has just broken the poor boy's heart, because Santa was his conception of God. Since the little boy's religious beliefs have been shattered he will become an atheist, eventually start a new religion and become known in later life as the second Jesus Christ.

In scoring the destruction of beliefs category note that:

(1) A mere questioning of beliefs is not scored unless it is clear that some change results.

(2) The belief can be in various things, as for example, Santa Claus, religion, the profession of law. Such statements as "has lost all faith in himself" would be scorable but not "a father disillusioned with his son" because the meaning of the word disillusioned is unclear. However, Imagery would be scored if the father states "I believed my son was good but now I am disillusioned."

Major assault on well-being generalizes to figures close to the figure under press:

A young man is visiting an elderly friend of his. The elderly friend could possibly be his mother and the younger the mother's son. There has been a crisis in the family, therefore, the son came to visit his mother. His father has been struck with a heart attack and the young fellow is telling his mother the bad news. They are thinking of all the enjoyable experiences that they spent together when the boy was young. They want to recall those experiences and they want to be rid of the crisis. The father will become healthy again, and the family will be together again! and all will be happy.

The specifics of this last set of presses are admittedly vague but we might say that in a broad sense they constitute themes of a paranoid nature. Someone or something is trying to "get" the central figure in a story.

Nervous breakdowns are included in this category, since they are considered a major assault on well-being. However, a statement of psychological problems is not scorable unless something else is present.

Particulars regarding the major assault on well-being category include:

(1) Major assault is not scored for animals, only humans.

(2) Major assault must be *physical*, or *mental* (in the form of nervous breakdown or some other mental illness)., Bankruptcy, or a man's house being vandalized does not constitute a major assault.

(3) Senility and natural death as the result of old age are not scored as major assaults because they are part of a natural course of events. (Consider, however, that often a scorable "deprivation of affiliation" may result.)

(4) To qualify as a "major" assault, a sickness must be critical or severe. "Sick" or "pneumonia" alone would not be scored, but "very sick" or "exceedingly sick" would qualify because of the emphasis on the *degree* of the assault. Note, however, that a headache (or even a bad headache) is not scored. If a wife is sick, requires expensive medical treatment, and her husband is worried about her, a major assault cannot be scored because there is no comment on the degree of assault. Expense of treatment does not correlate with seriousness of illness, and worry is only a weak affect word. Major diseases (tuberculosis, pneumonia) may or may not be major assaults, depending on the elaboration or outcome of the story.

(5) Major assault can generalize only to family and close friends, not to a doctor unless he is part of the family or a close friend, too.

In addition to the above general categories, the following specific cases are scored.

(1) The character is *fired* from a job.

(2) He is *thrown* out of school or *flunks out* of school.

(3) Failure (in an achievement situation) with strong affect.

(4) All suicides (with inferred G-).
(5) Pain with affect.

There is often a question of how strong the affect with failure must be to be scored. "Disappointed," "frustrated," "worried," "concerned" are not strong enough, whereas "desperate" is usually strong enough.

The stories of this last category of imagery should not be taken to exhaust the possibilities. Rather, the general notion of catastrophic Press should be kept in mind as the guiding factor.

Imagery and all subcategories should be scored regardless of where they are found in the story, including the first and last lines. Statements written before an actual statement of the press can be scored only if *temporally* they followed the press. When there are two or more categories in one story scorable for Imagery, score the category which has the greatest number of subcategories. Remember too that one word or statement can be scored for more than one category and that both a G+ and a G— can be scored in one story, as can a Ga+, Ga?, and Ga—. However, Ir can be scored for + or — but not both.

Need Press Relief (N). The N category is scored when someone in the story being affected by Hostile Press makes an overt statement of Need for relief, withdrawal, or escape. The following examples are taken from the stories above.

Our friend does not want to go to the dentist tomorrow.
The man is wanting to get out of there as soon as possible without having any punishment.

Note that this category may be scored for persons on whom a major assault generalizes, e.g., a young boy *wants* his very sick father to get better. Also, one can assume Need if a short answer is given in direct response to the protocol question "What is wanted?", e.g., the response "Out." Other statements lacking a specific need word can also be scored, as for example, in the case where a ballet dancer breaks a leg and will be crippled (major assault) and exclaims "If only I could dance again!"

Instrumental Reaction to Press (I+ or I—). Ir is scored when the figure under Press is moved to take eliminative action against the Press, to withdraw from it, or to adjust to it. The author may attribute such actions to the figure under press. Ir may be scored

(+) or (—), depending on the outcome of the instrumental activity. The subcategory Ir? is not scored.

> The boy is wondering how he can convince father to let him marry the girl without being disinherited.
> [They] are attempting to blot out thought and reorganize their tissues.

Success or failure of the instrumental activity is not determined specifically by the final outcome of the *story*, but by the outcome of the instrumental activity relating to the specific *press* for which the story was scored, regardless of whether new presses occur at a later time. For example, if a worker is reprimanded by his boss and quits his job, he has escaped the specific press of the reprimand. It is immaterial whether he finds another job and is happy or becomes a drunken bum.

Affect Reaction to Press (G+ or G—). Affect (G) is scored when the figure under Press reacts with some statement of emotional feeling. Again, the author may attribute affect without the figure under Press making an actual statement. Usually this is negative since positive affect to Hostile Press would be quite rare. At the moment we also score positive affect resulting from instrumental reactions to the press since they are Press related.

> Obviously, aside from being embarrassed. . . .
> . . . has just broken the poor boy's heart. . . .

G— is always inferred from the occurrence of a suicide. G— is also scored for the bottom 10 percent of all possible outcomes for the figure under press.

To be scorable, words like "awful" must refer to how the person feels, not to what type of situation it is. Score "he feels awful about the situation," but don't score "it was an awful situation;" score "he felt humiliated" but not "he was humiliated."

"Worried," "mad," "bitter," frustrated," "nerves are shot," "can't bear the strain," and "guilty" all suggest affect.

Remember too that a major assault can generalize to family and close friends, and their affects are scorable.

The bottom 10 percent category is one which we have used *very conservatively*. It applies only in the case of suicides or if the character explicitly states that something is the worst of all possible things which could happen to him. Dying, death penalty, nervous breakdown, or mental illness is presently not scored because it is not clear at this time that we can infer affect in such situations.

Goal Anticipation (Ga+, Ga?, Ga—). Paralleling the Goal Anticipation category of Need (for Achievement) systems, this deals with expressed statements of relief or renewed or additional Press. Ga may not be inferred. Relief is scored + and renewed or additional press is scored —. Ga is not scored for a simple statement of "afraid of" alone.

. . . he is worried because . . . it was threatened that he would be sent to the principal. (Ga—)
He is wondering if the gangsters will ever stop blackmailing him. (Ga?)

This last statement is scored ? since neither relief nor additional Press is explicitly anticipated.

As in the need Achievement scoring system, anticipation may be done by the person under press, or any other person in the story.

If a boy is worried about his very sick father, "worried" would be scored for both G— and Ga— because it is clear that in this case "worried" is an anticipatory word connected with the Press.

Press Thema (PTh). For the present, *thema will be scored unless achievement imagery is present.*

Task Press Imagery. No mention is made of the task concept in this scoring system. Perhaps we need another word. The general notion would be one of undefined or unthreatening Press—hence unscorable—but related to our Press thema rather than to some stated Need. We might also wish later to distinguish between unrelated Press and unrelated Need stories. Below is an example of a story which is undefined Press and at present scored zero.

I am in class and rather disgruntled with the situation. The teacher has digressed into a relatively unimportant argument. I am wishing we could get back to the discussion which the teacher had started before the argument. The class will argue, I'll be bored and finally before the end of the class the teacher will try to tell us what he had planned to teach this period.

We have answered the question, What do the low n Achievement *S*s write? They write Hostile Press themes in which the central figures strive to escape, adjust, or overcome. There is no sense that these figures are trying to accomplish something of their own, to express themselves, or to get somewhere.

VALIDITY STUDIES

The utility of the Hostile Press (HP) score was tested by determining its relation to the level of aspiration indices. Table 3.10 shows the association of the HP score and cautious behavior on the LA tasks.

TABLE 3.10. A COMPARISON OF LEVEL
OF ASPIRATION (D_1) GROUPS ON HP,
n ACHIEVEMENT, AND n AFFILIATION SCORES

Level of Aspiration	HP	n Ach	n Aff
Neg or Zero (N = 23)	4.35	.35	4.61
Mean	4.35	.35	4.61
S. D.	3.52	3.15	3.21
Low Positive (N = 16)			
Mean	2.50	4.38	2.14
S. D.	2.27	5.37	2.75
High Positive (N = 14)			
Mean	3.00	2.21	1.93
S.D.	2.46	4.26	2.22
Neg vs. LP — p value	.01	.01	.04
Neg vs. HP — p value	.05	n.s.	.01

Both the HP scores and the n Aff scores show a positive relation to caution on the LA task, while the n Ach scores are negatively related. The point was made earlier that the n Aff was associated with caution, and so the obvious analysis of HP and n Aff scores was done. Total scores show only a low positive association, but the reason for this emerges in the analysis of Table 3.11.

Here we see that the three basic types of imagery scored under the n Aff system have differential relationships to HP scores. Actively stated need for Affiliation is negatively related to Press scores, while imagery of deprivation of affiliation or companionate activity is positively related.

TABLE 3.11. THE RELATIONSHIP OF HP SCORES
TO THE MAJOR TYPES OF n AFFILIATION IMAGERY

		Number of Subjects Showing *Affiliation Imagery at Least Once*		
		Need	Companionate	Deprivation
Hostile Press	High	7	10	11
	Low	12	6	6

		Total Affiliation Score	
		Low	High
Hostile Press	High	13	17
	Low	15	8

Now we had a scoring system and had found that it related our level of aspiration indices in a way which made sense. The next step in the validation of this instrument, following McClelland et al. (1953) was to see if we could effect an increase in scores through the technique of "arousing" the motive.

The Effects of Failure on HP

The motive-arousal procedure followed that first used by Mc-Clelland et al. (1953). Subjects were drawn randomly from the population of eighth-grade students to control for possible sampling bias. Pretest or matching of groups on TAT scores is not wise where the same pictures must be used in the experimental condition (1953, p. 193). The Ss were randomly assigned to Control and Experimental groups. The Control groups took the TAT under the standard instructions. The Experimental group first took a test in mathematics, received false norms which had the effect of failing them, and then took the TAT before any discussion of the mathematics test could take place. Following the experiment the procedures were explained in full. The purpose of this design is to permit a comparison of TAT scores for the group experiencing test failure with the group not so aroused.

Subjects. The subjects were eighth-grade males and females in a public school system. There were two groups of *S*s, 60 per group, evenly divided by sex; the 120 were randomly selected from the total eighth-grade population of the system.

Testing Procedure. Under the Neutral condition the *S*s were given the modified TAT task using the standard instructions and administration developed by McClelland et al. (1953). There were four pictures in the battery: two from the McClelland series (Father-Son, Boy in Checked Shirt), and two new pictures used to elicit HP (Man at mirror, Man at Desk).

The Aroused condition required that the *S*s first take a test of mathematics administered as follows:

E: "Allow me to introduce myself. I am [NAME] * from Bucknell University. We are here to do an experiment for the psychology department and would appreciate your cooperation.

"This experiment consists of two parts. The first part involves your taking a standardized mathematics test, which will now be given to you." (Pass out the tests.)

"Do you each have a copy? Please keep them face down until you are told otherwise. Does everyone have a pencil?

"This test has been given to 8th-graders in different parts of the country. You will have ten minutes to do as many problems as you are able to do in the allotted time. Both speed and accuracy are important; therefore, work as quickly and accurately as you can. In division, work out to as many places as are in the problem. Where there are no decimal places, work it out to one place.

"Are there any questions? Turn your paper over. Put your name in the upper left-hand corner. You may now begin."

(Ten minutes later.) "Stop. Put your pencils down."

Papers are exchanged with fellow students and are corrected by the students as the *E* reads the correct answers.

E: "Put the number answered in the left-hand corner of the paper. Put the number correct in the right-hand corner of the paper. Hand the papers back to the original owner."

(About two minutes later.) "Pass your papers forward."

"Norms for this exam have been standardized (explanation of this term) on an 8th-grade population all over the country. The average 8th-grade student, that is one who falls in the 50th percentile, is able to answer 13 problems and get 11 of these correct."

The *E* then thumbs through the papers and tells the *S*s that some got more right than they really did: "15-12," "16-12," etc. In effect the *S*s were told they should have got more right than any of them had actually got. Thus each *S* was left with the impression that he had failed in this group.

E: "Part II of this experiment involves your writing stories about pictures you will see.

* We are indebted to Kenneth Altschul and Grace Kirkpatrick, who acted as experimenters.

"This is a test of your creative imagination. A number of pictures will be projected on the screen before you. You will have twenty seconds to look at the picture and then about four minutes to make up a story about it. Notice that there is one page for each picture. The same four questions are asked. They will guide your thinking and enable you to cover all the elements of a plot in the time allotted. Plan to spend about a minute on each question. I will keep time and tell you when it is about time to go on to the next question for each story. You will have a little time to finish your story before the next picture is shown.

"Obviously there are no right or wrong answers, so you may feel free to make up any kind of a story about the pictures that you choose. Try to make them vivid and dramatic, for this is a test of creative imagination. Do not merely describe the picture you see. We know what is in the picture; do not tell us that, but tell a story about it. Are there any questions? If you need more space for any question, use the reverse side."

Results of Experiment I. It was our hypothesis that the experience of failure on a mathematics test would produce increased amounts of HP. Table 3.12 shows the nature of the discrimination

TABLE 3.12. THE EFFECT
OF FAILURE AROUSAL ON HP SCORE

	Hostile Press		
	Below Median	Above Median	
Failure	19	41	60
Neutral	41	19	60
	60	60	120

$\chi^2 = 7.70$, $p < .01$.

effected by the increase in HP score under Aroused conditions. The data for the college students were obtained by scoring the protocols of the reading-speed experiment for HP. Now we find confirmation for our sense that differences between the groups did exist in the stories. Here we see the resulting chi-squared value reaches $P < .01$.

Inspection of Table 3.13 shows that the major increases in categories are those of a negative outcome or tone. The scoring system reported here embodies some modifications which account for the increase in I+ and I− found with the eighth-grade students.

TABLE 3.13. PERCENTS FOR
EACH CATEGORY SCORED UNDER CONTROL
AND AROUSAL CONDITIONS FOR TWO EXPERIMENTS

	COLLEGE STUDENTS (Reading Speed Exp: Failure condition)			EIGHTH-GRADE STUDENTS		
	Moderate	*High*		*Low*	*High*	
Arousal of Fear of Failure						
N	30	33		60	60	
No. of stories	180	198		240	240	
No. of HP Imagery	32	49		60	93	
Percent of HP Imagery	17.8	24.7		25.0	38.7	
Percents of			*Diff.*			*Diff.*
N	28	36.7	+8.7	20.	29	+9
Ga+	2	2	0	5	2	−3
Ga−	9.4	24.4	+13.0	.5	13.9	+13.4
G+	1.4	1	+4	0	2	+2
G−	18.8	42.8	+24.0	23	33.3	+10.3
I+	1.4	3.6	+2.8	0	20.4	+20.4
I−	−	−	−	0	15.0	+15.0
I?	31.	16.	−15.0	38.	5.	−33.
Th	62.5	75.5	+13	96.6	82.7	−13.9

The original practice of combining doubtful and negative instrumental outcomes yielded a negative predicting category, and the current analysis shows that this seems to be true of the doubtful category alone. The change in the instrumental plus (I+) category was to include withdrawal or escape as positive instrumental actions.

The data in Table 3.13 do not permit tests of significance because category tallies are not independent of the imagery category, and we cannot assume independence for each of the four stories written by each *S*. However, the findings of mean differences in group scores are given further illumination by the data in Table 3.13, since they provide some assurance that total scores are responses to shifts in several of the scoring system categories. Initial validation studies of n Power (Veroff, 1957), and n Aff (Shipley and Veroff, 1952) show about the same discrimination for their categories.

The demonstration that changes in antecedent conditions designed to produce fear of failure in achievement situations cause increases in the HP imagery of stories is taken as support for the contention that such imagery may reflect motivational disposition. McClelland et al. 1953 argued that such fantasy could be used as motivational signs if it could be shown to be sensitive to situational cues used by the culture to motivate persons. However, as we have seen, the discovery of the nature of the shifting imagery is an empirical task. Just as n Ach finally became defined as competition with a standard of excellence, so we are reporting that the same procedures have led us to define fear of failure imagery as assault on the well-being of the central figure by reprimand, affiliative-loss, natural forces, or personal failure.

We have shown that efforts to induce failure have resulted in increased HP imagery. Does this mean that Ss writing such imagery under neutral writing conditions will respond with fear-of-failure motivation when placed in achievement situations? Not necessarily. Our task is to learn when such co-respondence does occur. We know that imagery is overdetermined by picture cues, momentary personal conditions, task irrelevant cues, and the like. Research on the achievement motive has illustrated the tortuous manner in which construct validity must be attained by dozens of tests of hypotheses, some confirmed and some unconfirmed.

The remainder of this book is devoted to such study. Once we established the psychometric characteristics of the HP scores, we then set out to test for its value in illuminating fear-of-failure motivation. Our guiding assumption is that Ss who display HP imagery to pictures of tasklike situations where evaluation is possible will display avoidance behavior in achievement-task situations. However, we are by no means clear about the many varieties of avoidance we will encounter, and much of what follows reflects our effort to become more precise in our definition of avoidance behavior. Certainly there is no reason to expect that it will prove less complicated than the task of defining achievement behavior itself.

Reliability Characteristics of HP

It has been customary for scorer reliabilities to approximate +.90 with sufficient experience with the systems for n Ach, n Aff, and n Power. The HP measure has proved to be equally easy to master and score reliably. Students placed in study groups can usually reach agreement with the scoring manual of +.75 after one week, and by two weeks the +.90 criterion is met.

It has been possible to gather successive stories from the same *S*s over an extended period of time. A sample of 60 male college students shows that the HP coefficient of stability is +.40 for a two-week interval and +.55 for a six-month interval (N = 85 males; all coefficients calculated by the product-moment coefficient). These levels of stability also compare with those reported for n Ach and provide sufficient stability to permit research comparison of group differences. Obviously these stabilities are too low to permit use of the measure for individual personality assessment purposes.

Psychometric Correlates of HP

Given a number of self-report measures dealing with anxiety, one obvious first step is to do a series of correlation studies to determine the relationship of HP scores to these standardized measures. Table 3.14 provides a summary of the coefficients found since the HP system was constructed.

We could not be sure that avoidance imagery would fail to show a high correlation with self-reported anxiety simply because n Ach approach imagery has failed to correlate with expressed achievement interest. For one thing many of the items on anxiety questionnaires focus on the way the respondent views the world, rather than on his view of himself. Thus his TAT imagery might be similar to endorsement of various statements of perceived threat in the world. For another, it is possible that despite our failure to elicit statements of feelings of failure, the use of anxiety questionnaires rests on the willingness of the *S* to state that he usually suffers from feelings of anxiety in test situations, and this kind of statement might correlate with the presence of HP imagery. There is evidence for this possibility in the table.

Although HP proves unrelated to other current measures of fear of failure, such as the combination of French n Ach and TAQ used

TABLE 3.14. CORRELATIONS BETWEEN HP SCORES AND PERSONALITY TESTS

Measure	Citation	N	Sample	Statistic	Relationship	Comment
F Test (total)	Teevan-Hartsough	22	MCS	Spearman rho		
Scale C					+.23	Authoritarian tendencies
A–S					-.21	Conventionalism
A–A					+.28	Authoritarian-Submission
A–I					+.11	Authoritarian-Aggression
S–S					+.05	Authoritarian-Intraception
P–T					+.11	Superstition-Stereotypy
D–C					+.39*	Power and Toughness
P					+.67**	Destructive-Cynicism
S					+.27	Projectivity
					-.15	Sex
Allport Vernon SV						
T					-.05	Theoretical
E					+.34*	Economic
A					+.29	Aesthetic
S					+.06	Social
P					-.24	Political
R					-.02	Religious
MMPI	Teevan-Hartsough	49		Spearman rho		
F					+.29*	
K					-.20	
Hs					-.18	Hypochondriasis
D					+.25*	Depression
Hy					-.07	Hysteria
Pd					+.05	Psychopathic deviate
MF-m					-.10	Masculinity

Measure	Author(s)	N	Scale	Method	Statistic	Sig.	Description
Pa						-.07	Paranoia
PT						+.24*	Psychasthenia
Sc						+.23	Schizophrenia
Ma						+.25*	Mania
Si						+.39**	Introversion
L						+.30*	Lie
Ascendent-Submissive						-.10	
James-Phare						+.36*	External control
Manifest Hostility Scale						+.38*	Projected hostility
n Ach-n Aff (TAT)							
HL vs. LH	Teevan-Thomas	56	MHS	Chi Squared	3.80,	$p < .01$ neg.	
n Ach-TAQ							
HL vs. LH	Teevan-Thomas	43	MHS	Chi Squared	5.18 neg.,	$p < .05$	
n Ach	Birney-Rolf	99	MCS	Product Mo.		-.28	Negative relationship to n Ach
n Ach	Birney-Stillings	140	MCS	Product Mo.		-.19	Negative relationship to n Ach
Achievement Anxiety Test							
Debilitating	Birney-Rolf	99	MCS	Product Mo.		-.04	No relationship
	Birney-Stillings	140	MCS	Product Mo.		+.08	No relationship
Test Anxiety							
Questionnaire	Birney-Stillings	76	MCS	Product Mo.		+.11	No relationship
				Mean Diff.			
IPAT	Teevan-Stamps	56	MCS	High vs. Low HP			
Manifest Anxiety					$p < .065$	n.s.	L > H
Latent Anxiety						n.s.	
Defective Integration						n.s.	
Paranoid Insanity					$p < .05$		H < L
Guilt Proneness					$p < .01$		H < L
Frustration Tension						n.s.	

$*p < .05$
$**p < .01$

by Atkinson, and the Haber-Alpert Achievement Anxiety Test, it does show positive relationships to Siegal's Manifest Anxiety Scale, and James-Phare's Scale (predecessor of the Rotter Internal-External Scale), and a sensible pattern of MMPI, IPAT, and F subscales. Essentially these scales reflect the tendency to see the world as a hostile, powerful, disorderly place that produces depression and requires authority. For the most part the order of relationships is low positive, and not so high as to permit the conclusion that the TAT score is a duplicate measure. But these findings do suggest that the HP measure reflects a generalized avoidance reaction rather than a reaction to achievement-test anxiety alone. One possibility suggested by this interpretation is that this form of fear of failure is focused beyond the immediate consequences of task outcome. As we shall see, this interpretation is developed more fully as we proceed. Some support is provided by the finding that the correlation between HP and the Scholastic Aptitude Test Verbal score is —.039 or 117 male college students. The range of SAT scores was approximately 500 to 800. This absence of relationship contrasts with the negative relationships reported for the TAQ by Sarason (1960).

CHAPTER 4

Decision, Performance, and Motivation

GIVEN SUCCESS IN MEASURING FEAR OF FAILURE WITH THE HP score, our next step was to establish its construct validity. Although the studies reported in this and subsequent chapters were not carried out in the order here presented, we will offer them within the structure of our achievement-situation taxonomy for purposes of organization. In this chapter we present our findings regarding the role that fear of failure (HP) plays in the engagement, choice, and performance phases of participation in achievement settings. In general we shall be trying to answer the question, What can we expect of a high HP when he is faced with an achievement situation? Materials from other theorists, other data, and our own theorizing lead us to expect that he will orient himself in such a way as to avoid failure. There are many ways in which this can be done, depending partly on the individual personality and partly on the situation. We believe the situation to be the most important variable and shall attack it first.

The first decision a person must make when faced with an achievement situation is whether or not to become involved at all. The high-HP person is oriented to avoid failure. Since he cannot fail if he does not take part, we expect that he will avoid achievement situations whenever he can. Therefore, Hypothesis 1 states that if we ask that he volunteer for the achievement task and our request does not engage any other motivations, we expect him to refuse. If we force him into the situation but allow him a wide latitude of choice as to what he will do, we hypothesize that he may do any of several things which allow him to avoid failure. He may defend himself against a realization of failure by arguing that chance had a lot to do with the score; that he had a bad day; that the task is not a good one; that he didn't really try, etc. He may also set his level of aspiration so high that "no one could succeed" or so low that he knows he can exceed it. The idea here is that he will take part in the task at some level (because we do not allow him to refuse) but will find some way of avoiding the implications of his performance (as does the student who is physically in class but psychologically far away). Finally if we force the subject into the task and we set the performance standards of the task in such a way that none of these defenses is possible, then we hypothesize that the only way he will find left to avoid failure is to work hard and to "succeed," and that in this kind of situation the high-HP will do just this. The prime example here is the school situation.

We have carried out a series of researches designed to test the hypothesis set forth above. We begin with the situation in which the subject is asked to volunteer for a task which engages (as much as possible) only the motive to take part in the achievement task.

Teevan (1963), using as subjects all the males in an introductory psychology class, asked for volunteers for a task which he described as being "an achievement task in which you will have a chance to find out how good you are at throwing darts." He stressed the achievement nature of the task and the fact that the subjects would have access to the data so that they would be able to tell how well they had done in relationship to each other. The subjects were told that this had nothing to do with course grades and nothing to do with the instructor; that he was merely collecting the data for some other researcher and had no personal interest in it at all. In this situation it was expected that persons with high HP would *not* volunteer. The HP instrument had been given to the class approximately one month before the volunteers were asked to participate. As Table 4.1 shows, there was a significant difference between the number of high- and low-HP persons who volunteered in this situation. A median break on HP was used.

As part of the same experiment a second class in introductory psychology was asked for volunteers for the same task. Again the task was described as an achievement task in which the subjects would have an opportunity to see how well they did. In addition, however, they were told that the experiment was very important for the instructor and that he would appreciate it if people would

TABLE 4.1. VOLUNTEERS AND NON-
VOLUNTEERS FOR ACHIEVEMENT TASK VS. HP SCORE

		Volunteers	Non-Volunteers
Hostile Press	High	7	21
	Low	19	9

$X^2 = 10.34$, $p < .01$.

volunteer. The attempt here was to test the idea that the high-HP
person was person-oriented rather than task-oriented and that, with
the affiliation motive added, he would volunteer as much as would
the low-HP person. In other words, the prediction here followed the
null hypothesis.

TABLE 4.2. VOLUNTEERS AND NON-
VOLUNTEERS FOR COOPERATION TASK VS. HP SCORE

		Volunteers	Non-Volunteers
Hostile Press	High	9	15
	Low	12	12

$X^2 = .76$, $p < .05$.

Table 4.2 gives the results of this part of the experiment. Again
a median break was used on HP. The prediction is borne out: there
is no difference between high and low HP when affiliation is added
to the motivation for the task. This study suggests that high-HP
subjects are oriented towards people as rewarding rather than
towards situations as rewarding. It also suggests that the HP persons
will avoid situations which they perceive as achievement-oriented if
we allow them to do so. But what will they do if they are not allowed
to avoid the task? The next step, following the set of hypotheses set
up at the beginning of this chapter, is to find out what the high-HP
person will do when he is in a situation which cannot be avoided,
but in which he has a measure of control over the standards within
the task.

We have already reviewed the manner in which level of aspiration (LA) studies have contributed to theorizing about fear of

failure; and we have seen that it was the stories of *S*s with defensive LA patterns which led to the development of the HP scoring system. The subsequent validation of the system using experimental arousal of failure experience gives independent evidence for the validity of the HP score, but it follows that cross validation of the LA relationships as soon as possible would open up a valuable area for study. Therefore we chose to use LA measures in our study of the HP person who is constrained to perform in an achievement situation.

To set up this kind of situation, Thomas and Teevan (1964) used 105 male *S*s between the ages of 13 and 15 from a small-town high school. The principal apparatus was a commercial product, the Electronic Rifle Range by Emenee, Inc. This consists of a photoelectric cell mounted in a swinging pendulum and a rifle which shoots a beam of light. When the light strikes the cell, a light on the target lights and a buzzer sounds. The subjects were given the HP measure and, one week later, the rifle task. Each *S* performed individually. *S*s were instructed to aim at the center of the target and told that they would have five trials of twenty shots each. Before each trial they were asked for a level of aspiration, in terms of what they "expected to get." At the end of his trials, each *S* was asked how he felt about his performance and whether he felt the electronic rifle range was a good test of his ability to hit a moving target.

It was hypothesized that the high-HP *S* would (1) have defensive scores on the LA measure (D) and (2) show defensiveness on the questions having to do with how he felt about his performance, and on whether or not the rifle range was a good measure of his ability to hit a moving target. To test Hypothesis 1, the LA scores were divided into a defensive group (negative, zero, and extremely high D scores) and a nondefensive group (low and moderately positive D scores), and *S*s were assigned to groups according to their majority D scores. Table 4.3 shows that persons with high HP are more apt to defend than are the lows, thus bearing out the hypothesis.

Tables 4.4 and 4.5 set forth the data necessary to test the second hypothesis. Table 4.4 shows that persons with a high-HP score tend to feel that the rifle range is *not* a good measure and Table 4.5 suggests that the high-HP person is not as pleased with his scores as is the low.

TABLE 4.3. HP AND LEVEL OF ASPIRATION

		LA	
		Defensive	Non-Defensive
Hostile Press	Low	11	39
	High	21	25

$X^2 = 5.01, \ p < .05.$

In the above study the subject who was trying to avoid failure did so by setting unrealistic levels of aspiration and by casting aspersions on the task. In the eyes of an outside observer his behavior was "irrational" since the outside observer would expect him to be trying to "succeed." Atkinson's model (Atkinson, 1957) of achievement motivation has focused attention on risk-taking behavior and predicts that *S*s with fear-of-failure motivation will show an "irrational" pattern of risk taking, preferring extreme risks of

TABLE 4.4. RELATIONSHIP OF HP TO DEFENSE
QUESTION: "DO YOU THINK THE ELECTRONIC RIFLE
RANGE IS A GOOD TEST OF YOUR ABILITY TO SHOOT
AT A MOVING TARGET?"

		Rifle Range Question	
		Defensive	Non-Denfensive
Hostile Press	Low	4	52
	High	14	34

$X^2 = 7.29, \ p < .01.$

long shots or sure things. Although LA behavior is analogous to risk taking, we wished to study risk preferences directly to further establish the validity of the HP score. It is an empirical fact that some *S*s display preferences for extreme risks in choice situations. Would those with high HP scores be more likely to display this behavior? If so, the case for the validity of the HP measure would be further strengthened.

To test for this relationship, Hancock and Teevan (1964) drew

TABLE 4.5. RELATIONSHIP OF HP
TO DEFENSE QUESTION: "HOW DO YOU FEEL
ABOUT HOW WELL YOU DID TODAY?"

		Affect Question	
		Defensive	Non-Defensive
Hostile Press	Low	26	22
	High	35	12

$X^2 = 3.43$, $p < .07$.

sixty male subjects from a high school sophomore class. The Ss were stratified on the basis of course of study (college preparatory, commercial, etc.) and were randomly selected within each category. To test risk-taking behavior, battery-operated boxes with numbered push buttons, counters, and dials were used. Each box had a red light which went on when one of the correct buttons was pushed, and showed the odds chosen and whether the S won or lost on a given trial. Each S was seated in front of a box and told that he would take part in an arithmetic task. He was told that a $\frac{1}{6}$ probability meant that only one of the six buttons would light the light while a $\frac{5}{6}$ probability meant that five of the six buttons would light the light. The payoffs were reciprocally equated to the odds: thus a $\frac{1}{6}$ probability of success paid fifty cents, $\frac{2}{6}$ paid forty cents, etc. This procedure holds Incentive constant. The S could push only one button per trial and could change his odds choice after each trial. Immediately after the task the HP measure was given. The task was scored on the basis of "irrational" moves in odds after success or failure. If an S succeeded and moved to easier odds he was given a point for "irrationality." He was also given a point if he failed and moved to harder odds, or if he moved all the way from $\frac{1}{6}$ to $\frac{5}{6}$ or the reverse. In general, any behavior which departed from the "rational" way of doing things was given a point. The "irrationality" score for each subject was added and a chi-square was computed taking the risk-taking ("irrationality") score vs. the HP score, both using a median break. Table 4.6 gives the results of this breakdown.

Persons with high HP make "irrational" choices on a risk-taking task. These findings led Hancock and Teevan to conclude that

TABLE 4.6. HP AND RISK-TAKING SCORE

		Risk-Taking	
		Low	High
Hostile Press	High	19	11
	Low	11	19

$X^2 = 4.27$, $p < .05$.

though the fear-of-failure subjects seemed to be making irrational choices, these choices appear rational if it is remembered that the high-HP subjects are attempting to avoid failure rather than attempting to succeed.

We have already expressed our sense of caution regarding the interpretation to be placed on the behavior of the fear-of-failure *S* in risk-taking situations. The choice of the mid-range of probabilities is usually the best payoff strategy, though it was not so in the Hancock and Teevan experiment. The HP *S* might not understand how to maximize payoff, or he might understand but wish to defend himself against evaluation by using an "irrational" set of choices that signify nonparticipation. Birney and Rolf (1965) argued that the latter pattern is facilitated when the HP person can adopt a "game" set toward the task. They set out to control the game-cue variable by devising two risk-taking tasks having identical payoff formats, but differing in their alleged meaning to the *E*. They hypothesized that the HP *S*s would show irrational, optimistic risk preferences in the situation permitting the game set, and pessimistic, irrational risk preferences in the situation designed to eliminate game cues. This form of the hypothesis reflected the belief that the HP person wishes to avoid involvement at all costs. The *S*s were 113 male college students.

They wished to test the idea that one way to reduce the effects of failure is to take the attitude that the task is "only a game" and hence one can act more irrationally than one would if the consequences were a serious threat to the *S*. The implication is that the fear-of-failure *S* knows the rational way to deal with the task, but fearing that such strategy will lead to failure, redefines the situation so as to permit the use of irrational behavior.

Following a suggestion by Burdick (1965), the game task consisted of testing the ability of *S*s to predict their success in guessing the location of a particular card under conditions of known probability. The non-game task used the same format but different materials, and the *S*s were instructed that the *E* would interpret their performance as a sign of their personality structure.

In order to assure that all *S*s did, in fact, know the rational odds for success, the procedures required that the answer sheet contain blanks in which the *S* had to record the chances for success for each trial. A description of the first task follows:

The *Star-Odds* task consists of ten sets of cards having ten cards per set. For each set the *S*s are told there are either 1, 3, 5, 7, or 9 stars printed on the reverse side. The *S*s were told:

1. There will be 10 trials.
2. For each trial, 10 cards will be placed on the board in the front of the room. Each card will have a number.
3. For each trial some of the cards will have a star beneath them while the others will be blank.
4. On each trial you will be informed of the number of cards that have a star.
5. On some trials you will win a point if you choose the card with a star. On other trials you will lose a point if you choose the card with the star. If you pick a card that is blank, you will neither lose nor gain a point.
6. On each trial you will be told whether you will win or lose a point if you choose the card with the star.
7. On each trial you will select one card and write its number on the designated line.

The trial card format was as follows.

1. Do you expect to choose a card with a star?
    YES —————— NO ————
2. How confident are you that your expectations will be fulfilled? Using the scale below *circle* the number which most closely corresponds to your degree of confidence.

1	2	3	4	5
HIGH CONFIDENCE	MODERATE CONFIDENCE	SOME CONFIDENCE	LITTLE CONFIDENCE	NO CONFIDENCE

3. Choose a card and write its number on the line.

Fear of Failure

No information was given the *S*s about their trial success or failure, thus eliminating feedback effects of the strategies used. The request for confidence level was used to provide a more refined measure of risk preference. The *S* who strongly believes he has chosen the correct card under odds of 1 to 10 should receive a higher score than one who expresses little confidence about the same choice. By combining the odds and confidence measures as shown in Table 4.7, we generate a score distribution ranging from optimism to pessimism with the rational score set equal to zero.

TABLE 4.7. METHOD OF SCORING STAR-ODDS TEST

	\multicolumn{5}{c}{*Odds for Picking a Star*}
	1/10	3/10	5/10	7/10	9/10
A					
Win "Yes"	+5	+4	+3	+2	+1
"No"	−1	−2	−3	−4	−5
Lose "Yes"	−5	−4	−3	−2	−1
"No"	+1	+2	+3	+4	+5
B	*No*	*Little*	*Some*	*Moderate*	*Great*
Level of Confidence					
Assigned Value	0	1	2	3	4
(A × B) = Score					

The testing atmosphere in this situation was more or less relaxed though attentive. Occasionally in a session someone would ask if this was an extrasensory perception experiment. Obviously, previous studies of n Ach suggest that *S*s high on this motivation would not become involved with this task, since one's score is wholly a matter of chance. However, we argued that those high on HP would take the opportunity to display irrational estimates of successes as part of their "gaming" defense.

All *S*s together generated a score distribution displaced to the optimistic side of zero, the rational score point, and the mean score for the high-HP groups was significantly higher than that of the lows (t is 2.17, $p < .025$). Now for the second half of the experiment.

In this phase we needed a testing situation with the above format which would not permit the "game" interpretation. To obtain this we turned to ten sets of statements alleged to have been made by "disturbed" and "creative" persons in response to Holtzman ink-blots. The Ss were told: "It has been established that a close correspondence exists between the ability to identify these categories of responses and the balance of such dispositions in the subject." Each S worked alone in a cubicle, viewing each blot over closed-circuit TV. For each blot he worked on the items below, following E's announcement of the number and nature of items he was to identify. Here of course S did see the material, hence the need to classify each line, but the odds conditions were identical to the Star-Odds task, and the same confidence measures were taken. The win and lose categories do not apply, of course.

We hypothesized that on this task the HP score would be correlated with pessimistic strategies. This time the grand mean falls on the pessimistic side of the rational point, but the mean differences for the high- and low-HP groups do *not* confirm our hypothesis. The high-HP Ss show the most pessimistic stance, but not at an acceptable level of confidence. Rather, we settle for the observation that we have demonstrated that under the "non-game" set we find the high-HP group displaying *rational* rather than irrational estimates of risk preferences.

We feel this demonstration that the risk preferences displayed by fear-of-failure Ss may vary with the nature of the inferences to be made about performance is important to our understanding of avoidance motivation. Most of the risk-taking research reviewed earlier permits a game set to be adopted by the S. This condition changes when studies of vocational choice in college students are conducted. A serious answer by the subject cannot be interpreted from a gamelike point of view, but at the same time the questions deal with the hypothetical. Actual vocational choices are not being made. To the extent that the S takes the task seriously we would expect a greater degree of rationality in choice, and we are prepared to argue (see p.   ) that the data gathered about vocational choice may be interpreted as departing markedly from the Atkinson model. It is now our position that the relationship between motive measures and risk preferences depends in part on the way the S

structures the value of a particular risk-taking strategy as it serves his relationship to E and his self-esteem, as well as the task consequences per se. We must learn more about the unique conditions under which fear of failure produces rational, adaptive behavior.

For this we turn to situations where the subject is forced into the situation and the success and failure conditions are defined by the culture (or the experimentalist) in such a way that they cannot be easily avoided. It seems to us that the best example of this kind of situation is found in the schools. Since the person cannot avoid the situation (either because of public laws or, in the case of college, tremendous social pressure) and cannot avoid the implications of the success or failure (which is also defined by the culture) there would seem to be only one way out. To avoid failure—which is still his primary goal—he must work hard enough so that he can avoid failing by "succeeding." Another possibility exists, but because of social pressure, we would expect it to be used by but few persons. Even in this situation it is possible for the high-HP person not to try.

In such a case he would fail, and thus the defense of not trying would not work here. (Since he is externally oriented, we feel that the dropout or the person who fails in college through giving up is not the high-HP person. Research on this aspect is planned, but not yet carried out). Our prediction, then, is that the high-HP person caught in this situation will work hard and therefore we expect a positive correlation between HP and grades in school.

Teevan and Custer (1965) tested this hypothesis on fifth-grade male subjects in a medium-sized town. The HP measure was given under neutral instructions, and the grades were taken from school records. Both measures were then broken at their respective medians and the chi square in Table 4.8 emerged.

The hypothesis was also tested at the high-school level. Teevan (1962) used 82 male students in the eleventh and twelfth grades. Again the HP measure was given under neutral instructions and the grade-point data were gathered from school records. Both measures were broken at their respective medians and the chi square was used to test their relationship. Table 4.9 gives the results of the analysis. The hypothesis was again confirmed at a significant level of confidence.

Hancock (1964) tested the same hypothesis, using high-school seniors, and reported a significant difference in favor of the hypoth-

TABLE 4.8. RELATIONSHIP OF
ELEMENTARY-SCHOOL GRADES TO HP

		Grades	
		High	Low
Hostile Press	High	16	5
	Low	5	16

$X^2 = 11.2$, $p < .01$.

esis. People who score high on the HP measure of fear of failure also get high grades in both elementary school and high school.

Finally the hypothesis was tested at the college level by Hancock (1964), Teevan and Smith (1964a), and Teevan and Pearson (1965). In each case, there was a significant positive relationship

TABLE 4.9. RELATIONSHIP OF
HIGH-SCHOOL GRADES TO HP SCORES

		Grades	
		High	Low
Hostile Press	High	29	12
	Low	12	29

$X^2 = 14.0$, $p < .001$.

between HP and grade-point average. The results of only one of these will be reported. Teevan and Smith (1964a) used 92 male college students from a section of introductory psychology as subjects. The HP measure was given under neutral conditions and the grade-point data were secured from school files. The HP measure was given in the first week of the semester and the semester grade-point average was computed at the end of that same semester. Table 4.10 gives the results of the analysis.

If we assume that students in the college preparatory course in high school are, in general, better students than those in the commercial and industrial program, then another finding becomes rele-

TABLE 4.10. RELATIONSHIP OF
COLLEGE GRADES TO HP SCORE

		Grades	
		High	Low
Hostile Press	High	32	14
	Low	14	32

$X^2 = 14.0$, $p < .01$.

vant. In an earlier part of this chapter, we reported the risk-taking
study of Hancock and Teevan (1964). In this study the subjects
were stratified on the basis of course of study and were randomly
selected from within each course of study. In a chi-square analysis,
the subjects who were in the college preparatory course were
tested against subjects in all other courses with the prediction that
there would be more high-HP persons than lows in the college
preparatory course. Table 4.11 shows that there are significantly
more high-HP persons than lows in the college preparatory course
(median break on HP). This finding has been replicated by Loomis
(1963).

TABLE 4.11. RELATIONSHIP OF
COURSE OF STUDY TO HP SCORE

		Course of Study	
		College Prep	Other
Hostile Press	High	15	15
	Low	4	26

$X^2 = 9.32$, $p < .01$.

In this chapter we have shown the following.

(1) If a high-HP person is given a choice whether or not to
engage an achievement situation, he will choose not to so engage.

(2) If the high-HP person is forced to engage an achievement
situation, he will do whatever he has to do in order not to fail:

if he is forced into the situation but is allowed considerable freedom in standards of success and failure, he will use whatever defense he feels will allow him to escape the situation without having failed. The key here is that he is not trying to succeed; he is only trying not to fail.

(3) Along this same line, if he is forced into a situation and the only way out is to work hard to "succeed," since this is the only way not to fail, he will work hard in order not to fail.

The picture which comes from these studies is consistent with our other research and also with the statements made by other theorists about fear of failure. If we look upon the behavior of these persons in the light of the usual cultural norms, their behavior seems irrational; if we look upon it as behavior which is designed to keep the person concerned from failing, then it makes good, rational sense.

Most of the studies reported in this chapter were conducted early in our program of research and gave us confidence in the HP score as a measure of fear-of-failure motivation. Each of them was done to illustrate the coherence of avoidance behavior related to achievement situations, whether volunteering, task aspiration level, structuring of the task importance, or performance under constraint conditions. Each dimension of the achievement situation is sufficiently complex to suggest a research program of its own. From this point forward we had to concentrate on aspects of achievement behavior whose analysis we felt would make the greatest contribution to our understanding of fear-of-failure motivation.

CHAPTER 5

Level of Aspiration and Hostile Press

THE CONCEPT OF LEVEL OF ASPIRATION (LA) HAS INFLUENCED MUCH of our work to date. In this book we first discussed it in Chapter 1 in our review of fear of failure, and we have placed it under Performance in our taxonomy. In Chapter 3 it played a large part in the development of the HP measure and here, for the first time, we added a new concept—the "pleased" score—to the literature. In Chapter 4 we used the LA concept in reporting on the study by Thomas and Teevan (1964) which described what the high-HP person could do as one method of avoiding failure: he could use the "expect" score of the LA.

In this chapter we would like to enlarge the concept of LA once again. In research on this topic the usual practice is to have a subject perform on a given task and then ask him a question designed to reveal what he expects (hopes, etc.) to get the next time he performs the task. The subject gives a single score and this is taken as his level of aspiration for the next trial.

As long ago as 1930 Hoppe suggested that most subjects were able to distinguish a natural maximum and minimum for the level of aspiration which varied with the task. When one thinks of a subject being faced with a task, especially if he has had little or no experience with this task, it would seem likely that his level of aspiration would not be a single value but would rather be a range of more or less probable values (Mace, 1931). In such a case we hypothesize that the individual may set a lower level or baseline below which a performance will produce a feeling of failure because he feels he should be able to do at least that well. He may

112

also set a higher level above which a performance will give rise to a feeling of success because he would be surprised to do this well. (The derivation of this measure and its relationship to the "pleased" score of Chapter 3 now becomes obvious.) Between these two levels lies an area of adaptation, or a "confirming interval" (CI) within which the individual expects to perform. Performances within this CI should give rise to indifference or a slight positive affect because the prediction is correct ("I know my abilities").

Let us now follow this reasoning through with an example. Suppose we ask subjects to throw darts at a target and we set the target up in such a way that we can get only hits or misses. We now have two subjects who will engage in dart throwing. Subject 1 has never thrown a dart before, but Subject 2 has had much experience at this task.

We ask Subject 1 the level-of-aspiration question: "How many hits do you expect to get on the next trial?" His previous score was 8 out of 20 possible. He gives us an LA of 10. We now ask him what is the lowest score he could get without being surprised. Knowing nothing about his ability on the task, he would not know if the score he already had was mainly chance or not. Since it is the only anchor point he has, he will use it, but he will not be very confident about it. Therefore, he should go down several notches for his lower limit. Let us suppose he gives us 4. We then ask: "What is the highest score you could get without being surprised?" Again, for the same reasons already given, we would expect him to go up several notches and he might give us 12. In other words, we expect a person engaging a new task to have a wide CI due to his lack of experience with the task.

If we put Subject 2 in the same situation we would expect him, since he has had a lot of experience with the task, to have a narrow CI. If his previous score had been 14 and this fit with his past experience, he would probably give us 12 or 13 for his lower bound, and a 15 or 16 for his upper bound.

The idea of the CI leads to a number of specific hypotheses. Teevan, Smith, and Loomis (1964) set out to test three of these:

1. Subjects scoring above their CI's will feel pleased; those scoring within their CI's will feel neutral to slightly pleased. These predictions cover the heart of the idea of the CI. If the subject really feels that it is probable that he will get a score which falls

within the definition of the CI, then actually getting such a score should have a minimal effect on him. He should feel a little better if the score falls in the upper reaches of the CI than if it falls in the lower reaches, but in either case his reaction should be that this is what he expected and thus his affect should be fairly neutral. We feel that it might be slightly positive because he has at least known what he could do and has made a correct prediction. If he does better than he expected (above the CI) he should feel good about it, and if he does worse (below the CI) he should feel more negative about it.

It seems obvious that we have in mind here a distribution of probabilities. We feel that the "expect" score is the most probable score. It might be argued that this is not true in all cases and we know, as a matter of fact, that this is not true for all subjects. Since the high-HP person is using the "expect" score (in some cases) as a defense, he will not give us his most probable score. However, when we ask the usual subject for the score he *expects*, by definition this would seem to be the score he has chosen as most probable.

The probabilities should drop away on both sides of the "expect" score, reaching zero at some considerable distance from it. However, we are arguing that this dropping off is not a continuous function. We believe that there is some point (both above and below the expect score) at which there is a discontinuous change in the probabilities. Since the subject has no difficulty in giving us an upper bound and a lower bound for the CI, it seems necessary to assume that he can distinguish a point where the probability changes from, for example, 40 percent to 20 percent. This argument is not crucial to the concept of the CI. It is also possible that people have learned to set cut-off points at, for instance, the 75th percentile or the 25th percentile. Obviously, we have here an empirical question which we will, at some future time, be able to answer. For the present it is easier for us to think in terms of the probability jump so we will continue to do so until the shape of the probability curve is empirically derived.

2. The width of the CI (distance between upper and lower boundaries) will be reduced by experience with the task. As stated above, if we introduce the subject to a task with which he has had little or no experience, the range of scores which are probable should be large. As he gains experience with the task, the range of

probable scores should become smaller. We are sure that there is a plateau effect here, so that if the person already has much experience with a given task, his CI may remain the same. Thus it is necessary to use a task with which the subject is not familiar. This prediction seems obvious and may even seem trivial to some. However this fact will become important in later studies having to do with the HP system.

3. The classical "expect" statements of subjects receiving scores within their CI's will be closer to their actual scores than will those of subjects receiving scores outside their CI's (either lower or higher). It should take some time for the subjects receiving scores outside their CI's to adjust to the fact that their expectations are not being confirmed, thus creating a discrepancy between expectation and obtained score.

The subjects were 45 male ninth-grade students enrolled in a medium-sized high school. The principal apparatus was the Electronic Rifle Range (Emenee, Inc.). The range seems to consist of a photoelectric cell mounted in a swinging pendulum. However, the cell was covered and a wire and switch attached to the apparatus so that an experimenter seated at a control table could activate a light and a buzzer on the rifle range. Thus the experimenter, rather than the skill of the subject, controlled the number of hits received. The rifle was also modified so that when the trigger was pulled a buzzer on the rifle and a counter on the control table were activated.

A seven-point affect scale was presented to the subject after each trial and he was asked to mark off his feelings.

The subjects were randomly assigned to three experimental groups of 15 each. Each subject was tested individually on the rifle task. After the subject's name had been recorded and his group determined from a previously constructed random table, the experimenter read him the following instructions:

"As you can see we have an electronic rifle range set up here. We would like to have you do a little shooting for us as part of an experiment we are doing for the Navy. You must aim at the center of the area within the white circle on the target. When you pull the trigger, it completes an electrical circuit, and if your sights are lined up with the target, the target will light and a buzzer will go off. I will take a couple of shots to show you how it works." [The experimenter took two shots, missing one, hitting on the other.] "In a moment I will let you shoot 20 shots. First, though, I'd like to have you answer some questions for me. Think very carefully now. How many of the 20 shots do you expect to hit on? What is the most you could get without being surprised? What is the least you could get without being surprised? [After the subject answers the questions, the experimenter continues.] Be sure to pull the trigger all the way back on each shot and to let it all the way up after each shot. You should stop after each shot so that the man at the table can write down your score. Aim carefully and try to hit on as many shots as you can."

The subject fires the 20 shots which constitute Trial 1. *E* then gives him his score, using the following words:
"Out of those 20 shots you got _____ hits."

S is then asked to respond to the Affect Scale under the following instructions: "Each number on this card has a word beside it to describe how you feel. Look carefully at each number and the words beside it and tell me which one best tells how you feel about your score on the 20 shots you have just finished." The numbers and corresponding words on the Affect Scale are: 1. Very pleased, 2. Pleased, 3. Just slightly pleased, 4. Neutral (neither pleased nor displeased), 5. Just slightly displeased, 6. Displeased, 7. Very displeased.

Each subsequent trial was conducted in the same manner as Trial 1. For the first three trials, subjects in all groups were randomized into three experimental conditions:

CONDITION A: Subjects received 7 hits on Trial 1, 9 on Trial 2 and 10 on Trial 3.

CONDITION B: Eight hits on Trial 1, 10 on Trial 2, and 11 on Trial 3.

CONDITION C: Nine on Trial 1, 11 on Trial 2, and 12 on Trial 3.

The three conditions were selected to be near the center of the possible scores in order to minimize the possibility of very high and very low CI's. Three conditions rather than one were used to minimize the possibility of feedback to future subjects.

The first three trials having reduced the vagueness of the CI boundaries, differential experimental treatments were applied to each subject according to his experimental group (i.e., above, within, or below CI). On Trials 4, 5, and 6, subjects in Group I received scores which were three hits above the tops of their CI's. Group III scored three hits below the lower limits of their CI's. Group II subjects were randomized into two conditions: subjects under condition X received scores which were above their "expect" scores on two of the three trials and a score which was below their "expect" on the other; condition Y subjects received two scores below and one above their "expect" score and the appropriate boundary score. If a halfway point was fractional, the higher number was scored.

For all trials a table of random positions of hits was employed to determine on what shots the subject scored. To test Hypothesis 1, that affect would depend on score relative to the CI boundaries, the Affect Scale was divided into three parts: Pleased (choices of numbers one and two); Neutral (numbers three through five); and Displeased (numbers six and seven).

Table 5.1 gives the chi-square analysis of the appropriate trials.

TABLE 5.1. RELATIONSHIP OF AFFECT
TO EXPERIMENTAL TREATMENT ON TRIALS 4, 5,
AND 6 AS DETERMINED BY CHI SQUARE ANALYSIS

	Trial 4		
	Group I[a]	Group II	Group III
Pleased	15	9	0
Neutral	0	5	2
Displeased	0	1	13

$X^2 = 51.54$[b]

	Trial 5		
Pleased	15	8	0
Neutral	0	7	0
Displeased	0	0	15

$X^2 = 69.15$[b]

	Trial 6		
Pleased	15	8	0
Neutral	0	6	0
Displeased	0	1	15

[a]Group I: Ss receiving scores above CI; Group II: Ss receiving scores within the CI; Group III: Ss receiving scores below the CI.
[b]Significant at the .01 level.

The hypothesis was confirmed. In group I (above CI) all subjects responded with positive affect on each of the three trials. Most subjects in Group III (below CI) gave negative responses. Group II tended to make responses of Pleased slightly (but not significantly) more than of Neutral or Displeased.

Hypothesis 2 stated that there should be a reduction in CI width with experience. This discrepancy score was obtained for each subject on each trial and the mean CI width of the combined groups ($N = 45$) for each trial was compared with the mean for each other trial (Table 5.2). Since an analysis of variance proved significant ($F = 61.9$), t's were computed. The results show that in mean width for Trial 1 is significantly different from Trial 7. Other differences are not significant, though all but one (Trial 3 vs. Trial 4) are in the predicted direction. Width continues to decrease on the last four trials even though the subjects were being run in differing experimental conditions.

Hypothesis 3 was concerned with the relationship between experimental treatment and LA discrepancy score (D). The t test was used to compare separately the means of the LA discrepancy scores of each of the outside CI groups with those of Group II (within CI) on Trials 4–5, 5–6, and 6–7 (Table 5.3). All t's were significant at or beyond the .01 level, the outside CI groups having greater discrepancies (D-scores) than the within CI group. Thus the hypothesis was confirmed.

This experiment led us to believe that the CI as a measure of level of aspiration was on solid ground. The next step was to research the relationship of the CI to our HP measure of fear of failure. As we have seen, a subject who has had little experience with a task tends to have a wide CI. The wider the CI the less chance there is of receiving scores outside of it—in other words, the less chance there is of either succeeding or failing, the more chance there is of confirming one's expectations. Following this reasoning, it becomes obvious that one can use a wide CI as a defense in this kind of situation. One can use a wide CI to avoid failing. Giving a wide CI cuts down chances of success, but a wide CI practically guarantees that one will not fail. Since the person with high HP is seen as oriented toward avoiding failure, it would seem that people with high HP should also have wider CI's than persons with low HP.

This hypothesis was tested by Teevan and Smith (1964b). These

TABLE 5.2. CHANGE IN CI WIDTH AS A FUNCTION OF EXPERIENCE OVER SEVEN TRIALS

	Mean CI Widths		
Trials	A[a]	B[a]	t
1 vs. 2	9.47	9.24	1.70
1 vs. 3	9.47	7.40	2.97[b]
1 vs. 4	9.47	7.53	2.80[b]
1 vs. 5	9.47	7.18	3.09[b]
1 vs. 6	9.47	6.84	3.56[b]
1 vs. 7	9.47	6.24	4.13[b]
2 vs. 3	9.24	7.40	1.15
2 vs. 4	9.24	7.53	.96
2 vs. 5	9.24	7.18	1.38
2 vs. 6	9.24	6.84	1.79
2 vs. 7	9.24	6.24	2.53[c]
3 vs. 4	7.40	7.53	.022
3 vs. 5	7.40	7.18	.033
3 vs. 6	7.40	6.84	.082
3 vs. 7	7.40	6.24	1.65
4 vs. 5	7.53	7.18	.054
4 vs. 6	7.53	6.84	1.01
4 vs. 7	7.53	6.24	1.84
5 vs. 6	7.18	6.84	.047
5 vs. 7	7.18	6.24	1.26
6 vs. 7	6.84	6.24	

[a]Column heads A and B simply indicate the mean of the earlier and later trial compared in each instance.

[b]Significant at the .01 level.

[c]Significant at the .05 level.

authors used 44 male students from an introductory psychology course. The subjects were required to participate in the experiment as part of their course requirement.

HP was measured as usual; the measurement took place in the first two weeks of the semester. To measure the CI a scrambled-words test was constructed. It consisted of one hundred words of

TABLE 5.3. RELATIONSHIP OF MEAN
LA DISCREPANCY SCORE TO EXPERIMENTAL
TREATMENT ON TRIALS 4 THROUGH 7

Trial		I	—	II	II	—	III
				Experimental Groups[a]			
4 − 5	Means	−2.13		1.73	1.73		5.73
	t		−16.36[b]			−10.39[c]	
	F		1.43 $(s_1 = s_2)$			2.23 $(s_1 = s_2)$	
5 − 6	Means	−1.20		2.0	2.0		6.13
	t		−9.25[c]			−8.69[c]	
	F		3.48 $(s_1 = s_2)$			1.46 $(s_1 = s_2)$	
6 − 7	Means	−.80		1.0	1.0		3.53
	t		−5.45[c]			−5.88[c]	
	F		2.42 $(s_1 = s_2)$			1.46 $(s_1 = s_2)$	

[a]Group I: Ss receiving scores above the CI; Group II: Ss receiving
scores within the CI; Group III: Ss receiving scores below the CI.

[b]Significant at the .001 level.

[c]Significant at the .01 level.

[d]The appropriate correction was made.

the Lowell (1949) Scrambled Words Test and another one hundred words drawn by the present experimenters from the Thorndike-
Lorge (1944) Word List. All words were common four-letter
words and all were scrambled.

Twenty scrambled words were placed in two columns on each
of ten pages. The same three questions mentioned above were used
to get at the CI. The subjects received the following instructions:

"The test you are about to take tests your ability to perceive particular
types of linguistic relationships. To the extent that this ability is a
function of intelligence, your score on the test will be a function of
intelligence. Now read the instructions on the cover of the booklet
while I read them aloud: "On the following pages you will find common
words that have been scrambled by changing the order of the letters.
There are twenty such words on each page. When the signal to begin
ie given, turn to page one and answer the questions at the top of the
page [the CI questions]. Then attempt to unscramble each set of letters
to make a word and write your answer in the space on the right.

When the time is up for each page, you will be told to stop and will then be given the correct answers.' "

Subjects were then instructed to check their answers and place the total number correct in the upper right corner of the page. The above procedure was repeated for each of the pages of the test, though the first block of instructions was omitted and the others abbreviated.

The mean CI width across all trials (pages) of the scrambled-words test was found for each subject and the width then correlated with HP, using a rank-order correlation. A positive correlation of +.25 was found. A t test for the significance of this correlation yielded a t of 1.70 which is significant beyond the .05 level of confidence (one-tailed). Thus the hypothesis was confirmed; persons with high HP also tend to have wide CI's.

Further confirmation of the preference of Ss with high HP scores for wider CI's comes from a study by Birney and Rolf (1965) using a maze task of considerable difficulty. Two hypotheses were tested using the maze speed test. These were that (a) HP scores are negatively related to scores on the maze speed test, i.e. trials to solution, and (b) HP scores are positively related to size of CI taken prior to each maze problem.

The maze speed test required the S to sit before a box having a sloped, glass writing surface. The maze problems were displayed on a rolled sheet passing under the glass. Behind the sheet was a light bulb of standard size which provided sufficient illumination to permit S to see the pencil maze. Illumination was provided for one second intervals, forty exposures per maze. The S viewed the maze projected on the tracing paper over the glass during the light periods and traced the correct path through the maze during the dark periods. The number of exposures that it takes the S to correctly trace the correct path becomes his score.

For each maze after Maze 1, the four following questions were put, asking for the S's level of aspiration. How many exposures were required to solution? How many exposures for Maze [next number] would be an unpleasant surprise? How many exposures to solution would be a pleasant surprise? How many exposures do you expect solution to take? This type of task was devised in the belief that it would produce a sense of urgency, demand precision, and require the Ss to overcome an unfamiliar working situation. One limitation

Fear of Failure

of such speeded tasks is that none of the standard ability tests can be used to control for ability differences. The Ss worked in cubicles, alone and directed by E over the intercommunication system. They could signal for assistance if instructions were not understood. There were six mazes in all and the analysis is based on data from the last five mazes. The mazes became progressively more difficult, and the Ss were told to expect this.

For the analyses performed in this study the distribution of HP scores was divided at approximately the 65th percentile. One third of the Ss received scores of zero, and one third scores of 4 or less. Accordingly it was decided to contrast the upper third of the distribution with the remainder. Given a normal distribution of total scores obtained for all six mazes we obtained a difference between means that is significant at the .005 level, see Table 5.4.

TABLE 5.4. MEAN NUMBER OF EXPOSURES
PER MAZE FOR HIGH AND LOW HP SUBJECTS

	High HP	(N)	Low HP	(N)	Mean Diff.
1	15.23	(26)	13.62	(48)	1.61
2	16.14	(26)	11.92	(51)	4.22
3	23.87	(23)	21.83	(48)	2.04
4	14.16	(25)	12.37	(51)	1.79
5	20.84	(25)	22.44	(50)	1.60
6	30.29	(24)	22.75	(49)	7.54
Total	122.45	(22)	102.2	(43)	20.25
S.D.	26.23		32.00		SEDiff. 7.54

$t = 2.69$, $p < .005$.

Our hypothesis was that the HP score would be positively related to the CI. This was tested for each maze by using the test of significance for various ratios. Table 5.5 shows that for every maze the variance of CI scores was greater for the high HP Ss than for the lows.

This finding means that the high HP Ss used either very narrow or very wide CI intervals. Inspection of the distributions shows that the majority of the deviation was toward the wide interval. Recall

TABLE 5.5. THE SIGNIFICANCE OF VARIENCE RATIOS
FOR CONFIRMATION INTERVALS OF HIGH AND LOW HP

Maze	HP Score	N	M	S^2	F	df	p
2	High	27	17.8	128.47	2.36	26/47	< .01
	Low	48	12.7	54.48			
3	High	26	13.8	111.95	10.87	25/49	< .005
	Low	50	11.8	10.30			
4	High	23	16.4	115.54	3.98	22/46	< .005
	Low	47	12.2	29.02			
5	High	22	17.1	106.76	2.39	21/48	< .01
	Low	49	12.8	44.62			
6	High	24	14.7	117.95	1.87	23/47	< .05
	Low	48	13.7	62.96			

that one must say he would be pleasantly surprised to solve the maze in five exposures, and unpleasantly surprised if he took all forty exposures to receive a CI score of 35. Although the majority of Ss chose CI intervals in the range of 8 to 15, the very wide intervals in excess of 23 are the choice of Ss with high HP scores.

The traditional LA score of "expect" score for the next maze is not related to HP scores. Although the Ss high on HP show an average LA that is more optimistic than the lows on four of five mazes, the differences do not reach an acceptable level of significance.

As has been stated above, the more experience a person has with a task, the narrower his CI should become. It would also seem sensible to argue that, in general, the more important a task is to the individual, the more experience he would have with that task. Since much of our research has had to do with achievement, we became interested in whether this kind of reasoning would hold for abilities. If we translate directly, then we come up with the statement that the more important an ability is for a given individual, the more he would have thought about it and practiced it, and therefore the more he would know about it. From this comes the hypothesis:

The more important the ability, the narrower *the CI.*

For people in general, the above should hold. However, when one thinks about the particular kind of person who receives a high score on HP, then a different kind of prediction makes sense. We have argued that this person is mainly concerned with avoiding failure. We have shown that one of the mechanisms he can and does use to defend himself against failure is a wide CI. The more important an ability is, the more important it is not to fail in that ability. Therefore, we would expect the high-HP person to defend most strongly in situations which are most important. Following this line of reasoning we come up with the hypothesis:

For high-HP persons, the more important the ability, the wider *the CI.*

To restate the above: For the *general population,* the more important the ability the *narrower* the CI; for *persons high in HP,* the more important the ability the *wider* the CI.

Teevan and Myers (1965) tested the above hypothesis using 100 male subjects drawn at random from the 11th grade in a medium-sized city. The subjects all took the HP measure on one day. The following day they were given test materials (described in the instructions) and then were read the following instructions:

"Now I will give you the instructions for page one. When you have finished, please stop and wait for further instructions. While you are waiting, please do not talk so that everyone has a chance to finish without interruption. Page 1 is a list of 35 abilities. Notice, also, the other booklet we have given you. It is a list of definitions. Please read these over and refer to them as often as you like. They are written to help you better understand the meaning of these abilities. We would like you to rank the abilities on page one from 1 to 35. Number 1 would be given to the ability that is most important to you and a rank of 35 would be given to that which is least important to you. Remember, this is not the rank or the importance that your parents, your teachers, or your friends would assign to the ability, but it is the rank of importance that *you* think it has. Do you have any questions?"

After the subjects had finished the first part of the test, this next set of instructions followed:

"Now turn to page 2. The instructions that I am going to give you now are for the next six pages. When you finish these, stop. Now suppose someone is judging you upon these abilities. This judge knows you very well and has seen your school records and your entire case history. Now we want you to put down the score you would expect this judge to give you. We want you to place a number between 1 and 100 on each line in answer to these questions. The score may range anywhere from 1 to 100. Answer all three questions on each ability by filling the number in. [The three questions were the same as used before to define the CI, adapted to fit this particular situation.] A score of zero would mean that the judge thinks that you have none of that ability. A score of 50 is about average, and a score of 100 would indicate that the judge knows that you are very superior in that ability. Do you have any questions?"

A rank order correlation was computed between the average rank and confirming interval for each ability. The correlation was a negative —.34. The *t*-value of this correlation was 2.07, whiclh gives us a *p* value beyond the .05 level of confidence. For the total sample, then, the more important the ability the narrower the CI. The first hypothesis was confirmed.

Breaking the population of HP scores at the median gave a population of 50 subjects who were above the median on HP–high-HP persons. The hypothesis regarding these people was that the more important the ability, the *wider* the CI would be. A rank-order correlation between average rank and confirming interval for each ability for this population was performed. The correlation was plus +.38, *t*-value 2.23, which gives a *p* value beyond the .05 level of confidence. As hypothesized, for high-HP persons, the more important the ability the wider the CI.

We interpret the results of these studies as support for the use of the CI as an important measure of aspiration strategy. The ease with which *S*s follow these instructions and the sensitivity of the CI measure to motivational differences suggest that various preferences for aspirational adaptation do reflect approach-and-avoidance tendencies as used by the *S*s. Traditionally the LA "expect" score has been shown to vary primarily with schedules of reinforcement provided by the obtained score. The CI limits, however, are not so obviously related to reinforcers, since positive reinforcement for a within interval estimate may be balanced off by negative reinforcement associated with moving closer to potential error. Thus the CI shows considerable variance that may be due to motivational effects rather than task-outcome effects.

CHAPTER 6

Conformity and HP

IN SEVERAL PLACES IN THIS VOLUME WE HAVE SUGGESTED THAT THE person who scores high in HP is oriented towards people rather than towards situations. It has seemed to us that he is less certain of the anchors within himself by which to judge success and failure, and therefore he looks outwards for such standards. One finding which we have already mentioned along these lines is the positive correlation between the James-Phares Scale (James, 1957) and HP which indicates that high-HP persons externalize their shortcomings, so that they perceive their failures as due to sources outside themselves (i.e., fate, other persons, etc.).

To further explore this variable, Teevan and Fischer (1966) designed a questionnaire specifically to see how the high-HP person perceived the definition of success and failure. They hypothesized that the person who scored high on HP would perceive success and failure as being defined externally—by other people rather than by themselves. The subjects were 44 male students in introductory psychology who were required to participate in an experiment as part of their course work. The HP measure was given at the beginning of the semester. The measure of success and failure definition was a questionnaire designed by the experimenters. The questionnaire contained five questions which were neutral and five questions which were designed to test the hypothesis. The five "experimental" questions were these:

1. Failure is primarily the inability to meet standards set by other people. (True)

2. Failure is primarily the inability to meet your own standards. (False)
3. My own evaluation of my performance is more important than an evaluation made by other people. (False)
4. I consider myself independent of other people when trying to determine how successful I have been in any given endeavor. (False)
5. Success and failure are determined by self-evaluation rather than external evaluation. (False)

We have put in parentheses the answers which we felt the high-HP person would give (the "external" response).

The first analysis used only persons who answered *all* of the experimental questions either in terms of the "external" response or in terms of the "internal" response. Table 6.1 gives the data for these 18 Ss. It shows that low-HP persons answer in "internal" terms while high-HP persons answer in "external" terms. This confirms the hypothesis.

TABLE 6.1. FISHER EXACT TEST
OF EXTERNAL VS. INTERNAL CRITERIA
FOR SUCCESS AND FAILURE VS. HP SCORE

		External	Internal
Hostile Press	High	4	3
	Low	1	10

$p < .05.$

The authors also split the HP scores at the median and did a *t*-test on the means of External scores. They gave the subjects one point for each "external" answer and then averaged the scores for high and low HP. Table 6.2 gives the results of this analysis. Again the hypothesis was confirmed. Persons with high HP tend to perceive standards of success and failure as being determined externally to themselves.

This evidence suggests that the high-HP person is oriented to the external world for standards and rewards. If this is true, then we would expect that he would tend to conform to the opinion of

TABLE 6.2. *T*-TEST ON "EXTERNAL"
MEANS OF HIGH AND LOW HP PERSONS

Group	N	$\bar{X}$	t	df	p
High HP	21	1.86	1.701	42	< .05[a]
Low HP	23	1.09			

[a]One-tailed.

others. The first test of this was made by Teevan and Loomis
(1964). They used a small *N* for a pilot test and found that "expert" opinion changed the opinions of high-HP persons more than
that of low-HP persons. The stimuli were paintings and historical
figures. McGhee (1965) followed this pilot with a study relating
conformity, as measured by the Crutchfield (1955) apparatus, to
HP and found no significant differences between high and low HP.
Stamps and Teevan (1966), trying to resolve the contradiction
in the studies cited, felt that there might be crucial differences between the situation in which the Crutchfield (1955) apparatus was
used and a situation in which there was more direct relationship
between the subjects themselves and also between subjects and the
experimenter. Since there is evidence that the high-HP person is
externally oriented and that he perceives his standards of success
and failure as being set by others, a conformity situation which allowed direct contact should exert a maximum influence on him.
Therefore Stamps and Teevan predicted, following McGhee (1965),
that there would be no difference between high- and low-HP subjects in the Crutchfield (1955) situation, but that high-HP subjects
would show more conformity in an Asch (1956) situation. This
should be true because in the Asch situation the subjects sat in
plain sight of one another; each subject could actually see who was
making what response; and the experimenter was also in plain
sight and seemed not at all shocked by the responses of the stooges.
To test the above prediction, Stamps and Teevan (1966) used
63 male college students. The subjects were required to participate
in the experiment as part of their course work. The HP measure
was given and a median break on the measure was carried out.
Half of the highs and half of the lows were assigned randomly to
each conformity condition (Asch and Crutchfield). Then the sub-

jects were run in the two conditions. The Crutchfield apparatus was composed of five booths such that the subjects could not see each other. Critical trials were interspersed with noncritical trials. Critical trials were those in which the subjects were fed incorrect information to see if this information would induce them to conform. The subjects thought the information they were receiving about the choices of others came from the other subjects; in actuality all information came from the experimenter who operated from a control booth out of sight of the subjects. On critical trials each subject had four reports which were incorrect before he had to make his own choice. These four incorrect reports, of course, agreed. A fuller description of the Crutchfield apparatus may be found in McGhee and Teevan (1965) or in Crutchfield (1955). The Asch situation was set up with five stooges who agreed unanimously on the incorrect solution to the problem before the actual subject made his choice. The stimuli were lines of the type originally used by Asch.

Table 6.3 gives the results for our expectation that there would

TABLE 6.3. MEAN CONFORMITY SCORES
FOR FF AND HS Ss IN THE CRUTCHFIELD SITUATION

Group	N	$\bar{X}$	t	df	p
Above HP Median (FF)	15	4.73	.47	29	> .05
Below HP Median (HS)	16	4.38			

be no difference between high- and low-HP subjects in conformity in the Crutchfield situation. Such is the case.

Table 6.4 shows the results pertaining to the main hypothesis.

TABLE 6.4. MEAN CONFORMITY SCORES
FOR FF AND HS Ss IN THE ASCH SITUATION

Group	n	$\bar{X}$	t	df	p
Above HP Median (FF)	16	6.19	3.097	30	< .01
Below HP Median (HS)	16	2.38			

High-HP subjects will conform more than will low-HP subjects in an Asch situation. This hypothesis was confirmed.

Further confirmation of the dependency relationship suggested by HP scores is found in a study by Birney and Rolf (1965). Arguing that a situation where one's performance is evaluated directly by others for group purposes would be threatening, they predicted that Ss high on HP would have their work "underchosen" in such a situation. It was assumed that differences in actual originality of response to Holtzman inkblots would not be related to HP scores, and this proved to be the case. Three-man groups were then composed of one S high on HP and two Ss who were low. They were instructed to consider the thirty responses they had among them, and to choose the "most creative" response of the three for each blot. This situation was devised because it was felt that the S with high HP would not want to defend his work nor wish the responsibility of having his work represent the group. Thus the straightforward prediction was made that HP Ss would be chosen below the expectancy level established by random processes. Table 6.5 shows that the prediction was confirmed.

TABLE 6.5. CONTINGENCY TABLE SHOWING THE FREQUENCY OF HIGH AND LOW HP Ss CONTRIBUTING LESS THAN THE EXPECTED NUMBER OF CREATIVE RESPONSES OR THE EXPECTED NUMBER AND ABOVE FOR THE GROUP IBT

	Frequency of Subjects	
	Less Than Expected	Expected and Above
High HP (N = 18)	9	9
Low HP (N = 36)	7	29

$X^2 = 5.373$, $p < .03$.

Here we see that the HP S seems willing to give up his right to credit for achievement in return for a secure place in the group. Thus cooperation can be at some cost in task accomplishment.

By conforming to the judgment of others, the S with high HP is less likely to fail in their eyes. It would seem, therefore, that this kind of person has no real choice in a social situation. Even if he is sure that he is right (in judging something like the length of lines) he cannot very well stand up against the judgment of others because it is precisely the judgment of others which is crucially important. We have no evidence that being right for its own sake constitutes a reinforcement for these people. It is being right in the eyes of others which is important. McClelland et al. (1953) have made the point that people with high need for achievement are competing with an *internal* standard of excellence. These people are actors: they perceive a need and they do something to satisfy it. People with high HP seem to have set their standards of excellence outside themselves. They operate in terms of *externals*. They are reactors rather than actors. For them the distinction between intrinsic reward and extrinsic reward may very well not exist; *all* rewards are extrinsic.

Prisoner's Dilemma

In the Asch situation, conformity to the majority requires that the S behave in an irrational way on the perception task he is asked to perform. But we should not expect that all such social conformity is necessarily so irrational. The hypothesis that HP reflects motivation to avoid evaluation suggests that Ss high in HP will avoid competition if they can. But what of the situation where cooperation produces the greatest payoff? Should we hypothesize that HP leads to an avoidance pattern, due to the possibility of evaluation, and hence a refusal to work cooperatively, or will it lead to co-operation of the Asch type and possible success as well?

Birney and Stillings (1967) set out to explore the above questions. Given the literature on Achievement motivation it seemed clear one must predict that the Ss with high n Ach would play to maximize their scores. However, the literature also contains numerous references to the requirement that the achievement situation be competitive and not cooperative. Again it is possible to put game strategy against social conditions and not be wholly sure what the net effects will be.

The achievement game situation which permits us to couple cooperation with game success is Prisoner's Dilemma. Rapoport (1962) had already observed: "In general we are led to suspect that individuals have cooperative or non-cooperative patterns of behavior that might be related to measurable personality patterns. This is a subject for future investigation" (p. 58). Deutsch (1960) had shown that the two-person nonzero-sum game, when used in single trial tests having nonsimultaneous choices, focused on the tendency to display trustworthiness and degree of trust in others, which was negatively related to F-scale scores. Rapoport had found that some Ss refused to adopt cooperative strategies of trust for many trials despite continuous score losses. It seemed to us that the Prisoner's Dilemma situation would provide an excellent opportunity to study the effects of n Ach and HP on strategy adopted.

A pretest revealed that the context in which the matrix is presented seriously influences the S's choice of strategy. Thus describing the task as similar to that faced by two businessmen produced competitive behavior by the entire sample of fifteen Ss. Similarly, Evans and Crumbaugh (1966) have since demonstrated that the form of the matrix presentation can produce complete cooperation. We needed a situation that would permit the motivational factors to influence the choice, and for this we found that it was best to require the S to fill in a questionnaire showing that he understood the matrix and then to describe in writing the strategy he chose to pursue before actually making the choice. This gave a control over instructional effects and permitted a first session assessment of the division between cooperation and competition.

Two types of games were used, counterbalanced for order, with all Ss. In the first a replication of the Deutsch game was used, except that the two trials were held simultaneously (though each featured nonsimultaneous choice). The same payoff matrix was used, and approximately the same fifty-fifty division between cooperation and competition was found. The n Ach and HP scores were divided at their respective medians to provide pattern analysis and *no* relationship to game behavior was found. The incentive portion of the instructions to S reads as follows:

"Your welfare as expressed in points is partly determined by this other person, and his welfare is partly determined by you. Thus you and E are faced with the problem of sizing up each other as best you can and doing as well as you can under the circumstances. For this purpose it is best that you think of the points in the matrix as representing money or personal satisfaction. You're trying to get as many and lose as few points as possible. You don't want to help the other person by making foolish sacrifices, but you aren't necessarily out to beat him either, especially if this unduly jeopardizes your own welfare."

In a situation of this type there is no opportunity for the Ss to influence each other. Rather, one's choice reflects a certain belief about others, since there is no way for anyone to know his opponent. In the serial-game situation all these conditions changed. The E played the role of opponent by responding to each move by the S from the central control room. The S knew he had about half an hour (though this was deliberately vague) in which to try to influence the E. However, the instructions for this session attempted to produce competition between Ss and not between S and E. The key instruction read as follows:

"Remember: The experimenter's choices are not prearranged and not determined by probability. He is playing each of you individually and will follow different strategy considerations for each of you depending on his own record of your choices. *Your job is to get as many points as possible given E's strategy.* [Then, just before play began:] At the end of the experiment your score will be compared *with the scores of the other subjects.*"

In fact E played a passive role for all Ss, permitting them to determine whether the strategy would stabilize, and if so whether it would be cooperative or competitive. The former would thus maximize the scores of S and E. This strategy by E gave the Ss maximum freedom to experiment, and the wide array of patterns followed shows that they did so.

Because the Ss had written a description of the strategies being followed after the play, it was possible to combine their remarks and patterns of play into coding indices that permitted classification of 90 of the 105 Ss into the three categories of Competitive, Defensive, and Optimal. Competitive Ss said they attempted to defeat E and their plays showed this. Defensive Ss maximized their scores with a minimum of experimental play, using either a Balance of Terror strategy or a shift to Defensive noncooperation after accumulating score. Optimal Ss were those who made no reference to E's strategy, showed a steady cooperative style of play, and gave rational reasons for it. Approximately one third of the Ss fell into each group. Table 6.6 shows the relationship between the Competitive vs. Noncompetitive groups and the motive pattern groups. The findings are quite striking.

It is the high-n-Ach–low-HP Ss who show the Competitive pattern. These Ss ignored the instruction to maximize scores for group

TABLE 6.6. THE RELATIONSHIP OF
MOTIVE PATTERN TO COMPETITIVE GAME PLAY

HP	High	High	Low	Low	
n Ach	High	Low	High	Low	N
Competitive Sequential Game Play	4	7	17	6	34
Non-competitive Sequential Game Play	23	19	10	19	71
N	27	26	27	26	105

$\chi^2 = 15.8$, $p < .01$.

competition, and instead chose to defeat *E*. However, those high on HP and low on n Ach accepted the instruction, cooperated and followed the Optimal strategy. The high-high group was not competitive, but it did include a majority of those who maximized and then shifted to the Defensive style of play. Table 6.7 shows this breakdown.

TABLE 6.7. THE RELATIONSHIP OF
MOTIVE PATTERN TO DEFENSIVE GAME PLAY

HP	High	High	Low	Low	
n Ach	High	Low	High	Low	N
Defensive Sequential Game Play	13	3	2	4	22
Non-defensive Sequential Game Play	14	23	25	21	83
N	27	26	27	25	105

$\chi^2 = 15.28$, $p < .01$.

These results illustrate quite clearly the manner in which cognitive variable (strategies available) interact with motivational variables to affect behavior. It is not correct to assert that fear of failure produces irrational problem solving, conformity, etc., without careful consideration of the terms set forth by the task situation. In contrast to the Asch situation, the Prisoner's Dilemma makes cooperation the maximizing strategy under certain conditions, and when this is the case it is the fear-of-failure *S* who follows the rational course, and the competitive n Ach *S* who is "irrational."

Finally, we have evidence that relates the HP score to behavior of a highly social nature which is free from achievement cues and which places the *S* squarely in the minority opposed to the majority on a question of great social importance. The behavior is active participation in movements aimed against the role of the United States in the Vietnamese conflict. It seemed to us that many of those protesting against the Vietnam policy expressed anxiety about the future, displayed aggression against authority seen as threatening, and generally perceived the environment as hostile. Thus the imagery of the protest movement seemed to be that of HP. However, the behavior of protest, though it requires nonconformity to society at large, requires conformity to the protest movement itself. Given this assessment Teevan and Stamps (1966) hypothesized that those protesting would display higher HP scores than a control group. They argued that the small-group conformity would overbalance the less personal nonconformist position. The *S*s were 99 undergraduates at a large state university. Sixty were chosen on the basis that they were not members of any protest groups. The other 39 were active members of protest groups which had actively demonstrated against the military involvement of the United States in Vietnam. The HP measure was given under neutral conditions. Table 6.8 gives the *t*-test on the means; the hypothesis was confirmed.

TABLE 6.8. MEAN HP SCORES FOR
PROTEST AND NON-PROTEST GROUP MEMBERS

Group	N	$\bar{X}$	t	df	p
Protest	39	4.85	1.9	97	$< .05$[a]
Non-Protest	60	3.68			

[a]One-tailed test.

The series of studies described in this chapter provide evidence for the interpretation of the HP score as a measure of fear of failure. But they also show that avoidance behavior cannot be simply categorized as irrational, maladaptive, and inefficient. Under achievement conditions where the *S* must work alone, provide his own standards, and submit to personal evaluation, we do find that avoidance motivation produces defensive behavior ill suited to task success. But if the situation is a social one, emphasizing the need to cooperate and permitting dependence or the standards of others, we find adaptive behavior as the accompaniment of avoidance motivation.

CHAPTER 7

Genesis, Implications, and Speculations

IN THIS CHAPTER WE SHALL TALK ABOUT THE GENESIS OF HP IN theoretical terms and then discuss some research bearing on this topic. We shall then discuss HP in terms of the implications we see for the person and for our culture. In doing this we will attempt to point out roads for future research to fill in the many gaps which will show up from our discussion.

There are many ways in which to talk about the achievement situation in terms of parent and child interaction. Among many variables that contribute to the way the child will act and feel in such situations, we have chosen to accent two: (1) the outcome of the situation and (2) the effort the child expends in the situation. We will discuss these variables in their relation to the reinforcement pattern which the parent brings to bear on the child. Assuming that the parent may reward, punish, or be neutral to either trying or not trying, and to succeeding or failing, we face a total of sixty-four possible patterns of parental reaction to both effort and outcome. Most of these pattern are bizarre—e.g., the parent punishes trying and success—and they are of concern only to those interested in pathological modes of child rearing. However sixteen of the patterns seem quite possible to us and these appear in Table 7.1.

Basically these patterns consist of combinations of reward alone, punishment alone, the use of neither, and the use of both. Pattern 1 indicates parental neutrality for both effort and outcome. This might be the parent who simply ignores achievement behavior. No

TABLE 7.1. VARIETIES OF PARENTAL REIN-
FORCEMENT OF ACHIEVEMENT EFFORT AND OUTCOME

EFFORT		OUTCOME		PREDICTED MOTIVE
Try	Not Try	Success	Failure	
1.	Neutral	Neutral		Non-achievement
2.	Neutral	Reward	Neutral	High HS-low HP
3.	Neutral	Reward	Punish	?
4.	Neutral	Neutral	Punish	High HP
5. Reward	Neutral	Neutral		?
6. Reward	Neutral	Reward	Neutral	High HS-low HP
7. Reward	Neutral	Reward	Punish	Mod HS-mod HP
8. Reward	Neutral	Neutral	Punish	Mod HP ?
9. Neutral	Punish	Neutral		?
10. Neutral	Punish	Reward	Neutral	Mod HS-mod HP?
11. Neutral	Punish	Reward	Punish	Mod HP
12. Neutral	Punish	Neutral	Punish	High HP-low HS
13. Reward	Punish	Neutral		?
14. Reward	Punish	Reward	Neutral	Mod HS
15. Reward	Punish	Reward	Punish	High HS-high HP
16. Reward	Punish	Neutral	Punish	High HP-high HS

accent is put upon it at all, and we would expect the child to have
no achievement motivation of any kind. Specifically we would expect this child to be low in HP. Since we sometimes talk about low
HP in terms of high Hope of Success and thus in terms of a positive approach to achievement situations, we must explain that this
is not the appropriate reinforcement pattern. This person is low in
any kind of achievement motivation and thus is a "false low" on
HP. We think such patterns exist, probably increasing in frequency
as we move down the socio-economic scale.

Number 2 is the pattern which defines pure Hope of Success.
Success is rewarded and everything else is neutral. No one cares
how success took place. An achievement situation is one in which
it is very possible to win (be rewarded) but not at all possible to
lose (be punished). This person should seek out achievement situations. His HP score should be low, and in terms of the Hope of
Success definition, this is a true low.

Number 3 defines a condition in which the effort variable is not relevant, but success outcomes are rewarded and failure outcomes are punished. It matters not how success is achieved, but it must be achieved, since failure entails punishment. The idea of the means justifying the ends may come from this kind of pattern. Cheating and other types of behavior of its type may well be engendered in this way. The important thing is to succeed and not to fail—the means is irrelevant. At present, we do not know how to predict to HP from this pattern.

Number 4 is the pattern which we believe gives rise to the high-HP person. There is no reward for succeeding; there is only punishment for failing. Since there is no reward or punishment for trying or not trying, this person would be expected to avoid achievement situations when it is at all possible. As we have seen (Chapter 4) this is what the high-HP person does. This pattern places accent on achievement behavior, but only in a negative way. It defines an achievement situation as one in which it is very possible to lose, but in which it is not possible to win. In terms of outcome, this is the pattern we predict for the high-HP person.

Number 5 says that the parent rewards the child for trying and all else is neutral. In a sense, this is a message which most parents subscribe to. How many times do we hear, "Just try your best. If you do that, it is all we can expect of you"? This seems to be a cultural ideal. However, we do not know if it really exists either. Is it possible to ignore outcomes in this culture? Even if the parent is sincere about this pattern, the teacher, the scout leader, etc., proceed in terms of outcomes. It is difficult for the child to believe the statement that only "trying" counts when others are going on to other things and he must stay back—either in school or in the yard.

Patterns 6 and 7 both emphasize reward for striving and outcome and should lead primarily to a Hope of Success orientation as long as the tasks are fitted to the child's ability so that he receives positive reinforcement much of the time. Pattern 8, where trying is rewarded and failing is punished, is the kind of pattern one might see in families where achievement by the child is necessary to the welfare of the family. The immigrant family that sensed the importance of school success without knowing what it might be would be such an example. Today among the middle classes such patterns should be rare. Pattern 9 is a more extreme variant of 8, since the child is punished for not trying without regard to outcome.

The pattern of punishment for not trying and reward for success (Pattern 10) should be moderately successful at keeping the child in the situation, but it is difficult to guess its effect on motivation. Depending on the relationship of outcome experience to effort experience we might get moderate levels of both Hope of Success and Fear of Failure. However with Pattern 11, where success is rewarded and failure punished, the emphasis on punishment of effort and outcome should produce moderate levels of HP.

Pattern 12 says that the parents punish not trying and also failure. They are neutral to trying and to success. This person must try so that he is forced into the achievement situation where he encounters no reward for success and only punishment for failure. We are afraid this pattern really does exist and would expect it to lead to pathological behavior of some sort. We do not expect to find many of these cases in college populations. They should have extremely high HP scores. We do not think there have been many of these in our samples. We predict that high-HP persons should not volunteer for achievement situations. If these people have been punished for not trying, would they feel compelled to volunteer to show that they were trying, or would trying only occur after they have been constrained to the achievement situation? At present we have no idea.

Pattern 13, which calls for reward and punishment of effort but neutrality toward outcome, seems too improbable to deserve further comment. But Pattern 14 with its emphasis on rewards in both effort and outcome should produce at least moderate levels of Hope of Success. And Pattern 15 seems to be a very informative and realistic way of defining reality for the child. It provides major discriminations for the child and defines success and failure for effort, which is under self-control, as well as for the task outcome, which is contingent on reality demands. We would expect this pattern to give rise to both Hope of Success and Fear of Failure at high levels. This person should be most motivated of all. Since there is reason to predict Fear of Failure, we would expect this person to be reasonably high on HP as well as n Ach.

We have very little empirical data relating to the aforegoing material. Two studies have been done which apply directly to the reinforcement patterns of high-HP persons. Nothing has been done as yet in regard to the effort variable.

Teevan and McGhee (1966) tested two hypotheses having to do

with the genesis of HP. (1) There is no relationship between earliness of expected independence and achievement behaviors and HP. (2) Children whose mothers report punishing the child for not performing up to expectation will have higher HP scores than children whose mothers report rewarding behavior which comes up to expectation and neutral behavior when the child does not come up to expectation. (This is the outcome pattern found in numbers 4 and 2 of Table 7.1 and the rationale is given in the explanation of the table. We are making the prediction in terms of number 2).

The subjects were 41 male high-school juniors and seniors from a middle-sized high school. One hundred questionnaires were sent out to mothers of juniors and seniors; 41 were returned; all were used.

The HP measure was given in high school classes. Most of the 20 questions in the questionnaire which was sent to the mothers to be filled out were the same as those in Winterbottom's (1958) questionnaire on Mother's Standards of Training in Independence and Mastery. The questionnaire listed a series of expected behaviors. The mother was asked to check the items which they had expected of their son and also the age at which they expected it. The questionnaire also contained lists of alternative reactions of the mother to the child's behavior in situations such as those listed in the questionnaire. The mother was to indicate which reactions were most typical of her in relation to her child. References were made specifically to examples of children's behavior which, generally speaking, were related to achievement of one sort or another. Out of six possible responses to their sons when the sons had succeeded, three responses were characterized as "neutral": "Do nothing at all to make it seem special," "Show him you expected it of him," "Show him how he could have done better"; and three as "reward": "Kiss or hug him to show how pleased you are," "Tell him what a good boy he is; praise him for being good," and "Give him a special treat or privilege." Out of six possible responses to a son when the son's behavior has fallen short of the mother's expectations, three maternal responses were again characterized as "neutral": "Don't show any feeling about it," "Point out how he should have behaved," and "Just wait until he does what you want"; and three as "punishment": "Scold him or spank him for doing it," "Show him you are disappointed in him," and "Deprive him of something he likes or expects, such as a special treat or privilege." Each mother was asked to indicate her first, second, and third most characteristic responses to her son under each of the two conditions (success and failure of the child). The mothers were led to believe that the questionnaires would be anonymous so that their answers would be more honest. Questionnaires were actually coded in such a way that the mother and son combination could be made.

The expectation of no difference in the earliness of expected independence and achievement behaviors between high and low HP was disconfirmed. A chi-square test, shown in Table 7.2, indicated that mothers of high-HP subjects expect such behaviors earlier than did mothers of low-HP subjects. Children of mothers who report expecting independence and achievement behaviors early tend to be in HP.

TABLE 7.2. ACHIEVEMENT AND
INDEPENDENCE BEHAVIORS EXPECTED[a]

		Early	Late
Hostile Press	High	11	8
	Low	5	16

$$x^2 = 4.80, \; p < .05.$$

[a]Mothers were said to expect achievement and independence behaviors early or late on the following basis: a mean age was computed for each behavior, taking into consideration all mothers who reported expecting that behavior. If the age reported by a particular mother was below the mean, she was categorized as having expected that behavior early; if it was higher than the mean, she was categorized as having expected it late. Then, taking all 20 items into consideration, if more of her expectations fell in the early category, she was said to have expected these behaviors of her son early; if more fell in the late category, she was said to have expected them of her son late. If an equal number of early and late expectations were made, she was placed in neither category.

To test the second hypothesis, mean HP scores were computed for (*a*) children whose mothers had reported punishing the child for not coming up to expectations but being neutral when the child did come up to expectations and (*b*) children whose mothers reported rewarding the child when he came up to expectations and being neutral when he did not. Table 7.3 gives the analysis of the two means in terms of a *t*-test.

TABLE 7.3. MEAN HP SCORES FOR
REWARD-NEUTRAL AND NEUTRAL-PUNISHMENT GROUPS

Group	N	$\overline{X}$	t	df	p
Reward-Neutral	16	2.13			
Neutral-Punishment	4	4.50	2.41	18	< .05

The difference is significant at beyond the .05 level. Neutrality, when the child comes up to expectations, and punishment, when he does not, seem to favor the development of high HP. This finding has been replicated by Teevan and Fischer (1967).

The question then arose concerning the child's perception of his mother's responses to him in achievement situations. Was his perception of his mother's response type similar to the way in which she would have described it? If this was so, we would expect that when students were asked to fill out a questionnaire about their childhood similar to the one used by Teevan and McGhee (1966), any high-FF student would be classified as Neutral-Punishment as opposed to Reward-Neutral in terms of the way in which he perceived his mother's responses to him in achievement situations.

Such a questionnaire was administered to 123 male students at Bucknell University enrolled in the introductory psychology course during the fall semester 1966-67. The questionnaire asked each S to choose the characteristic response of his mother (1) when his behavior satisfied his mother's expectations and (2) when it did not. In each case there were six possible responses to choose from which were essentially the same as those used in the first study. The Ss were instructed to number their choices in terms of the first, second, and third most characteristic responses made by their mothers.

Out of the 123 Ss, 45 were classified as Neutral-Punishment in terms of the way they stated their mothers responded to them in achievement situations, and 22 were classified as Reward-Neutral. (Forty-four Ss were classified as Reward-Punishment and 12 as Neutral-Neutral.) Table 7.4 represents a chi-square analysis of the N-P and R-N groups in terms of a median split of HP scores. This analysis yields a chi-square value of 6.41, which is significant at p less than .02.

TABLE 7.4. THE EFFECT OF OUTCOME R IN-
FORCEMENT PATTERNS ON HOSTILE PRESS SCORES

	Success-Neutral Failure-Punishment	Success-Reward Failure-Neutral	Total
High HP	25	5	30
Low HP	20	17	37
Total	45	22	67

$X^2 = 6.41$, 1 *df.*, $p < .02$.

The data thus indicated that *S*s who characterized themselves as N-P in terms of their mother's responses have higher HP scores than those who characterized themselves as R-N. This finding can be seen as supporting Teevan and McGhee's (1966) finding, and also as an indication that the child's own perception of his mother's responses to him in achievement situations is crucial to the childhood development of fear-of-failure motivations.

It would seem that if our research and thinking about the genesis of HP is valid, there would be some implications for how one would go about changing people on this variable. If a child became high in HP because he received punishment when he did not come up to expectations in achievement situations but received only a neutral reaction when he did come up to expectations, there might be some suggestion that a changed reinforcement pattern would change the orientation towards achievement. Suppose we gave a child rewards for succeeding in achievement situations and made sure that he did not fail. Would this have the effect of changing his HP score? We believe it would, but we have not yet done the research to bear it out.

There are certain problems in the above idea. Is there a point beyond which irreversibility sets in? It may be that a changed reinforcement pattern would work for a seven-year-old but not for a ten-year-old. Only empirical research can answer the question. It would seem to make sense to conduct this kind of research in school systems, since the high-HP child is forced into the situation and should be looking for ways to defend against failure. A promising technique to assure success and guard against failure would seem to be the use of programing. A program for a given set of material can be pretested so as to give the desired amount of success and failure. It would also give control over the amount of material or the amount of time spent in a way that conventional teaching methods could not match.

Another matter to watch would be the combination of fear of failure and hope of success. As a value judgment one might not want to change HP scores, because this might mean subtracting motivation in school situations. Finally, we must repeat that these initial studies have not focused on the patterns of reinforcement used for effort, and we suspect that research here will shed further light on the origins of HP.

However, there is another facet of high HP which must be considered when we are talking about change and the value of change. One might suggest that, in an achievement oriented culture, a negative approach to achievement could very well lead to poor adjustment. A feeling that one cannot win but can only lose in situations which the culture defines as exceedingly important would not seem to be a healthy feeling. It is also true that the use of defenses as the main procedure in these situations may be taken as indicating a less than ideal situation. If a person is acting only to avoid failure in situations where the culture places a great accent on succeeding, his satisfactions would seem to be minimal.

Looking at matters from this viewpoint, we would expect that the high HP person would have a self-image which might well be quite discrepant from what the society recommends, especially in the area of achievement behavior. The theorizing of Rogers (1951, 1959) becomes very relevant here. He argues that the discrepancy between the perceived (actual) self and the ideal self (self as the person thinks he should be) is a measure of mental health, the person with the larger discrepancy being seen as more disturbed.

In studying this problem, Smith and Teevan (1964) stated three hypotheses: 1. There is a significant negative relationship between HP and congruence of the perceived and ideal self-concepts. 2. There is a significant negative relationship between HP and the congruence between the perceived and ideal ratings of achievement-related items or traits. 3. There is a significant negative relationship between HP and adjustment.

The subjects were 49 male college students who were required to participate in the experiment as part of their course material. The HP measure was given under neutral conditions. The perceived vs. ideal self-concept was measured by use of the 100-item

Butler-Haigh Q-sort (1954). The second hypothesis having to do with the achievement items was measured through the use of the Brownfain (1952) Self-Rating Inventory as used by Martire (1956). The achievement-related items were ranked by the subjects twice: once for real and once for ideal self.

To test Hypothesis 1 a rank-order correlation was used. The correlation found was —.29. A *t* was calculated for this correlation and came out to be 2.31, which is significant at the .025 level, one-tailed. Hypothesis 1 was confirmed: there is a significant negative correlation between HP and perceived-ideal self-congruence. The high-HP person has a larger discrepancy between his "real" and his "ideal" self.

To test Hypothesis 2, the Brownfain Self-Rating Inventory items were ordered from one to five for each subject, and a rank correlation was computed between the SRI items and HP. The correlation was —.45, which yielded a *t* of 3.31. This *t* is significant beyond the .005 level, one-tailed. In the achievement area, then, the high-HP person has a larger discrepancy between "real" and "ideal" self than has the low. Hypothesis 2 was also confirmed.

To test Hypothesis 3—that HP is negatively related to adjustment—an adjustment score was computed from the Q-sort. This score was first devised by Dymong (1953), who had clinical psychologists divide the items of the Butler-Haigh (1954) Q-sort into those the well-adjusted person would say are like him and those he would say are unlike him. An adjustment score can thus be calculated for each subject by summing the items that he placed in the well-adjusted categories. When these scores were computed and correlated with HP scores, the correlation was —.20. The *t* computed from this correlation was 1.41, which is significant beyond the .10 level. The finding was in the predicted direction but did not reach the .05 level of confidence; yet the authors felt that the hypothesis had received some confirmation.

Although the above study is the only one in the field, and thus needs replication, we feel that it fits our other researches and theorizing well enough that we can say that high HP, in this culture, leads to certain psychological problems. This gives more urgency to research on methods of changing the patterns of HP in children.

CHAPTER 8

Integrating the Study of Fear of Failure

EARLIER IN THIS BOOK WE ALERTED THE READER TO THE FACT THAT our research was one of several programs currently being pursued. We made the point that the term "Fear of Failure" was an area term, used in a variety of ways, and that such multiple usage was unfortunate but unavoidable at this stage of research. Any construct term serves to denote a set of relationships for summary purposes. It is obvious that the researchers in this area are using a variety of measuring operations and are looking for the effects of the measured construct in a wide variety of dependent variables. Nor can we attempt to bolster the reader's confidence in any particular measure or procedure by claiming that it is firmly rooted in some broader theoretical context. This has been a program which borrows freely from behavior theory, psychoanalytic theory, and utility theory alike, wherever the experimenters found them useful. We prefer to think that still another form of theory is emerging—call it motivation theory if you like—which reflects operations devoted to content analysis, whether the content be assent or denial to questions put to the S, or stories he has written about pictures. Such operations are sufficiently unique in character that they do not easily lend themselves to theories having other data bases. At any rate, we take it as no accident that researchers interested in a particular type of avoidance behavior, i.e., Fear of Failure in achievement situations viewed as a matter of individual differences, adopt similar research strategies and similar construct language.

Turning to the problem of measurement, it is obvious that the term "Fear of Failure" gives little guidance to the type of motive measure to be used. There is a literature reviewed in Chapter 2 where researchers employed objective techniques to subject *S*s to failure or the anticipation of failure by falsifying scores, employing negative reinforcement schedules, or making the tasks progressively more difficult. This method does not use a measure of individual differences in strength of fear, but rather, contrasts groups treated in differing ways. There are several literature reviews of these studies which summarize their findings, and essentially they report as follows (C. G. Costello, in Sysenck, 1964):

1. Overall, regardless of task or *S* ability level, praise produces greater increases in output than blame.
2. For many tasks, especially those where *S* has some prior experience, blame may cause a decrease in performance.
3. For tasks quite new to the *S*s, blame may be as effective as praise, but neither may produce much in the way of improvement.
4. Failure or success sometimes affects variability instead of level of performance, and it is not unusual for the treatments to have no effect at all.
5. Both failure and success effects may generalize to other tasks similar in nature or associated in time.

Very few of these findings have been the product of sustained programmatic research by the same researchers with the same populations across time. It is very difficult to abstract from this literature any firm generalizations about the effects of failure on performance and experience. The best we can suggest is that the failure operation derives its effectiveness from the degree of ego involvement that the task evoked from the *S*, and that its effect varies with the degree of experience that *S* has had in dealing with similar failure in the past. It appears that with high ego-involvement, failure may produce increased effort which may in turn cause a deterioration of performance. Praise seems to produce a more modulated increase in effort that permits efficient functioning. This all adds up to a statement of the conditions under which the Yerkes-Dodson law may hold for human *S*s.

Obviously the general findings for praise and blame do not acknowledge the presence of individual differences in motivation toward the task situation, and only by introducing such measures will more precise estimates of the determinants of behavior become possible.

If we look on Fear of Failure as a special case of general anxiety we may immediately inquire whether the literature of anxiety scales will prove helpful. The research done on the Manifest Anxiety Scale, MAS (Taylor, 1953), and the Test Anxiety Questionnaire, TAQ (Mandler, Sarason, 1949) has been reviewed by Atkinson (1954). He shows very clearly that the chief interest of the Iowa group in the MAS is to provide a measure of drive level that will prove useful for more refined study of learning processes. In none of the many studies recently reviewed by Spence (1964) is there a concern for anxiety level as a contributor to choice or initiatory behaviors. The emphasis has been on eyelid conditioning, serial learning, and paired associates learning. Even here it develops that the presence of "threatening" stimuli seems to contribute to the appearance of depressed performance for the Ss reporting high anxiety levels. From our point of view the concentration upon issues of learning, even the important theoretical question of whether anxiety is best viewed as general drive level vs. a stimulus to anxiety-reducing responses, has not provided us with findings relevant to motivational questions.

We are impressed that Ss who report feeling highly anxious in test situations can be so identified by raters having no knowledge of their test scores (Mandler and Sarason, 1952). But our view is that Ss may become anxious from a variety of motivational bases of which Fear of Failure may be just one. Thus we are prepared to find that Ss high in MAS or TAQ may display some behaviors similar to those high in HP or FF, but there is no necessary reason to argue that these measures reflect the same motivation. As summarized by Sarason (1960), the MAS findings show (*a*) S's performance "is detrimentally affected by verbally administered highly motivating communications" (p. 411); (*b*) that, as task complexity increases, the disadvantages of high to low anxious Ss appears to increase" (p. 411); and (*c*) that no firm relationships have been established between general anxiety scores and intelligence scores or physiological indices. This pattern is not incompatible with the findings reported in this book for the studies of Ss high in HP.

A second literature of more direct interest to us is that generated by Atkinson and his associates using the combination of n Ach and TAQ scores to proved patterns for which the presence of Fear of Failure may be inferred. Thus Atkinson argued that low n-Ach–high-TAQ should be the pattern most characterized by Fear of Failure, or as he phrases it, avoidance tendency. In other words, the S who reports test anxiety and does not produce imagery emphasizing approach motivation to achievement situations is most likely to be in an avoidance condition. In the absence of a projective scoring system for Fear of Failure, Atkinson chose to proceed with the combined projective and self-report scores. The dependent variables used in these experiments reflect Atkinson's model for motivation which uses Motive $\times$ Expectancy (success-failure) $\times$ Incentive, with the special assumption for achievement motivation that the E $\times$ I relationship is reciprocal (1957). Thus these experiments concentrate on aspiration, memory, choice of task, and choice of task difficulty.

By combining the TAQ with projective measurement of n Ach, Atkinson was able to generate a wide array of relationships, as we will see. From our point of view, of course, the question remains: What did the low-n-Ach *S*s write in their stories? There is little doubt but that in the most general sense the low-n-Ach–high-TAQ *S*s were behaving in a generally avoidant fashion. Their performance suggests that they are not comfortable in achievement situations which test for individual proficiency. Certainly much of the LA data and choice of task data suggest defensive behavior. Yet there is no necessary reason to suppose that Fear of Failure projectively measured will show high positive correlation with TAQ scores. Again, we repeat, high TAQ might occur in response to a variety of avoidance motives.

This position is supported by Sarason's own theorizing about test anxiety.

Central to our conception of this problem is the assumption that anxiety is a danger signal indicating that the situation has increased the strength of certain ideas, wishes, or phantasies which, if allowed conscious expression and elaboration, might result in behavior towards and from others which would seriously endanger the child's well-being (p. 13).

Following the psychoanalytic view of repression of hostility as the source of the anxiety producing impulses, Sarason then argues that

Sullivan's conceptions and description, moreover, serve as a basis for specifying that the anxious reaction has been engendered in the child in part because the behavior of the parent explicitly or implicitly threatens the child with loss of parental approval and love, i.e. a threat to the stability of the child's self-system which cues off anxiety (p. 38). . . . [These strategies of the parent are thought to] communicate in various ways to the child an attitude which has two major effects: (1) it devalues the adequacy of the child's behavior or performance, and

(2) it renders the child relatively incapable of expressing overtly the hostility engendered in him" (p. 18).

This second requirement is seen as separable from the first, and should avenues of expression be open, the child ought not to become anxious. The key to the presence of anxiety is the presence of guilt over the hostility toward the de-valuating other.

Given the above theory, it follows that the effect of test anxiety will be to interfere with performance and that the test situations in which the child is given ample support in his efforts—i.e., his dependency requirements are met—will produce anxiety-free performance.

Sarason and his associate (1960) have produced experimental studies of school children which suggest that the theorizing has merit. Children confessing to physical symptoms of test anxiety, dreams of failure, and phantasies of escape from testing situations are found across the entire range of measured intellectual ability. They perform well when they are permitted time to focus their efforts without penalty for error and perform less well than their low-anxiety peers on speeded or error-penalty tests. Since most tests of aptitude and intelligence are of the latter variety, we find negative correlations between measured test anxiety (TASC) and IQ scores derived from the Otis Alpha, Otis Beta, Pintner-Cunningham, or Kuhlmann-Anderson group test. The values fall in the —30's and are subject to variation by sex and by administration conditions as well as the type of IQ measure.

More recently, Kogan and Wallach (1964) and (1967), used the debilitating scale of the Alpert-Haber (1960) Achievement Anxiety Test (AAT) in combination with the Marlowe-Crowne (1960) to test for "moderating" effects of these measures on correlations between performance measures of risk taking, post-decision satisfaction, scholastic aptitude, and confidence obtained from college undergraduates. Here the strategy is to search for variation in association between performance variables which is differentially effected by patterns of personality measures. For instance, they report that "in those cases where the decision-making task is embedded in a format suggestive of an intelligence or aptitude assessment, the test anxiety moderator becomes more critical and defensiveness [need for approval] assumes more of a background role" (p. 68). Using a measure of risk taking, they also found that males who were high on test anxiety showed conservative play only if they were high on verbal ability, but risky play if they were low in verbal ability. This leads to the suspicion "that general risk-taking tendencies influence behavior in both test-taking and decision-making contexts" (p. 9). Those who are conservative and test-anxious show caution when guessing and thus enhance their score, while those who are risk-takers and test-anxious depress their scores with poor guesses. The authors also suggest that Ss high on both test anxiety and need for approval are more concerned with decision-making strategy than with the actual outcomes, since in tests of skill the less they win the more satisfaction they express with their bets. Presumably this means they see the use of risky bets as more reinforcing than the actual accumulation of winnings possible with more conservative betting.

These studies assumed that test anxiety would be a "motivational disrupter" (which is what the test items ask the Ss to report) and that the Marlowe-Crowne need-for-approval scale would reflect "an excessive concern with image maintenance." The patterns of behavior they report for Ss high on these measures do suggest avoidance behavior in achievement settings as well as behavior whose instrumental value seems to be that it might preserve the self-image. The source of these two dispositions is not suggested in the pattern of these findings, however, since it was the author's intention to concentrate on the pattern of behaviors displayed across a variety of task situations where risk was a consideration.

From Sarason's point of view, test anxiety represents a failure of defense, and as such produces directly experienced affect of a disturbing kind which renders the child "more aware of his own covert responses than he is of the nature of the external stimulus situation, which includes, of course, the stimulus task and accompanying instructions" (p. 20). Thus the interference and loss of performance or, in the case of the highly intelligent child, a heightening of tensions follows.

The theory that guilt over hostility toward the threat of abandonment constitutes the origin of the anxiety response suggests that the TAT themes of such Ss might be filled with the kind of hostile press imagery we have found in our studies of fear of failure. However the role of such phantasy, or more precisely, the role of such a world view, might also be to guard against anxiety attacks. We are struck here by the similarity of the task-situation behaviors found for those with HP and FF to that described for the high TAQ scorer, and by the dissimilarity of correlations with aptitude measures as well as the absence of correlation between the measures.

A comparison of the task behavior found for Ss with high test-anxiety scores with those displaying HP or FF shows them to be quite similar. But as we see in Table 8.3, there is no relationship between these measures. We interpret Atkinson's findings with the TAQ as quite consistent with Sarason's theory, rather than his own view that low n Ach and high TAQ reveal a disposition to inhibit achievement approach tendencies (see pp. 149-150 for this discussion).

The theory that guilt over hostility toward the threat of abandonment for failure constitutes the origin of test anxiety unfortunately does not lead to clear or obvious predictions concerning the content of associated phantasy. Presumably the phantasy could serve either to express the hostility directly, in which case themes of aggression by the hero might dominate, or to express the hostility in disguised forms such as power or dominance themes; or the phantasy might be equally repressive and hence highly symbolic. Our finding that Ss who write themes of hostile press following the failure experience also display avoidance in achievement situations, without necessarily reporting test anxiety, suggests that projective measurement and self-report devices need to be integrated into research designs so that we can develop more refined statements of our hypothetical constructs.

At this writing it is simply not possible to state with confidence that, for instance, a common type of childhood experience with task situations produces ways of thinking about such situations and tendencies to experience negative affect which produce similar task behaviors despite a disassociation of thought and affect. It does appear that HP and FF signify greater adaptive tendencies and higher thresholds against the disruptive effects of task anxiety, since they show no correlation with IQ measures and a positive correlation with school achievement.

The most obvious hypothesis to pursue may be that early hostility toward parents may produce a low threshold for test anxiety, and in time, this produces various defenses in the form of attitudes and beliefs about the world which contribute to the imagery found in apperceptive methods. If some children succeed in such constructions, they may be much less prone to the effects of test anxiety, providing the imagery is securely associated with those stimuli which produce the anxiety reaction. Only careful exploration of the types of achievement situations usually encountered can shed light on these associations. This also suggests that not only the fact of parental threat but the form of imagery in which it is stated should be investigated. Sarason gives us a hint of the type of data to collect when he describes the mother of the high-anxiety child as "one who responds to and evaluates the behavior of her child not in terms of his capabilities (e.g., inhibiting aggressive or other strong feelings) or age-appropriate needs but in terms of standards and values which reflect her dependence on the attitudes of others" (p. 232). One wonders what type of rationale she communicates to the child in justification of her evaluation—especially what view of the world's standards of evaluation.

We can offer the tentative hypothesis that some of our patterns of reinforcement of effort and outcome discussed in Chapter 7 may be more likely to produce test anxiety than others. Sarason's comment above suggests that the mother of the high test-anxious child is one who reinforces outcomes more than effort. Conceivably the key to understanding the variations of avoidance behavior found in achievement situations will be in the analysis of the reinforcement patterns used in these situations by parents.

The implications of the research with the TAQ and the appercep-tive methods suggests we may be faced with the old distinction between thought and feeling. The TAQ items mix this language, e.g., "Do you sometimes dream at night that you are in school and cannot answer the teacher's questions?" versus "When the teacher says she is going to find out how much you have learned, does your heart begin to beat faster?" But the majority of the items inquire about worry, fear, trembling, crying, funny feelings, and the like. In contrast the scoring systems of HP and FF, while definitely using statements of affect, also score for actions, needs, and circumstances (imagery) which constitute a construction of a situation. We see that to a considerable extent these two approaches signal the same class of avoidance behavior in achievement situations. Essentially this means that persons with negative thoughts about situations act in a manner similar to those who feel disturbed by the situation. The differences in relationship to school achievement and IQ tests suggests further that the presence of negative views about tests of achievement may lead to adaptive behavior when there is time for preparation or when the subject can defend against the anxiety itself.

A number of combinations of these measures suggest themselves for future research. One can imagine that some *S*s report positive thoughts about achievement striving while confessing to debilitating anxiety. These are the students who have learned to value ideas, respect learning, appreciate task success, and at the same time suffer from anxiety decrement in their work. Or we might find the opposite, those who have nothing but negative views of achievement striving, perform adequately in order to serve other motivational systems, and are anxiety-free.

Since test anxiety interferes with performance, there is no question but that it should be counterconditioned where possible. To the extent that it has originated in parent-child relationships which have produced strong hostility toward the parents and associated teachers, such counterconditioning will prove difficult, as we all know. Since fear of failure also interferes with performance, it too should be eliminated if possible. But here we deal with a way of evaluating the world and its power (HP) or the possibility of suffering public shame or experiencing guilt (FF), and these views will require change in belief or attitude. One can sense here the sources of difficulty in trying to frame procedures for reducing the effects of fear or anxiety. Not until we have a clearer picture of the patterns to be diagnosed can we make a start at change procedures.

A Comparison of HP and FF

Turning to the projective systems for measuring Fear of Failure, we have already seen that three main groupings of literature exist. One grouping centering on studies done in the United States with college and elementary school samples has concentrated on using the Fear of Failure scoring systems as dependent variables. However, in the work of Heckhausen (1963) we have an extensive program on research using subjects at all school levels in a variety of behavioral situations. We have already said that Heckhausen's system scores for themes of concern over achievement failure, i.e., direct expression of failure imagery. An exhaustive review of his work is not possible here. Concentrating on the same behavioral domain, however, we summarize as follows (Birney, in press):

In situations where clear information is available HS Ss overestimate failures while FF Ss overestimate success. These reactions reverse themselves as the feedback becomes ambiguous. On simple tasks requiring no special ability he finds the HS students slow and disinterested but they display good study habits, work more quickly on complex problems, and respond to mild time pressure for problems requiring planning with better solutions than under no pressure. The FF students work speedily and well on simple tasks, show poor study habits, take more time on complex problems, and show a deterioration of solutions as time pressure increases. On maze problems the HS *S*s show the greater gains with practice.

Certainly these findings reflect a pattern of avoidance behavior, but this time they are the correlates of *S*s whose fantasies show a preoccuptaion with failure and its effects. Heckhausen calls his scoring Fear of Failure and Hope of Success with justification. And yet, as we have seen, we have generated a similar pattern of findings using a projective scoring system that is composed of generalized threat and hostility which we call the Hostile Press (HP) score. Obviously there are some major differences in our work. Heckhausen has devised his own set of pictures, and his population is German. But we too have produced new pictures. The key may lie in the populations, since it is perfectly possible that Fear of Failure is treated differently in the two cultures.

A joint research program with Heckhausen and his associates has been initiated to study fear of failure on a comparative basis. Results from an initial study will be reported here, followed by a brief description of the current work in progress.

Given the differences between pictures, scoring codes, and populations in the German and American programs, the initial study was designed to permit an assessment of the role played by each of these sources of variance. Since each program had emerged empirically in an effort to establish the construct validity of a fear-of-failure measure, we began by trying to interpret the obtained differences. The scoring codes for Heckhausen's FF emphasize direct expression of Need to avoid failure, Anticipation of possible task failure, Negative affect over failure, Instrumental action to avoid or recoup failure, and Thema preoccupation with task failure. In a preliminary effort Birney had concluded that the incidence of such imagery in his American college sample was too low, even when using pictures of students in academic test situations. Inspection of the German pictures suggested the presence of an authority figure whose role it was to evaluate task performance. By contrast the American scoring code emphasizes the hostile threat of nonachievement forces, and the pictures emphasize solitary figures or pairs of figures whose authority relationships are somewhat ambiguous.

This initial reading of the differences between the codes and pictures suggested that we were faced with a cultural difference.

We took as our guiding hypothesis the proposition that differences in child-rearing practices lead to German youth being reinforced for the direct expression of fear of failure, while American youth receive negative reinforcement. If we assume that the American youth were encouraged to remain optimistic about success in the face of actual failure, it seemed plausible that the phantasy associations of achievement task failure would take on a vague, generalized character in which explicit achievement references tend to be omitted.

On the other hand it was our impression that German task masters see value in having the learner experience a sense of personal shame and defeat when he fails. Such an expression is taken as a sign of involvement, and unless some such expression is made the teacher or parent may feel that the failure has not been recognized. Therefore the child may be reinforced for expressing feelings of fear and of failure.

We have no evidence to offer for these assumptions at this time beyond our personal experience with the American and German cultures, but in dealing with students of college age, one is struck by the emotional tension to be seen in German students who are being evaluated by an instructor and their willingness to take full blame or credit for the performance. In contrast it has often seemed to us that failure for the American students is seen as a block or source of frustration which has appeared in the environment. They speak of having "trouble" with the course or instructor who is "giving me a hard time." The affective language emphasizes being upset, disturbed, irritated, or angry rather than humiliated or ashamed.

Given these intuitive observations we felt a "repression" hypothesis had some merit. One might question whether we are justified in speaking of repression when we assert that the American has been taught to deny personal feelings of shame and humiliation. But we are holding that during the earlier age of competence training the young child does have such feelings which are subsequently trained out of his expressed imagery and given the overlay of "hostile environment" imagery which comes through on the stories.

We must bear in mind that FF and HP predict very similar behaviors in achievement settings. It is for this reason that we argue for the identity of construct validity between the two as related to their respective cultures. In other words, we feel that the two cultures are sufficiently alike that fear-motivated behavior in achievement task settings will be very similar. This line of argument leads to the con-

clusion that those *S*s who do show the imagery of the other culture
will not show similar avoidance behaviors. Thus the American who
writes FF and the German who writes HP are not expected to behave
like their cultural counterparts. The American may be one who can
accept his fear, express it, and use it to further involve himself in
achievement striving. And the German may be one whose HP imagery
signals social withdrawal rather than task withdrawal. At this point
we can only assert that we expect to find a rather different set of
behavioral relationships, and hence a different hypothetical construct
for these findings.

Obviously the first fact to establish is whether or not the respective
populations would maintain their thematic preferences when faced
with pictures from the other culture. Since neither population had
had its stories scored by persons who were expert in using the codes,
it was quite possible that picture differences and scorer differences
accounted for the population differences discussed above. Should this
be the case, the collection of data on matched populations whose
stories were expertly scored might yield identical levels of the two
scoring codes, i.e. Germans might write HosP to the American pictures, and Americans might write FF to the German pictures. Although we have been referring to pictures as a battery, the pictures
used do permit a more refined matching for achievement cue value,
and we stated our hypotheses accordingly (see below).

The second analysis to be performed is to determine the extent
of correlation between the two scoring systems within the populations. Our major hypothesis suggests that these values should be of
zero order.

Finally we were prepared to face a third and more complicated
possibility. Conceivably a comparison of the FF written by Americans
with that written by Germans might show context differences, i.e.,
might be contingent on as yet uncoded features of the stories whose
presence up to now has been implicit. Once again there would be
no assurance that the same score would imply identical behavior for
the two cultures.

To review the possibilities, we could find that each sample does
write material codable by the opposite scoring system to their own
picture battery. In this case the "repression" hypothesis is shaken,
and we must learn what the behavioral correlates of the systems may
be cross-culturally. Or we could find that the samples write the
foreign material only to foreign pictures; in which case we must
ask two questions. First, are the picture differences themselves due

to cultural effects? And second, do such scores have any predictive value? Or finally we could find that each sample writes only its own imagery regardles of pictures, which would correspond to the strong case of the "repression" hypothesis.

The experimental design adopted for the comparison of the scoring systems used samples of American and German students of college age. The American sample (*N* is 132) ranged from 18 to 21 years with a median of 19, and a majority of the students came from the upper-middle-class and lower-upper-middle-class strata. These students were given the story-writing task during a regular laboratory period in the introductory course in psychology. The German *S*s were 31 female students and 41 male students at the Psychological Institute of the Ruhr University, enrolled in the basic experimental course. The social strata are predominantly middle class, and median age, 21 years. Unlike the American research, there have been no major sex differences in the German findings. Hence the German sample includes both sexes.

Both administrations used the Neutral instructional set. Four groups of approximately 35 *S*s each were used in the American testing. Each American group received eight pictures—four German and four American. The German administration used two successive administrations, one week apart, beginning with the German set of pictures. Table 8.1 lists the pictures in each battery with their primary cue designations.

Scoring was done by experts with scoring reliabilities in the +.90's.* The German stories were translated into English before being scored for HP by Birney.

Analysis of the Cross-Cultural Study

A review of the distributions of scores for the samples by picture battery revealed that the overall level of scores, especially HP, is too low to permit the use of parametric indices; i.e., too large a proportion of the *S*s had zero scores. Therefore a more appropriate test of the hypotheses was made by treating each picture separately and using contingency statistics. Table 8.1 shows the proportions of *S*s scored for the respective Fear of Failure systems for each picture.

Hypothesis 1 holds that German *S*s will write more FF than American *S*s, on both picture batteries, with the effect strongest on German pictures D, E, and F. We see that this hypothesis receives support

---

* We are indebted to H. Gotzl and F. Beisenbuch for the FF scoring.

TABLE 8.1. PERCENT FREQUENCIES OF Ss SCORED FOR GERMAN (FF) AND AMERICAN (HP) FEAR-OF-FAILURE INDICES FOR PICTURES IN THE GERMAN AND AMERICAN TEST BATTERIES.[a]

German Pictures	German FF	American FF	X^2	German HP	American HP	X^2
A (HS) Smiling student	32	27	—	3	0	—
B (FF) Director's door	51	57	—	26	25	—
C (HS) Shop workers	37	29	1.28	26	23	—
D (FF) Teacher-pupil	90	68	9.68^b	6	26	8.00^b
E (HS) Man at desk	29	13	5.12^c	6	5	—
F (FF) Lab workers	51	26	12.50^b	22	32	

American Pictures	German FF	American FF	X^2	German HP	American HP	X^2
A (HS) Shop workers	67	62	—	2	6	—
B (HS) Father-son TAT 7	21	24	—	32	28	—
C (HS) Boy in class-room	67	59	3.26	29	18	1.28
D (FF) Man at desk (bufferin)	45	70	12.50^b	23	49	13.52^b
E (FF) Streetlight TAT	9	13	—	14	22	—
F (FF) Man at mirror	4	23	7.22^b	8	5	—

[a]German number of Ss for German pictures is 78; for American pictures, $N = 67$; American Ns range from 57 to 132 across pictures.
[b]$p < .01$.
[c]$p < .05$.

from four of the six pictures, with pictures D, E and F yielding significantly higher FF scores for Germans than for Americans.

Hypothesis 2 holds that American Ss will write more HP than German Ss on both picture batteries, with the strongest effect on American pictures D, E, and F. This hypothesis receives support from American picture D alone. More over, the Americans show more FF on this picture and on picture F, which means that American Ss do write FF to their own pictures.

Taken together, we find that Germans and Americans do write the others' imagery, but do so rather differently on Fear-of-Failure-cued pictures. Achievement-cued pictures pull equal amounts of each.

Hypothesis 3 (or expectation 3) was that FF and HP would not be correlated. Table 8.2 shows the correlations for each picture battery by sample, including the German sex groups. None of the values reach significance; thus our expectation gets support.

TABLE 8.2. CORRELATION OF FF AND HP BASED ON GERMAN AND AMERICAN PICTURE BATTERIES

	German Pictures	American Pictures
German males and females	+ .19[a] (N = 78)	+ .07 (N = 66)
American males	− .03 (N = 68)	+ .08 (N = 68)

[a] $p < .02$.

Picture Effects. The chief picture effect occurs on the Fear-of-Failure-cued pictures and seems to hinge on the authority-subordinate relationship portrayed. German picture D, the teacher-pupil picture, shows high FF and low HP for German Ss and a tendency for the oposite for American Ss. The same pattern appears for picture F, in which the laboratory workers are often seen as master and apprentice. Picture C fails to show a significant HP dominance by the German sample, but in this picture the younger worker is often seen as the authority, thus confounding the usual relationship. Within the German picture battery the German Ss give the least FF to pictures A and E, which are solitary figures. Picture B shows a solitary figure standing attentively before a door marked Director. Both samples of Ss write FF to this picture, and as we shall see below, there seem to be context differences within the stories for the two samples. The German Ss also write here of "boss-to-clerk" relationships.

When we consider the American failure-cued pictures which emphasize solitary figures—the man at the desk, the figure under the streetlight, and the man at the mirror—we find the German Ss writing lower levels of FF and HP. Thus it appears that the German Ss respond with FF to the authority-subordinate relationship in a way that Americans do not, and Americans are more sensitive to suggestions or loss or abandonment.

The American sample presents a rather different pattern. Failure-cued pictures both of solitary figures and of authority relationships elicit HP, and FF tends to be associated with solitary figures in work situations, i.e., pictures B (German), C (American), and D (American), as well as the teacher-pupil picture D (German) and the two inventors, picture A (American). This pattern suggests that the Americans are not particularly sensitive to the authority-subordinate dimension, but rather to more general task situation cues. The high level of FF obtained was not expected, and offers the opportunity to examine the FF scoring system more closely. The German picture B, showing the man at the director's door, elicited FF from over half of each sample and offers excellent material for comparison.

A reading of the stories by both samples strongly suggests that the FF written by Americans has a different context from that written by the Germans. This amounts to saying that additional scoring codes could be devised to supplement the FF codes which would discriminate between the samples. Such codes do not now exist, but samples of what we mean can be provided. Again, the context seems to involve the authoritarian relationship. The Americans treat the authority figure differently, and the FF material scored originates in a thematic source quite different from that of the Germans. Consider the following German story:

> An anxious bookkeeper is standing in front of the manager's door. He found a mistake in the registration and knows that it will have an immense effect on the calculation. Now he thinks how he can tell it. At the moment he cannot think clearly, merely parts of sentences he prepared previously. His expectations will be fulfilled. He will leave the room dejected, humiliated.

Under the FF scoring system this story received a score of four for action, and negative outcome. A similar American story reads as follows:

> With pipe in hand docile Ralph approached the Director's door, paused a moment, then knocked. Ralph has been reprimanded about his mistakes in filling orders. He had just made another mistake. "Boy, I'll catch it this time. And on his personal order too." The Director asks Ralph in. Ralph nervously tells of his mistake showing the order

form. The boss recognizes that *he* had made the mistake and forgives Ralph, but doesn't say why.

This story is also scored for negative affect, and negative anticipation, but there is something about the hero's use of "catch it" as well as the discovery that it is the Director himself that is at fault, that renders the personal involvement of Ralph much less intense than that of the figure in the German story. The two stories were chosen to illustrate our feeling that even nearly identical circumstances have a different ring. One possibility here, which must not be overlooked, is that the American sample reflects a social strata effect, since the Americans tend to come from higher strata than the German sample.

Further inspection of the stories to this picture suggests that the American Ss write more about people of little talent who keep trying to succeed and do not, or about underlings who find their bosses in compromising circumstances, or about little men who see themselves as failures and accept it, much the way one accepts a chronic disability. There is affect in all these stories, but it seems to lack the personal sense of responsibility so common in the German stories. Despite the high incidence of FF scored for each sample to this picture, we are left with the distinct feeling that German FF may not be American FF. Only the development of additional scoring codes can shed light on the possibility that even here the personal-vs.-environmental dimension distinguishes the cultures. Heckhausen has observed that there is freedom in structuring the relationship to a superordinate person behind the door, so the FF by Americans may avoid the threat reflected in HP, and vice versa for the Germans.

Summary of the FF to HP Relationship. Viewing the findings as a whole, we find that two of the three failure-cued pictures in the German series show significantly more FF written by the German students than the Americans. The third picture shows fairly high levels for both groups. In one case, the teacher-pupil picture, the Americans also show significantly more HP than the Germans. The Hope-of-Success-cued pictures gave low levels of both HP and FF for both. groups. However, on the two pictures showing German preference for FF imagery, the Americans gave 65 percent and 26 percent levels for FF, which are not low. We do find what appears to be a cultural effect, however. This impression is reinforced by the percentages obtained using the American pictures.

The failure-cued pictures in the American series show that one of the three pictures yields an HP level which is significantly greater for the American sample, but two of these pictures show significantly more FF for the Americans. Thus it appears that pictures showing solitary figures in darkened settings produce more FF and HP from Americans than from Germans. Again the success-cued pictures show fairly high levels of both scores for both groups.

This pattern of findings is complex. German pictures favor German imagery (FF) by German Ss, but American pictures favor German imagery (FF) by American Ss most strongly; and American imagery (HP) by American Ss is favored on one picture from each series.

We have found that each sample writes the other's imagery; hence there is no support for the "repression" hypothesis. However, there is a cultural effect operating in the picture differences, which, on inspection, seems to hinge on the presence and nature of the authority cues present in the pictures. We also found no correlation between the two systems, sugesting they might develop from different sources of experience. Finally, there is some reason to suspect that each system may require still more codes before we can be certain each sample is writing the other's imagery.

Further Studies of FF and HP

Under the auspices of the Psychological Institute at the Ruhr University, Bochum, Federal Republic of Germany, a series of experiments was conducted using both the FF and HP measures. Without presenting the designs in detail, our basic strategy can be outlined. Essentially the aim was to gather task-performance and level-of-aspiration measures to permit validity comparisons using performance measures whose relationships to the motive measures have been previously established. Next, the ideas presented in Chapter 9 were used to design situations in which opposite forms of behavior were predicted from the two measures. In particular, FF was viewed as implying sensitivity to internal affective states of a task-related nature, and HP was hypothesized to reflect sensitivity to external sources of threat to the self. Efforts to vary conditions of public and private performance, source of evaluation, and the like, were designed to test for differences in the behavior of the two fear-of-failure groups. A similar series of experiments is being initiated with American samples, in an effort to shed more light on the nature of fear of failure in the two cultures. At this writing, analysis of the data is in progress and we have no further findings to report beyond the picture study.

Summary

We opened this chapter by suggesting that Fear of Failure was an area term. We close by suggesting that the area referred to is that which includes self-reported test anxiety, as well as apperceptively measured hostile-press imagery and fear-of-failure imagery. One measure we have not discussed at length is the Achievement Anxiety Test scale of Haber and Alpert (1960) which provides the subject with an opportunity to report that physical symptoms of arousal facilitate his performance as well as cause debilitating effects. Two scales are taken from the instrument, and they provide the subject with an opportunity to contrast the effects of anxiey on his perform-ance. The debilitating scale (AAT—) shows substantial correlation with the TAQ, and we favor the AAT over the TAQ for the added information to be gained from the AAT+ scale. However, Table 8.3 shows the absence of correlation found between measures which have proved their ability to predict various avoidance behaviors in achievement situations. This table includes only correlations found for samples of Ss tested in our own research. Additional correlations may be found in the tables of Chapter 9. It is clear that these are independent measures with similar predictive validities. We have made some suggestions about testing for relationships between these measures, especially regarding possible childhood origins of thought and feeling. But for purposes of researching hope and fear in the achievement situation, it seems essential that efforts be made to incor-porate both self-respect and apperceptive measures in common re-search designs. Sarason's demonstration of lower anxiety scores on a second administration of the TAQ, as well as of experimenter effects, alerts us to control for possible interactions between measures and/or test situations. As we will see in the next chapter, the findings thus far suggest that avoidance behavior in achievement situations varies markedly with the nature of the achievement setting—a con-clusion supported by the work of Kogan and Wallach (1964). Given such a wide array of possible effects, it is critical that future research

TABLE 8.3. INTERCORRELATIONS
OF MEASURES OF FEAR OF FAILURE

	Apperceptive	*Self-Descriptive*		
	FF	TAQ	AAT−	AAT+
HP	+ .13 (1) + .08 (1a)	+ .11 (2)	+ .08 (2a) + .04 (3)	+ .02 (3) + .01 (2)
FF		+ .01 (1) − .15 (1a)		
TAQ			+ .58 (2a)	+ .02 (2a)
AAT−				− .37 (2)

(1) *N* is 23 German males, German pictures.
(1a) *N* is 68 American males, American pictures.
(2) *N* is 77 American males, American pictures.
(2a) *N* is 105 American males, American pictures.
(3) *N* is 69 American males, American pictures.

concentrate on selected patterns of independent and dependent variables with an eye to learning as much as possible from critical contrasts.

We are left with the position that each of these measures has generated its own hypothetical construct under the general term, Fear of Failure. In time we will learn more of how they may be combined most coherently.

CHAPTER 9

Current Theories of Fear of Failure

THE PRECEDING EIGHT CHAPTERS HAVE REVIEWED OUR RESEARCH OF Fear of Failure motivation. We have tried to present our work as descriptively as possible with a minimum of theorizing to support our guiding hypotheses. We have already made reference to the work of others on the same problem, and in this chapter we turn to a consideration of the theoretical issues which now surround the findings. The reader must bear in mind that many of the differences so clearly apparent at this writing were slowly emerging over the years covered by this report. Ideas change and adjust to fit the findings as they emerge. Hopefully, they will continue to do so. But it was never possible to come to a firm decision in favor of some particular theoretical formulation. Rather, the formulation has itself emerged, and with it a better understanding of the ideas of others and the difference between approaches to be reviewed here.

We stated earlier that the area phrase, Fear of Failure, was initially suggested by a behavioral pattern of performance and aspiration (see p. 2). We chose to strive for a motive measure by following the technique used by McClelland to test for the effects of failure experience on fantasy as displayed in short, structured TAT stories. Given the measure, Hostile Press, it has been possible to conduct a series of studies to learn how persons given to such fantasy behave in achievement situations. Meanwhile Atkinson, using the n-Ach–TAQ measure of resultant achievement motivation, and Heckhausen, using empirically refined codes for scoring Hope of Success and Fear of Failure in TAT stories, have also been conducting studies to test for the correlates of their Fear of Failure indices in achievement situa-

tion behaviors. At this writing these three programs rest on somewhat different theoretical assumptions about motivation and the
function of Fear of Failure in achievement situations. We deal first
with the Atkinson position because it was clearly stated in 1957
and has been subject to refinement since that time. Given its impact
on the research being done on this problem, we must make clear
the basis for our decision to reject Atkinson's theoretical position.
After stating our own position, we will then consider the position
taken by Heckhausen (1967), with particular attention to the additional issues raised by trying to integrate interpretations made from
work conducted with populations of another society.

Atkinson's Theory of Fear of Failure

In 1957 Atkinson published a model of behavior in achievement
situations. Defining motive as "a disposition to strive for a certain
kind of satisfaction, as a capacity for satisfaction in the attainment of
a certain class of incentives," he moved away from the earlier definition of McClelland et al. (1953) which emphasized anticipated
change of affect rather than striving for it. Presumably the satisfaction referred to is that of achieving the anticipated change in affect,
but the new statement places the term "incentive," which means
some objectively definable event, in a central position. Motive as a
dispositional state requires a definition of the actualized state, and for
Atkinson the actualization occurs in the presence of objective cues
which produce an expectancy of incentive attainment. Thus we have
motivation, or we say someone is motivated, when Motive, Expectancy of Incentive, and Incentive combine to produce behavior. This
behavior is characterized by initiation of directed, selective striving
toward a particular class of goal objects or conditions, attainment of
which ends the striving. Turning to the achievement motive, the more
specific statement is that the achievement motive is "a disposition
to approach success" (p. 360). Expectancy then becomes the Probability of success (Ps), and Incentive becomes the value of success
(Is). Success here means objective success as defined by the task.
However, the satisfaction which it brings is said to be pride in accomplishment. Conversely, Atkinson states: "The aim of another
class of motive is to minimize pain. . . . An avoidance motive represents the individual's capacity to experience pain in connection with
certain kinds of negative consequences of acts. The motive to avoid
failure is considered a disposition to avoid failure and/or a capacity

for experiencing shame and humiliation as a consequence of failure" (p. 360). It remains only to combine the Expectancy for failure (Pf) and Incentive (failure) (If) to complete the model for fear of failure.

At this writing Atkinson's Motive term had the properties of variation in strength, and of disposition toward a certain class of satisfactions and away from a certain class of annoyances. Thus it combines the energizing property of Drive with the directive properties of Habit as set out in the writings of Spence (1958) and Brown (1961). By 1964, however, Atkinson had modified his views on the nature of fear of failure. Comparing the treatment of anxiety given by Drive $\times$ Habit and Expectancy $\times$ Value theories he concludes that " 'fear' should not be conceived as the exciter of avoidance responses, but as a symptom that an animal is already performing a response with an expectancy of a negative consequence" (p. 289). From this it follows that fear of failure must be given a definition as a disposition to *inhibit* one's achievement striving on penalty of pain. Indeed, the avoidance motive is one of being disposed to inhibit achievement striving so that fear of failure will not occur. Strictly speaking, since the term fear is given to the outcome state, and not the anticipation of it, we now have the failure avoidance motive, where failure is objectively defined. The effects of making this distinction, between the disposition to act and the experience produced by the action, will soon become apparent. But note that the same revision could be undertaken for the need for achievement. One could say that by need for achievement we should say the success motive, which when activated creates the sense that one's strivings will bring success, and with that sense a pride in one's actions. The ghost of the James-Lange theory of emotion haunts this formulation because it asserts that the emotive side of motivation occurs in course, following the activation of action, and the motive itself is stripped of its emotional dimension.

Atkinson has moved into this position to avoid having to assert that the motivation to avoid failure "might sometimes function to instigate (or excite) achievement-oriented performance" (1966, p. 19). He wishes to avoid saying this because the form given to the relationship between Motive, Expectancy, and Incentive seems to dictate these definitions. That form asserts that values for the three variables combine multiplicatively, and also that values of Incentive are inverse to values of Expectancy. This model is offered as a theoretical case, and by changing the motive from approach to inhibition of approach we get values for resultant approach and avoidance motivations which are exact opposites; conditions of maximum approach become conditions of maximum inhibition and conditions of minimum approach become conditions of minimum inhibition. In effect, the two motive dispositions operate in direct opposition to one another and produce opposite behaviors in persons dominated by one or the other.

This strategy of theorizing has led Atkinson and his co-workers to a degree of theoretical sophistication which tends to outrun the power of their measures. The model provides sufficient variables for a great variety of behavior patterns to result in theory. Unfortunately it is not possible to prove or disprove the model at the moment. However, it is a fruitful source of ideas. For instance, since it has the effect of emphasizing approach dispositions, it forces us to consider what Incentives other than pride of accomplishment may serve to support achievement striving. Atkinson is quick to concede that should the approach and the avoidance tendencies be equal, and the person continue to strive, we must postulate that another positive motive has become dominant, such as social approval. The model also suggests that repeated failure in achievement situations in which the child is constrained to keep trying may result in an approach motive to please authority which is quite distinct from task accomplishment, such that the child will be motivated to strive to achieve excellence under authoritarian demand, but never for himself. In the more immediate design of research, this type of model challenges the psychologist to product the conditions which the model says will yield a particular behavior. This has tended to be the course of research followed by Atkinson and his co-workers.

The reader is aware that we have not used the Atkinson model in planning our own research. In view of the terms in which we describe our research, it may now be clear why we have not. We have preferred a less rigorous model, a somewhat less theoretical approach, and a somewhat more empirical wait-and-see attitude toward the data. This was especially true in the beginning of our work. By continuing to define a motive as an anticipated change in affect, we felt that fear of failure was such an anticipation and might be changed by a wide variety of actions, of which inhibition of striving might be only one. That is, we kept open the possibility that fear of failure might lead to increased achievement striving, under certain conditions, just as Atkinson had originally suggested (1957). We see no reason why the conception of the anticipatory goal reaction as a stimulus to action should not be applied to fear of failure. That is, we accept the point made by Brown (1961) that from the viewpoint of Hullian learning theory we are studying special classes of habits learned associatively. We prefer the "anxiety-reduction" model of Mowrer, 1939, and Miller, 1948, since it permits us to speculate on the possible reinforcing value of various behaviors which might be fear-reducing. Motives as anticipated changes in affect may be considered a special class of habits if this view proves useful. The important feature is to preserve the view of motives as internal states capable of change which may produce learning. Atkinson initially suggested that under fear of failure the person constrained to the achievement situation would find "only one path open to him to avoid failure—success at the task he is presented. So we expect him to manifest the strength of his motivation to avoid failure in performance of the task. He, too, in other words, should try *hardest* when Ps is .50 and less hard when the chance of winning is either greater or less" (1957, p. 364). As we have seen this view is explicitly repudiated in 1966. The subject's behavior "is to be understood in terms of what he is trying not to do" (1966, p. 261). But it is the 1957 view that we have wished to maintain and have found useful in guiding our research. We attempt to understand what the subject is trying to do.

From the outset we have questioned the requirement that the terms Motive, Incentive, and Probability be viewed as independent of each other. To view them so we would require that the extensive literature on wish fulfillment, as well as that dealing with various defensive distortions of reality due to fear, be set aside. We were prepared to find that variation in Motive or Incentive might cause distortion of Ps; e.g., at high levels of Fear of Failure the perceived values of Ps might be distorted upward. And we were concerned that some achievement situations might offer Ps values with no clear objective statement of If at all, thus permitting the Ps estimate to distort or even define If; e.g., "if the task is this easy, the penalty of failure must be quite great," vs. "the penalty can't be much because the task is too hard." We could even imagine achievement task situations in which the value of the Is was *positively* related to Ps, e.g., a gentleman's C, which is easy to get, is still worth more, as a Pass, than a high B, which is fine for those who get B's. This type of criticism adds up to saying that we find the decision to use just three variables related in a precise fashion to be arbitrary and restrictive in research on Fear of Failure motivation. We view the identification of key variables as still open, the relationships between known variables as yet to be determined, and the problems of researching avoidance motivation as distinct from those of approach motivation.

Another important reason for not adopting the Atkinson model was our reservation regarding the assumption that Probability and Incentive are inversely related. There is no doubt but that the relationship affects behavior, but we were not persuaded of the wisdom of confining the relationship to even the set of inverse orders, let alone the exact condition that Is equaled (1-Ps). Essentially this constitutes a narrowing of the attribute of Incentive to task difficulty alone. For Fear of Failure, this amounts to saying that persons show avoidance out of a sense of the difficulty of the task facing them. On intuitive grounds we felt that the definition of incentive should be kept open and not confined to attributes of the task itself. (A similar reservation is voiced by Feather (1965) regarding the achievement motive.) Atkinson later suggested that if Incentive is *invariant* with regard to Ps we have the usual conditions served by the law of effect. Applied to fear-of-failure motivation, this suggests that if the penalties of failure are equally great for an easy and for a difficult task, the subject might be best advised to choose a difficult task in the hope of minimizing social disapproval. As we shall see shortly, one could argue that some studies show this. The point of this discussion, however, is that we felt we should treat the Incentive-Probability relationship as a researchable condition rather than a theoretical one. There is no question but that the relationship is important, but its nature could easily vary depending on various situational conditions, and we wished to be free to accept this variation if it appeared in the research.

Finally, we chose not to use the Atkinson model because we held a broader view of the achievement situation than the model permits. Rather than treat Incentive and Probability as task-defined, we wanted to explore which aspects of achievement situations caused variation in the attributes of the Incentive influencing the subject. Given our content analysis of the Hostile Press scoring system, it seemed to us that for these subjects Fear of Failure did not mean fear of task failure according to personal standards of excellence, but rather fear of being a failure in the eyes of others according to their standards. What we question here is the wisdom of confining the definition of the chief variables in the situation to task attributes alone. However successful this appeared to be for studies of the achievement motive, it was our view that fear of failure would prove much more socially sensitive. Our research shows the influence of this view. We have been prompted to contrast solitary to social situations of task performance. We have explored for personality-test correlates of Hostile Press, and we have tried to learn under what conditions persons with high fear of failure scores perform best.

A Critique of the Atkinson Model

Our reservations above have been presented without citation of the literature. Here we present selected findings which we feel give support to the position we have taken. At the outset let us be clear that we do not see this as a closed matter. It is still too early to state flatly that the usefulness of a "strong assumption" model at the outset of research is less than the more literary theory we present in Chapter 10. All that we want to do here is review the literature beyond our own which we feel supports our strategy of definition and hypothesis formation.

At the outset the Atkinson model defined the values of Is and Ps objectively in task terms. However, it was soon apparent that these values did not fit the results obtained (Atkinson and Litwin, 1960) in studies of risk preference. Obviously, some estimate of the subjectively perceived Ps values was required beyond the objectively experienced success with the task in practice trials. Next it was found that if Ss were asked to commit themselves to a particular set of estimated Ps values prior to performance, there was danger that the task had changed from one requiring success to one requiring accuracy of Ps judgment (Litwin, 1958). Hence the view that asking Ss for Ps judgments contaminated the usual achievement situation. The question of the relationship of subjective Ps values to objective Ps values continues to be troublesome. Indeed, there is some evidence that in fact Ps judgments differ, between those with approach and those with avoidance motivation (Brody, 1963; Feather, 1965). In general, the findings for the achievement motive show a preference for risk which is somewhat more extreme than the model predicts. But for fear of failure, defined according to the n-Ach–TAQ combination, there has been practically no support for the model. Rather, the consistent result has been that these Ss show a preference for moderate risks, extreme risks, and low risks, in that order (Atkinson and Litwin, 1960), or a preference for intermediate risks that is less extreme than that of the hope-of-success Ss (Moulton, 1965).

Studies of persistence have been more in line with the predictions of the model, but also permit more than one interpretation (Feather, 1961). Persistence at an unsolvable task which one has been told is difficult may reflect a fear of loss of social approval ("one must not be a quitter!") just as lack of persistence at an unsolvable task which one has been told is easy may reflect the same fear ("you expected me to solve this problem quickly and I am not doing so. Please give me another"). Persistence, especially under conditions of failure, is probably almost solely social in origin. If the subject is task-oriented he will act as the hope-of-success subject does, persisting at easy tasks and dropping the difficult when both are unsolvable; but the subject who is socially oriented may do just the opposite.

Studies of expressed level of aspiration (LA) have tended to show that fear-of-failure *S*s display more willingness to make extreme aspirations, including atypical shifts away from the direction of the previous outcome, than do the hope-of-success *S*s (Martire, 1956; Clark, (Riciutti, and Teevan, 1956; Robinson, 1962). This may be interpreted to mean that a preference for extreme Ps values for the next trial signifies a maximization of avoidance motivation around the values implied by the performance itself. Thus the *S* who succeeds and raises his LA somewhat, as the hope-of-success *S* does, is moving into a more challenging range of difficulty. So too, the movement downward following failure moves one toward the intermediate range. However, once again the data are most clear for the hope-of-success *S*s, and more equivocal for the fear-of-failure *S*s. The latter show distributions of LA's with greater instances of extreme behavior, or atypical reaction, but the obtained distributions do not fit the predicted curve of the model. Furthermore the alternative interpretation of LA behavior as socially determined is equally tenable. If we assume that such behavior has been reinforced in the past, we must ask what such reinforcement might have been. Since it could not be task success itself, as a rule, we must consider that setting high aspiration or being excessively modest may have been socially reinforced. And if this is the Incentive being pursued, the behavior makes sense.

It is not possible to re-interpret each of the studies generated by the Atkinson model in this space, nor is it necessary. Our point is simply that the model, in our judgment, has not been often satisfied by the data where Fear of Failure is concerned, and where it has been satisfied, an alternative interpretation based on a consideration of what the S is trying to do can be made. Notice that some of the possibilities for relationship between Ms and Is and Ps mentioned earlier have appeared in the research program. Although most Ss report subjective Ps values in excess of the objective ones, the hope-of-success Ss are more optimistic than the fear-of-failure Ss prior to any direct experience with the task. M can effect Ps.

Evidence for interactive relationships between M and Ps and Is does exist. We have already seen that Ss distort Ps judgments, usually optimistically in laboratory achievement situations. If we consider this distortion to be a form of wish fulfillment, we may argue that we would expect such distortion to be at a maximum either when the Incentive is of little importance to the S or when it is of maximum importance. That is, as the importance of the Incentive increases, we expect wishful distortion to give way to reality estimates until the importance reaches a level where the reality of possible loss cannot be borne and optimistic distortion occurs.

Fig. 9–1 displays this hypothetical function for the objective Ps level of .50. Filling in with figures from various studies, we see that a possible interpretation of the findings to date is that most of the laboratory tasks used must be judged as in the low importance range.

Exploration of this hypothetical function is being carried out by Burdick and his co-workers. Beginning with trivial tasks of guessing at chance events, Burdick varied the instructions given, in an effort to show that as performance was defined as increasingly important to the experimenter's judgment of the subject, the distortion of the Ps estimates decreased. A study by Irwin (1953) had demonstrated that college students who were told the number of "win" cards in a deck, and were asked to earn points by guessing whether a drawn card was a "win," gave a higher proportion of Yes responses than was dictated by the objective proportions facing them. Irwin had used an individual testing procedure, but Fig. 9–1 shows that Burdick's classroom procedure yields substantially the same results. Across twenty trials without feedback, the Ss had to guess whether they had chosen a "win" card from decks varying in composition from 10 percent to 90 percent "win" cards. The extent to which a set to "win" influences results also appears when we consider what happens when the S is told he must not pick a "lose" card, and is then asked if he has done so. The "lose" responses are

Fig. 9–1. Hypothesized degree of Ps distortion as a function of incentive importance.

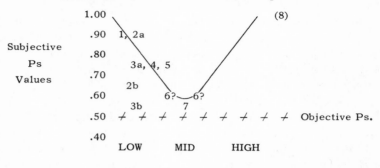

Incentive Importance

1. Guessing under chance conditions to win points (Irwin, 1953)
2. a. Replication of Irwin, group testing (Burdick, 1964)
   b. Same as 2a except aim is to minimize losses.
3. a. Guessing under chance conditions to score high on Social Sensitivity (Burdick, 1964)
   b. Minimize losses.
4. Guessing under chance conditions to achieve accuracy (Irwin, 1953).
5. Estimated Ps for ring toss game lines (Litwin, 1958).
6? Estimation of season record by Varsity debaters (Birney, 1964). *Note:* We place the Varsity debaters' estimates at two positions because we cannot be sure they are more or less motivated than the Novices. This illustrates the need for independent measurement of Incentive Importance.
7. Estimation of season record by Novice debaters (Birney, 1964).
8. Hypothetical value for contestants at world Championship level.

closer to the objective odds in both studies. If distortion occurs under the "lose" test condition, we expect the *S* to deny losing even when the odds predict that he most probably has lost. This too occurs.

Burdick (1965) next set out to structure the card-guessing task in such a way that he could vary the importance of the task using instructions alone. He repeated the card-guessing format precisely, but told the *S*s:

Last year during orientation week we asked all the members of the incoming freshmen class to indicate how they would like to have the cards marked. Although there were differences in their choices, there were clear preferences for certain patterns. Is it your task to guess what those preferred patterns were. If you are able to play the role of another, your guesses should be better than chance. It is this ability to play the role of another that indicates social sensitivity. It is this type of test that psychologists have been using for many years to measure social sensitivity.

The aim of this instruction was to convince the S that he was facing ten cards each of which had been voted on to receive a "win" mark. Given one such card in the .10 condition, could he pick it? After choosing a card, the S was asked whether he thought he had been successful in matching the choice of the last year's freshmen. By telling the Ss that this ability to match the choice of his predecessors was a sign of important social skill, it was hoped the task would take on more importance for the S, and it was predicted that he would move closer to the objective odds in each case. Again the condition was run for both "win" and "lose" conditions.

The classroom procedure used was as follows. Thirty-two students in an introductory psychology class were used as subjects. Each subject was given a packet of 11 sheets: a cover sheet and one sheet for each of the 10 trials to come. The cover sheet, on which the subject wrote his name, explained the procedure of the game. Each trial involved 10 cards which were hung, face hidden, on a board in front of the class for about 40 seconds. During this time the subjects read on their individual trial sheets (1) whether they would win or lose a point if they chose a marked card, and (2) how many of the 10 cards were marked. This information (as to winning and losing, and the number of marked cards) had been randomly combined within each individual packet; all Ss had the same 10 trial sheets, but not in the same order. In five of the trials the S was told he would win a point, while in the other five he was told he would lose a point if he chose a marked card. The win and lose conditions each had ostensibly 1, 3, 5, 7, or 9 marked cards. Actually, none of the cards was marked, but the Ss did not know this. [The Ss in the first study were told that this was a pure guessing game and that there would be no real basis for making a given selection. The Ss in the second study were told it was a test of social sensitivity.] For each trial the S indicated whether or not he believed he would choose a marked card and the degree of his confidence in his choice. He then selected a card by marking down the designating number.

The key comparison to be made in the data shown in Fig. 9–1 is between the "guessing" condition and the "Social Sensitivity" condition. At the critical .50 level, we see, the proportion of those saying they did pick a "win" card has dropped from .91 to .74. At the same time the proportion denying the choice of "lose" card moves from .69 to .57. Both movements are in the predicted direction, though admission of loss shows less effect of instruction.

These studies of Ps distortion introduce the notion of "importance" as being a distinctive attribute of Incentive that is not the same as difficulty. This is the key point we wish to make with these studies. Incentives have importance or value for the subject which go beyond the Ps value of the task being faced. Given objective Ps values for task success, it is possible to vary the meaning of the task to the S, using instructions, so that his subjective Ps values vary as well. The function in Fig. 9–1 could be taken to mean that given an objective Ps value .50, a change in behavior must reflect a change in Incentive. Thus the obtained subjective level of Ps $= .91$ implies an Is of .09, while the second level of .74 implies an increase in Is to .26. This may be so, but in that case it makes more psychological sense to say that Ps is a function of Is, such that Ps $= 1\text{-Is}$. This says that it makes as much sense to argue that Ps is distorted by Is as it does to say that Is is distorted away from the objective values by Ps alone. We prefer to treat Ps and Is independently, subject to situational variation and capable of a wide variety of relationships.

One possibility in Fig. 9–1 is that the inverse relationship of Ps and Is may vary across the "importance" attribute of Is. As stated, the model uses a perfectly inverse set of values for the two variables, regardless of "bias."

Suppose Atkinson is right that the difficulty Incentive value is perfectly inverse to Ps, but suppose Ps varies with the importance of Is, which is independent of Ps. Then we get two classes of achievement situations, those of little importance, such as laboratory games, and those of great importance, such as championship contests, where the greatest resultant motivation values come at objective Ps levels of .20 to .30. To the extent that fearful persons show less positive distortion, and in the moderate value ranges perhaps even show negative distortion of Ps, we can expect them to show the greatest resultant avoidant motivation at the *easier* objective levels of .60 and .70, and a preference for the more difficult levels of the task.

It must be pointed out that this formulation differs from that offered by Atkinson (1957) to account for the tendency of Ss to bias their subjective Ps estimates above the objective values. Atkinson assumes that it is the strength of M which produces this effect. In particular he states:

The assumption to be made seems a reasonable one: the relative strength of a motive influences the subjective probability of the consequence consistent with that motive, i.e., biases it upwards. In other words, the stronger the achievement motive relative to the motive to avoid failure, the higher the subjective probability of success, given stated odds. (1957, p. 367).

We prefer to speak of variation in Is or If values rather than Ms or Mf because we doubt whether the latter variation can be demonstrated. A person with a high Fear of Failure score can be placed in game settings, examinations, and championship contests, and there is no doubt his resultant motivation will vary, but it is the situational index related to Incentive that gives us our estimates of variation, not changes in his Fear of Failure score.

Unfortunately, not even this modification of the model yields predictions congruent with the obtained findings for Fear of Failure Ss. These Ss show a preference for difficulty levels in the Ps = .20 to .40 range, and a relative avoidance of .90 to .70, as the bias assumption suggests. However, it is yet to be demonstrated that these Ss have the greatest avoidance tendencies at the middle range, relative to the extremes. The findings obtained are best fitted by assuming that Fear-of-Failure Ss see the Incentive relationship of Pf as much more extreme than a simple inversion. This requires that we drop the determination of If values from Pf, treat them independently, and, given the objective Pf values and resultant motivation scores, solve for If values. When we do this we find that Fear of Failure Ss apparently fear failure at Pf .10 far more than at Pf .50, which in turn is only slightly worse than Pf .90. Thus we are left proposing not only that Incentive affects subjective Probability but that the relationship between Probability and its

Incentive component differs for approach and for avoidance motivation.

Obviously, we feel that the study of the Ps-Is relationship is important. There can be no question but that in many achievement situations, especially competitive ones, the objective amount of reward to be obtained is inversely related to the objective degree of difficulty of the task. One intriguing possibility before us is that achievement situations might be classified according to the objective relationship between Ps and Is or If. Thus we might classify those situations according to whether the relationship is inverse, null, or positive. The null case means that Is is invariant with respect to Ps. The child who enters a swimming class and strives to win his certificate is not given a certification that records the degree of difficulty he had to overcome to obtain it. The reward is constant regardless of variation in Ps among children. There are probably many such work and school achievement situations where a more or less absolute standard of excellence is applied, and the individual must match it. Here we may find that Heckhausen's emphasis on the time gradient leading to success is quite important. People may differ in the amount of time or effort that they will invest to pursue a particular standard of excellence whose eventual achievement, given the investment, is never in doubt. And there may be situations where Ps and Is have a positive relationship. The greater reward may come on the easier task and diminish as things become more difficult. This may be a condition which can occur only after a period of inverse relationship. That is, the individual who begins to master one of the performing arts begins under the familiar condition that the greatest rewards are given for the most difficult achievements, but the public definition of extreme difficulty may not challenge his capability. And as he attempts to reach the limits of his talent he may find that less and less public reward is offered for his achievements. He must depend on personal standards and self-reinforcement, and without some reference group or appreciative audience he finds himself alone. These speculations suggest that we may have to focus more of our attention on the relationship between the objective values of Ps and Is and the subjective values. Perhaps it is the subjective values that usually take some form of inverse relationship, rather than the objective values. We say "some form," because as we have shown, it need not be the perfectly inverse set of values used in the Atkinson model. It may be that it would be more profitable in studies of risk taking to write the Ps-to-Is relationship according to the empirical values obtained, and compare the objective value relationship with those obtained from subjective estimates of Ps taken from control groups. This line of study would permit the emergence of differences between Hope of Success and Fear of Failure dispositions, if there be such. It also tends to remind us that subjective estimates reflect prior experience with achievement tasks, and we might be encouraged to study the effect of reinforcements which vary inversely with difficulty of response acquisition. Conceivably, fearful *S*s are much slower to master tasks providing such reinforcement than are Hope of Success *S*s.

These suggestions for further work are offered to show that we see great value in the studies generated by the Atkinson model. The findings are suggestive of important issues remaining to be resolved, and as they are resolved we expect to see the model modified and expanded.

Heckhausen's Theory of Fear of Failure

In 1963 Heckhausen published a summary of a research program which is still in progress. He, too, was interested in hope of success (HS) and fear of failure (FF) in achievement situations. Working with populations of German students, workers, children, and soldiers, he had developed TAT codes for HS and FF using the empirical methods of item analysis. Starting with a priori definitions of HS and FF references, and avoiding the restricting scoring convention that subcategories must not be scored without Imagery scoring, he returned to the coding index strategy of Murray (1938) and attempted to isolate the categories which proved to be correlated with realistic vs. atypical level-of-aspiration patterns. Subsequently he also conducted an arousal study to show that his scores were sensitive to achievement cues (1964).

Summarizing his ideas (1967), Heckhausen states,

Potential and actual motivation should be differentiated. [Potential motivation is substantially what he means by "motivation."] Potential motivation is a normative state which determines, as does a frame of reference, how (in relation to the self) a given category of life situations has to be constituted to be satisfactory for a certain person. Actual motivation (or an aroused motive) consists of an expectation linking present and future state of being. The strength of the motive arousal corresponds to the steepness of the expectation gradient which is determined (1) by the size of the discrepancy between the present and future states of being within the frame of reference of the normative motivational state, and (2) by the psychic distance between the states of being over time (p. 3).

Fear of Failure thus becomes a potential state of dissatisfaction or dis-ease which becomes actual in the face of impending events leading to it. This definition has the virtue of focusing on what the person expects will be his future condition and is congruent with Atkinson's view of anxiety. It leaves open for study and further definition the alternative normative states which may be activitated to avoid the failure condition. Heckhausen chooses to work with the basic ideas of goal discrepancy, psychological distance, and psychological time. For him

Achievement motivation, can, therefore, be defined as the striving to increase, or keep as high as possible, one's own capability in all activities in which a standard of excellence is though to apply and where the execution of such activities can, therefore, either succeed or fail (1967, p. 5).

These definitions point to the areas in which systematic investigation must be done. If persons are concerned about standards of excellence, we need to know more about their sources, structure and origin. As we shall see in the next chapter Heckhausen has done research on these problems. So, too, we might expect that fearful persons have a different time sense than hopeful persons about achievement outcomes, a different structuring of the past, etc. For Heckhausen, Fear of Failure centers on the fear that one will not meet the standards of excellence appropriate to the task at hand. The story content scored for FF focuses on this motive. Much of it comes in Need thema stories of achievement striving, or in task-completion stories where performance has been demanded by an authority figure. There is fear both of personal shame and public dishonor. Scoring for this type of content suggests that achievement situations be analyzed for the nature of the failure possible, and suggests the need for comparative research to learn more of the attributes of achievement situations within and between societies. We have already described the steps being taken in this direction.

A Final Comment

This review of the guiding theoretical ideas behind the three programs of research on Fear of Failure attempts to clarify their positions. From our point of view, Heckhausen is using the most general set of definitions and guiding assumptions, but is most sensitive to the situational and psychological dimensions left untouched by Atkinson's group and our own. We see ourselves as being somewhat more restricted in our thinking, trying to deal with several important sources of variance, both personal and social, in fear-reductive, reinforcement terms. Atkinson's group is vigorously researching the utility of a highly restricted model and strives to maximize economy of definition and variable relationships.

We have concentrated on the differences between us in order to sharpen our sense of the common problems being analyzed. Hopefully such emphasis also clarifies language. We choose to hold off for now from any effort to resolve our differences in measurement procedures for Fear of Failure. Since all three techniques continue to produce sensible findings, we see them as reflecting distinctions that remain to be understood and researched in their own right. Beginnings in this direction have been described in Chapter 8. Finally, we wish to make it plain that it is possible, and even wise, to treat the findings from these programs as one body of literature rather than separately. We so treat them in the next chapter.

CHAPTER 10

A Summary of Research Findings for Fear-of-Failure Motivation

IN THIS CHAPTER WE WILL SUMMARIZE THE EMPIRICAL RELATION-ships reported between measures of Fear of Failure and a wide array of dependent behaviors. Using our taxonomy, we will review the work of Atkinson and his co-workers, Heckhausen's work with German populations, and our own work.

We wish to put before the reader each set of distinctive findings, accompanied by a description of the circumstances in which it appeared, so that we may estimate the extent to which findings agree. As any psychologist knows, replication of findings has not been central to the development of psychological science, as it should be. Most of our groupings of studies do not involve exact replication. But if in our judgment the conditions are sufficiently similar in the abstract, we will consider the relationship replicated. The reader will recall that in Chapter 1 we quoted in full Atkinson's summary of the "failure threatened personality." At the end of this section we offer our version of this portrait as we see it emerging from the three programs viewed together.

Engagement

Obtaining a sample of *S*s for laboratory research raises serious problems for the study of motivation. Factors which would introduce no bias whatsoever in studies of perception, or some types of learning, may seriously affect a study of motivation. We have known this for some time (Burdick, Harry, 1955) and the usual practice has been to use all members of a particular course of study, fraternity group, etc., in the hope that the factors influencing course election, etc., will not have sufficient penetrance to affect the closely controlled laboratory work.

At the same time we have theorized that Fear of Failure motivation should lead the S to avoid engagement in achievement situations where possible. At this writing only our own study of volunteering shows the reluctance of FF's to engage in achievement tasks of an experimental type (see pp. 99-100).

It is our opinion that the proper studies of the engagement phase of achievement behavior have not yet been done. Subsequent work suggests that the attractiveness of achievement situations can be varied in such a way that some types of tasks, such as those involving teamwork and shared credit for achievement, may have the most appeal for fear-of-failure Ss. The careful definition of task attributes which the fear-of-failure S finds appealing remains to be done.

Choice of Task

Under this heading we deal with the behavior of the fear-of-failure S who is constrained to perform in the achievement situation, but is free to choose a task from several offered. This category thus includes one study of risk preference in which the chief distinguishing attribute of the tasks is probability of success or failure, and studies of expressed preference for achievement situations such as vocations and course of study.

It is perhaps a bit strong to assume that having to declare a career choice is a constraint achievement situation: many motives may dictate a particular choice. But in the experimental setting where the S knows he is being asked to share his intentions, the sense of being judged on the basis of one's choice must surely be present. Thus it is the judging situation itself which is the constraint achievement situation being studied in these reports. We find that there is fair agreement that the FF Ss show an optimism about their personal qualifications that seems extreme. The use of absolute vocational values also suggests that despite this optimism they are more cautious in their range of choices. We are left wondering whether these Ss simply have no basis for choice—i.e., have no plans, do not have a future time perspective—or whether they experience anxiety of social evaluation of their choices and defend accordingly.

The Isaacson and Weiner-Rosenbaum studies used more imme-

TABLE 10.1. CHOICE: VOCATIONAL AND Ps (INITIAL)

Source	Sample	Measure of FF	Dependent Variable	Relationship
Mahone, 1960	MCS	75 n Ach-AAT-	Clinically estimated realism of vocational choice	FF Ss overestimate measured ability, prefer vocations above or below perceived ability, prefer vocations judged unrealistic, usually optimistically
Burstein, 1963	MCS	35 n Ach-MAS	Choice of vocations ranked for difficulty	FF lowest ir absolute vocational aspiration, and lowest in "settle for" level of difficulty
Issacson, 1964	MCS	108 FnAch-TAQ	Honors-nonHonors by difficulty of courses chosen	FF non-Honors Ss choose difficult courses, and FF honors choose easy.
Weiner-Rosenbaum, 1965	MCS	199 n Ach-TAQ	Choice of picture rating task vs. puzzle solving at Ps .30, .50, and .70.	FF prefer picture task at .50 and .30.
Morris, 1966	MHS	94 n Ach-TAQ	Vocational choice within chosen career area	All Ss choose areas with high Ps, but FF then choose high Ps vocation if they are of low IQ

NOTATION for these tables is as follows: M or F—male or female; CS, HS, GS—college, high school or grade school students; n Ach—McClelland, FnAch—French. FFTAT is any TAT index used for fear of failure. All other letter abbreviations are consistent with the usage in the text.

186

diate achievement situations, and in general the FF *S*s seemed to choose away from tests of ability. Apparently the vocational area chosen has a high probability of success for all *S*s drawn from college populations. These *S*s can be presumed to have some information about job attributes. But within the area there is evidence that low-ability FF *S*s show the extreme preference patterns. Putting these findings together suggests that fear of failure about vocational choice may appear when *S*s have avoided learning sufficient information about themselves and job requirements, for whatever reasons, and find themselves forced to express choice. None of these studies has taken the next step to determine whether the FF *S*s actually do take jobs below their ability level, or keep trying to obtain jobs for which they are not qualified.

Performance

The performance of FF *S*s has been studied in several types of achievement settings. Whether such motivation facilitates or debilitates performance clearly depends on the task demands themselves. In general, it appears that unfamiliar, complex, speeded, and non-game (threatening) achievement settings show the FF *S* at a disadvantage. He does not master such situations rapidly, and his aspiration levels fluctuate in a manner having little to do with his actual performance. These findings are uniformly based on individual performance settings of a noncooperative nature, and these conditions may serve to increase the avoidance motivation of the *S*. Competition produces his worst performance. Individual tasks supported by rewards from *E* are better, as are tests of speed at easy tasks. Moreover, the same kind of pattern appears in game settings where the *S* seems more concerned with his relationship to the *E* than with maximizing his performance level. The one set of circumstances where the FF *S*s perform well are those involving cooperation with others. We would include the pursuit of academic success in this category, since so many aspects of academic progress involve compliance to the teacher's demands. Table 10.2 summarizes these studies.

Conformity

Sensitivity to social conformity can serve a person well or ill depending on the appropriateness of the conformity to the task

TABLE 10.2. PERFORMANCE

Source	Sample	Measure of FF	Dependent Variable	Relationship
Brown, 1953	162 MFCS	Mid-third n Ach	Einstellung effect water bottle prob.	Under aroused cond. FF's have lower proportion of success.
Feather, 1961	89 MCS	n Ach-TAQ	Persistence at unsolvable perceptual reasoning tasks—"diff" and "easy"	FF's persist at "diff" task and shift away from "easy"
Teevan, 1962	82 MHS	HP	Academic performance	FF's show positive relation
Birney, 1963	70 MHS	HP-n Ach	Debating performance	FF's deny preparation for debate. Extreme HS's or FF's perf. best
Heckhausen, 1963	74 MFCS	FF TAT	Additions Speed Test	FF's show greater effort
Heckhausen, 1963	47 MFCS	FF TAT	Time to complete homework	FF's take longer on homework
Berkun-Burdick, 1963	142 M-Army	n Ach-TAQ	Arithmetic reasoning under failure arousal	Ss showing FF following arousal work harder
Caron, 1963	241 MHS	n Ach-TAQ	Comprehension and rote learning tasks	FF's do poorly on comprehension
Bartmann, 1963	HS	FF TAT	Complex, speeded problems	FF's solve fewer problems under time pressure

TABLE 10.2. PERFORMANCE (CONTINUED)

Teevan-Smith, 1964	92 MHS	HP	Academic performance	Positive relationship
Hojo, 1964	Adults	FFTAT	Driving practices	FF's show fewer nondriving violations
Rolf-Birney 1965	69 MCS	HP	Complex paced maze task	FF's perf. poorly (trials to solution)
Teevan-Custer, 1965	42 5th grade males	HP	Academic performance	FF's show positive relationship
Bartmann, 1965	HS	FFTAT	Programed instruction of insight problems	FF's show least improvement
Weiner, 1966	195 MCS	n Ach-TAQ	Paired associate learning under success vs. failure feedback	FF's perform best under success feedback, do worst under failure
Ryan-Lakie, 1965	35 MCS	FnAch-MAS	Mirror maze task under solitary vs. competitive conditions	FF's are superior under solitary, improve least under competition.
Weiner, 1965	60 MCS	n Ach-TAQ	Persistence at digit-symbol task.	FF's perform better following success and persist longer
Feather, 1966	96 FCS	n Ach-TAQ	Performance and Expectation following success and failure	FF's make more "typical" Ps changes following failure than success

reality. We have seen that the FF *S* is susceptible to group pressure, so that his success with a task is contingent upon the appropriateness of the group suggestion. He apparently sacrifices task
success for social acceptability as he perceives it. Furthermore the
effectiveness of such social pressure depends on direct and close
interpersonal conditions, rather than abstract or impersonal conceptions of social sanctions. Table 10.3 summarizes these findings.

Aspiration and Risk Preference

Our review of the level of aspiration literature, and our use of
the technique, have convinced us that the role of aspiration and
its dependence on motivation are not well understood. We sometimes forget that almost nothing is known of the incidence of aspiration behavior. This means that when we ask *S*s to give us aspiration estimates, our *S*s may differ greatly in the amount of experience
they have had making such estimates, and the differences we find
between motive tendencies may be confounded by this uncontrolled
variable. The *S*s with Hope-of-Success motivation seem quite skilled
at making aspiration estimates which reflect their actual performance. On the other hand, the Fear-of-Failure *S*s give estimates which
initially seem quite out of touch with their performance and only
come in line with it slowly, if at all. We have chosen to suspend
judgment about the meaning of this finding. Under Fear of Failure,
*S*s may not aspire unless forced to. Under Hope of Success, aspiration behavior may provide a source of reinforcement which is under
personal control. Heckhausen's discovery that FF *S*s do not report
a long-range time perspective adds to the suspicion that they may
avoid aspiration itself.

We have established that *S*s can follow a great variety of re-
quests for aspiration, and give fairly reliable data, as shown by
Table 10.4. We think our Confirming Interval questions may mag-
nify motivational effects so that we may better study them. Yet
there is no question but that the *S*'s personal history of task reinforcement contributes greatly to his aspiration behavior, and in
general this is difficult to bring under laboratory control. The study
of vocational choice may prove an excellent area for estimating
such long term effects.

TABLE 10.3. CONFORMITY

Citation	Sample	Measure of FF	Dependent Variable	Relationship
Teevan-Smith-Loomis, 1964	45 MHS	HP	Crutchfield conformity task	No relationship
Stamps-Teevan, 1965	63 MCS	HP	Crutchfield and Asch conformity tasks	FF's conform under Asch, not under Crutchfield
Teevan-Stamps, 1965	99 MFCS	HP	Social protest activism (anti-Vietnam)	FF's are positively related to protest
Birney-Rolf, 1965	69 MCS	HP	Contributing to group product	FF's show subexpectancy contribution
Birney-Stillings 1966	105 MCS	HP	Prisoner's Dilemma: single trial vs. series	FF's show no relation to single trial; positive relation to point maximizing via cooperation in series.

TABLE 10.4. LEVEL OF ASPIRATION AND RISK PREFERENCE

Source	Sample	Measure of FF	Dependent Variable	Relationship
Atkinson-Litwin, 1960	49 MCS	n Ach-TAQ	Choice of ring toss distance	Low positive r to increased distance
Heckhausen, 1963	74 MFCS	FF-TAT	LA with knowledge of results	FF's do not adjust LA following onset of failure, initially high pos. or neg.

TABLE 10.4. LEVEL OF ASPIRATION AND RISK PREFERENCE (CONTINUED)

Brody, 1963	91 MCS	n Ach-TAQ (1/4iles)	LA confidence numerosity task	FF's take extreme confidence positions, slower to achieve confidence
Feather, 1963	126 MCS	AAT	Estimate Ps, post-task without knowledge of results, for Ps .20, .50, and .80.	AAT— correl. −.16 with Ps.
Thomas-Teevan, 1964	105 MHS	HP	LA electronic rifle range	FF's show extremes in LA
Teevan-Smith, 1964	44 MHS	HP	Size of CI on scrambled words task	FF's show wide CI
Hancock-Teevan, 1964	60 MHS	HP	Ps with expectancy value constant	FF's prefer extreme Ps values
Teevan-Myers, 1965	100 MHS	HP	CI by Importance to S across *ability*.	FF upper half shows r .38 with CI width
Feather, 1965	168 MCS	n Ach-TAQ	Initial estimated Ps at mod. difficult and easy tasks.	FF negatively related to Ps, difference with Hs greatest at mod. difficulty
De Charms-Dave, 1965	71 MGS	FF-TAT	Choice of basket shooting distance	FF-TAT's avoid personal mid-Ps range. No n Ach-TAQ effect
Moulton, 1965	105 MJS	n Ach-TAQ	Choice of Ps follows success or failure	FF's make atypical choices
Rolf-Birney, 1965	69 MCS	HP	CI under paced maze task. Est. Ps under game vs. personal threat	FF's have wider CI's. FF's prefer extreme Ps under game, prefer mod. Ps under threat
Weiner, 1965	60 MCS	n Ach-TAQ	Preferred difficulty at digit-symbol task	FF's show no modal difficulty preference

TABLE 10.5.

Source	Sample	Measure of FF	Dependent Variable	Relationship
Argyle-Robinson, 1962	59 MHS	Neg. n Ach	Reported parental demands	FF's have low positive rel. to parental demands
Kasserjian 1963	260 Male	Psychological and Social Failure Scales	Self-concept, Chicago Adjustment scale, Cornell Medical index	Psych. Failure shows −.60 rel. to adjustment and −.42 to medical index
Teevan-Smith, 1964	49 MCS	HP	Discrepancy between self and ideal Q sort	FF's have pos. rel. to size of self-ideal discrepancy
Ertel, 1964	26 MFCS	FFTAT	Semantic diff. for "IQ test" prior to test	FF's show Apprehension of "failure-despite-effort"
Teevan-Fischer, 1966	44 MCS	HP	Attribution of responsibility in achievement situations	FF's attribute responsibility to external sources

Subjective Experience in Achievement Situations

The use of questionnaires to solicit subjective reports from Ss about their performance and the situation they are in has not been widely practiced in research on fear of failure. This is regrettable, because the right questions can frequently provide considerable insight for the E as to what S thought was happening. Also, the Ss do think about their experience and their report of it is an important behavior in its own right. Our early efforts to produce failure feelings showed that Ss are quite capable of denying any such effects, choosing instead to devalue the task or the attribute measured by the task or to invoke chance as the explanation of their performance. One study suggested that such cognitions are a defense against fear of failure, which, when they fail as defenses, then appears (reading speed in Chapter 2). Our exploration of the psychometric correlates of HP suggests that FF Ss do report the sense of falling far short of the ideals they hold, and that the world is a hostile place which may affect one's efforts in arbitrary and capricious ways.

Table 10.5 shows the little we know about the cognitions in these situations. We suspect that suspension of knowledge of results may permit variation in self-esteem expression in the face of task experience, but once an outcome is known there seems little prospect of chance in self-esteem. Under conditions of variation the fear-of-failure person may be more conservative about himself. So little is known about this facet of the achievement situation, that we can only assert that we must learn more, because it seems certain that self-esteem estimates influence task choice and engagement behaviors, if not performance itself.

There have been a fair number of studies done to investigate the memory and perception of persons who are high in fear of failure. These studies are summarized in Table 10.6. Many speculations could be made about these results but the main conclusion, from our point of view, is that memory and perception seem to be used as defensive maneuvers. This can be seen most simply from the several studies done on the recall of incompleted and completed tasks.

Physiological Indicators

Two studies by Raphaelson and one by Heckhausen and Müscher (see Table 10.7) have shown the potential usefulness of physio-

TABLE 10.6

Source	Sample	Measure of FF	Dependent Variable	Relationship
			MEMORY	
Heckhausen, 1963	54 MFCS 68 MF teacher trainees	FFTAT	Estimation of past task success	Under feedback FF's underestimate success; without feedback, FF's underestimate success
Atkinson, 1953	83 MCS	Mid third of n Ach	Recall of interrupted tasks, relaxed vs. aroused	FF's shift ratio of completed over incompleted recalled under aroused conditions.
De Charms et al, 1955	81 MCS	Mid third of n Ach	Intentional recall of achievement stories	FF's show greatest recall
Moulton, 1958	24 MCS	FFTAT	Recall of interrupted tasks, relaxed and aroused	FF's show pos. relationship to recall of completed tasks
Gotzl, 1960	106 MFGS	FFTAT	Recall of tests, awaiting knowledge of results	FF's recall best those tests to be reported in one day vs. two weeks
Reitman, 1961	108 MCS	Mid third of n Ach	Recall of success, neutral or failure TAT stories after 30 min. of arith. and perceptual tasks	FF's recall failure stories under neutral cues, recall success-neutral stories under aroused cues
Vukosvich, 1964	93 soldiers and trade-school males	Lo-AM–Hi TAT	Memory preference for fantasy contents	FF's prefer achievement-related fantasy

TABLE 10.6. (CONTINUED)

Heckhausen, 1963	71 MF teacher trainees	FF-TAT	Recall of tasks solved	FF's recall more solved tasks

PERCEPTION

McClelland-Liberman, 1949	36 MCS	Mid third of n Ach	Recognition threshold for success and failure words	FF's show slow recognition of failure words
Heckhausen, 1963	52 MCS	FF-TAT	Knapp time metaphors	FF's prefer metaphors of time as "aimless, incessant stream of motion"
Teevan-Thomas, 1944	105 MHS	HP	Is the rifle range an adequate measure? How do you feel about your scores?	FF's deny adequacy of meas. FF's express displeasure
Meyer-Heckhausen-Kemmler, 1955	77 MGS	FF-TAT	Field Dependency Test	FF's are positively related to field dependency

TABLE 10.7. PHYSIOLOGICAL INDICATORS

Source	Sample	Measure of FF	Dependent Variable	Relationship
Raphaelson, 1957	25 MCS	n Ach-TAQ	GSR, across pre-task, task, and post-task	FF's are highest during task and post-task periods
Raphaelson-Moulton, 1958	25 MCS	n Ach-TAQ	GSR for task failure condition	FF's are low during task and HS's are high
Müscher-Heckhausen, 1962	33 MCS	HS-FF TAT	EMG (Muscle tonus)	AM pos. rel. to tonus in rest ($r = .41$) activity ($r = .38$) and total ($r = 41$)

logical indices as dependent or co-variant measures vis-à-vis fear of failure.

This work suggests that facing possible success or failure, the FF *s* is maximally engaged, while facing certain failure, he is not. This pattern is consistent with the findings presented in Tables 10.2, 10.4, and 10.6 showing best performance under success promptings, or without knowledge, and more rigid patterns of maladaptive behaviors following clear objective failure. One is reminded of Epstein's findings (1962) regarding the effect of experience (successful parachuting) on progressive loss of GSR arousal at the time of jump. Perhaps the FF *S* is one whose experience with failure has led to nonarousal in the face of failure certainty. This suggests still another distinction—between avoidance in the service of nonarousal and avoidance serving arousal. Some of the maladaptive behaviors we have reported seem consistent with nonengagement, while others seem to reflect supra-engagement. Physiological measures might prove useful as a way of testing for this distinction.

Reaction to Outcome and Subsequent Engagement

With the finish of a particular task and some kind of knowledge of results by the *S*, we may ask what the effect of the experience will be on subsequent task variables. Actually this question has not often been asked. For this reason we refer the reader to the few experiments already listed in the preceding tables. These are Weiner and Rosenbaum (1965) in Table 10.1 and Feather (1961, 1966) and Weiner (1965) in Table 10.2. In these experiments the *S* is offered an alternative task following a success or failure experience, or he is given a second round of performance for which new estimates must be made. We know of no experiments where the time interval between initial performance and subsequent behaviors is longer than a few minutes. These experiments might serve as models for the investigation of success and failure effects over periods of twenty-four hours or more, periods which seem much closer to common experience with achievement situations.

Further Aspects of Fear of Failure

Our taxonomy for the achievement situation does not encompass questions about the origins of fear of failure nor broader questions of how the approach-avoidance motivation system for achievement situations functions within the personality. We have reported just one study which we have conducted of reported parental practices which might contribute to the appearance of fear-of-failure motivation. Following the design used to study origins of need for achievement, Teevan and McGhee (1965) were able to show that mothers of sons high in HP report expectation of independent behavior by them earlier than mothers whose sons are low. This was not expected to be the case, and our initial efforts to study the pattern of reinforcements which the mother uses with her son give tentative support to their using punishment for failure and neutrality for success.

The fact that mothers report earlier independence training may mean that we have here a hint as to why *S*s with fear of failure become engaged by achievement situations at all, instead of simply remaining neutral or concerned solely about the objective consequences. At this writing we simply know very little about the origins of fear of failure.

An Expanded Portrait of the Fear-of-Failure Person

Early in the book, we presented Atkinson's portrait of the "failure threatened personality." In the light of the review just finished, we can verify most of that portrait and add to it. Atkinson's work concentrated on engagement, choice, and performance aspects of the fear-of-failure person, including his aspiration behavior. As we have seen, we have been able to replicate most of those findings. Thus, by addressing ourselves to achievement situations of a social, cooperative, and complex variety, we have learned something about the circumstances under which fear of failure can produce behaviors that are highly successful. This in turn has suggested which configurations of achievement situations the fear-of-failure person will approach rather than avoid.

Perhaps at this point the reader will accept an invitation to turn back to page 16 and read Atkinson's portrait once again. Then he can continue with the addition to it which we present here:

"Given constraint to perform in achievment situations, and sufficient experience with tasks for which the person has some aptitude, the fearful individual will show a preference for achievement situations which permit ample practice and development of skills, especially if the task contains requirements for cooperation with co-workers with whom success and failure credit is shared, and who can act as a source of positive social evaluation. Under these conditions the person's patterns of aspiration become more realistic and show sensitivity to the course of task outcomes. If the person is forced by the social situation to choose between rational task performance and conformity to the group as the source of social evaluation, he will choose the latter. He will sacrifice his mastery of task demands in order to maintain his social worth. Such sacrifice also brings its defenses, and most of his aspirational behavior is designed to leave his self-esteem on a particular task attribute untouched. Thus he may adopt a very wide range of performance levels on any given trial or task. Or more commonly, he may reinterpret the task situation as being a game rather than a serious undertaking, and hence gamelike aspirations become permissible. When he is confronted by situations which cannot be transformed into games and are clearly important, his aspiration becomes realistic or even pessimistic.

"In serious situations of achievement he seems most concerned with the social evaluation the testing authority will place on his behavior. Conceivably this reflects his early experience, in which he was taught that such situations are very important, but punishment for failure, in the form of derogation, was much stronger than the mild rewards offered for success. Given this orientation he gravitates toward the channels of vocational progress that emphasize order, gradual advancement, and diffused responsibility. Here he is quite safe from the judgment that his achievement task behavior is pathological."

(The discerning reader will note that we choose to suspend judgment about the circumstances which produce self-reports of anxiety in achievement situations, or fantasy of failure or of general threat.)

FEAR OF FAILURE: A RESTATEMENT OF THEORY

Conditions of Arousal and Effects on Behavior and Experience

Our own research and our reading of the research of others have led us to state and restate our current understanding of fear-of-failure motivation. Good research should lead to progressive refinement of definition and statements of relationship. We feel such progress has been taking place, and in this section we wish to offer our restatements of what we have presented in this book. The reader will probably choose to exercise his right to draw his own picture of where this work stands.

Failure can be initially defined as the nonattainment of a prescribed standard. But failure defined this way omits the quality of "invidious comparison" that makes failure an experience to be feared. Nonattainment by itself is merely a source of information about the level of the individual's ability and should not, in and of itself, produce any fear reactions. But the fact is that nonattainment can be unpleasant, and the possibility of nonattainment of an achievement standard can produce fear. If we are to understand why nonattainment is aversive, we must know what results from an episode of nonattainment.

Consequences of Nonattainment

Though nonattainment is essentially a learning experience and is not by itself aversive, it can develop a *secondary punishing characteristic*, becoming something to be feared, when it leads to an aversive experience. This experience may take any or all of three possible forms—(1) a lowered self-estimate, (2) the receipt of a nonego punishment, (3) a reduction in one's social value—in any given achievement situation.

Nonattainment fears will take three forms, corresponding to the three kinds of negative consequences. It is important to keep the three forms separated in our thinking because they may express themselves differently in the behavior of the individual.

Devaluation of the Self-Estimate: FF¹ *
we shall simply refer to them as Fear of Failure 1, 2, and 3.

One possible consequence of nonattainment is the information it carries regarding the *quality of the underlying attribute*. Thus if a girl is not chosen as a contestant in a beauty contest, this might indicate that she is not as pretty as her competitors. If a man sits down at the piano to play a song and all he produces is noise, then the evidence clearly indicates that he does not have the skill to make music. It would be an error to assume that such instances are always experienced as failures. If, however, the girl thought she deserved to be a contestant, and the person at the piano be-

---

* When we summarize the discussions, we shall indicate the factors affecting the magnitude of the failure fear in the form of propositions. Since there are three forms of the failure fear, we shall construct three propositions, each one pertaining to a particular form. Rather than engage in the clumsy procedure of spelling out the form of the failure fear in each proposition,

lieved he could play the song, then and only then would non-attainment create a sense of failure, or attainment a sense of success. This is the original definition of Hoppe (1930). Nonattainment is experienced as failure *when it is accepted as evidence that the self-estimate has been higher than it ought to be.* When this happens, the self-estimate is lowered and the process of lowering one's evaluation is experienced as failure. The more the self-estimate is lowered, the greater the sense of failure.

If nonattainment has no implication for a change in the self-estimate, then it does not produce this first kind of failure experience. If a person knows that he cannot broad-jump 20 feet, jumping less than 20 feet merely confirms his self-estimate; and since there is no implication for a reduction of the self-estimate, there is no failure. Another way of putting the matter is to say that non-attainment has meaning only when the probability of attaining the standard is greater than zero. If one considers the other side of the achievement coin, it follows that the attainment of a standard has meaning only when the probability of attainment is less than 1.0. In the extreme and rare instances when the individual knows with certainty that he can or that he cannot attain the standard, success and failure are no longer possible experiences. In such situations the individual stands to learn nothing new about his ability and in that sense we have no achievement setting. This is essentially the point Atkinson (1957) makes with his suggestion that when subjective probabilities of success are either 1.0 or 0.0, the motive to engage the task for achievement purposes is minimal.

Achievement situations are those in which the individual has the opportunity of discovering something new about the level of his ability. If he should discover that he is better than he thought, he experiences success; if he finds out that he is worse than he thought, he experiences failure.

In discussing self-evaluation as one outcome of the achievement situation, we have suggested that one form a fear of nonattainment might take is the fear of lowering the self-estimate. It may be, however, that there is also *a fear of the self-estimate change itself.* Not only do we like raising our self-estimate, we also like to maintain a *stable* self concept, and any information that suggests a change in the self-estimate could constitute a threat. It may well be that for a given individual the positive value of raising his self-estimate is more than offset by the negative value of having his self-estimate changed. We all know of cases in which a recommendation that one should raise his self-estimate has not been met with pleasure. A study by Aronson (1957) lends some support to the claim that information recommending a large increase in the self-estimate elicits the same sort of negative reaction as does any form of dissonance. Apparently, raising the self-estimate without maintaining an appropriate level of confidence or sense of "deserve" can be a source of much anxiety for certain people.

Although there are some fears about unprepared-for changes in the self-estimate, the primary fear in an achievement setting is that of having to *lower* the self-estimate. The failure experience, however, may be of such small magnitude that there is little to fear. We have said that our first form of failure is essentially the lowering of the self-estimate, but if the attribute on which the estimate is lowered is of no significance to the individual, the failure experience will have lost its sting.

Although the failure experience leads to behavior that must be explained and predicted, such behavior takes place *only after* the achievement episode ends and is essentially *not* achievement behavior. In order to understand what a person will do when faced with an achievement task, we must know the nature and magnitude of his particular anticipation of the failure experience. In other words, we must be concerned with the *fear* of failure rather than with the failure itself.

Whether a person will fear failure depends on the magnitude of the failure experience and whether or not he believes the failure will take place. Since attainment of the standard will avoid failure, fear will be present only when the individual is uncertain about the outcome. We all accept the fact that a plane crash is a pretty horrible experience, but if we do not *believe* we will be in a plane accident, there will be no fear when we buy our tickets.

The simplest assumption is that the magnitude of the fear increases as the probability of attainment decreases. However, there is a limit to this relationship because the individual may reject the standard as a basis for evaluation when the probability of attainment approaches zero. It is therefore necessary to assume that the person has accepted the standard as appropriate in order for the relationship to hold.

Even when the person has accepted the standard as appropriate, nonattainment need not result in a lowering of the self-estimate.

Nonattainment is merely a *recommendation* that the estimate be lowered, and this recommendation can vary in its persuasive force. So long as measures of the attribute vary in precision and reliability, the individual can dismiss nonattainment as an error of measurement. Furthermore, since standards vary in clarity, the individual can always convince himself that nonattainment was in fact attainment, or at least that nonattainment was indeterminate.

A necessary condition for nonattainment to carry persuasive force is the *acceptance by the individual of responsibility for the performance*. As McClelland (1961) has pointed out, in order for an individual to experience failure, he must consider himself responsible for the outcome. The meaning of responsibility for an achievement outcome is essentially the acceptance of the performance as being a direct expression of the underlying skill. When such factors as fatigue, distraction, chance, and lack of effort are introduced, responsibility for the performance is reduced (see Chapter 2). The importance of the responsibility factor is that it strengthens the implications of nonattainment for the self-estimate. We would therefore expect that the fear of failure would increase as responsibility increases.

In considering the fear of self-estimate loss, we have argued that the achievement situation was one in which the individual discovered his level of ability. If there is a desire to have a correct opinion about one's ability as Festinger (1954) has suggested, the reason for the desire may well rest on the fact that such knowledge allows the person to make decisions and take intelligent action. It is just such a point that Festinger makes when he shows that pressures toward uniformity (uniformity being one basis for believing that the opinion is correct) increase as the opinion increases in relevance for some action. In other words, the demand for knowledge about one's ability increases when such knowledge will permit future action.

When knowledge about one's ability is to be used, then even the discovery that one's self-estimate is higher than it is thought to be might be preferable to uncertainty and ignorance. Under such circumstances we would expect that the fear of self-devaluation would be reduced. On the other hand, if the loss in self-estimate cannot be used as information leading to action or decision, we would expect the failure fear to be increased. For example, it might be preferable to tell a cancer patient the truth about his disease if knowing the nature of his condition will permit him to put his spiritual and mental state in order. For many, however, the certainty of imminent death would produce nothing but panic and deep anxiety. These people, if they are at all suspicious of their health, ask for information in a way that also implies "Do not tell me if it is bad; I want reassurance or nothing." The doctor or relative who pays attention to the quality of the patient's question should have no difficulty in deciding whether or not to tell him the truth.

If teaching is the only trade a person knows, and discovering that he is a poor teacher serves no other purpose than to make him miserable, he would doubtless prefer "not to know." If, on the other hand, there is a decision at stake and the person wants to know whether to stay in teaching or to go into another line of work, the information regarding his teaching incompetence might help him decide the issue. In such a situation, even though teaching ability is important, his search for evaluation will not be opposed too strongly by a fear of failure. Although he would certainly prefer to discover that he is a capable teacher, knowing the truth would permit him to act in his own best interests. It is when the trait is very important, but the discovery that one is incompetent is *not instrumental* in permitting the person to make a decision in his own favor, that the fear of failure will produce the strongest force in opposition to the drive for evaluation. Doubtless both these forces increase with the importance of the trait, but it is our guess that the gradient is greater for the force generated by the fear of failure. This would be consistent with Miller's (1944) theory of approach and avoidant gradients and would explain why uncertainty would produce *searching behavior* when the issue is not important, and *avoidance of information* when it is. This is also consistent with Festinger's (1964) hypothesis that searching is increased when information is relevant to decision making.

PROPOSITION 1 The magnitude of FF[1] increases as (*a*) the probability of nonattainment increases, (*b*) the strength of the implication of nonattainment increases, (*c*) the importance of the attribute increases, (*d*) the degree of reduction in the self-estimate increases, and (*e*) the utility of nonattainment for decision decreases.

Nonego Punishments: FF²

In any community certain skills are valued, and the members of the group who possess the skills are rewarded accordingly. On the other hand, those who are deficient in the valued skills are punished by not being allowed to partake of the rewards. Few communities go out of their way to hurt the unskilled, inasmuch as the lack of reward seems to be punishment enough. But there are times when nonattainment of the prescribed standard does result in direct punishment. Thus, not clearing a fence will result in a punishing fall. Not solving a problem might be followed by an unpleasant electric shock in a psychology experiment. Losing a job, being imprisoned, and having to repeat a university course are also instances of punishment that can follow a demonstration of inadequate skill.

Although these punishments can have a strong effect upon the person's self concept, the effect is indirect. Thus the subject finds out he cannot do the problem when he feels the shock, and the student discovers he did not master the course when he is told he has to take it over again. Since there are ways of informing the person about the level of his skill other than through a punishment, the primary status of punishment is that of an aversive consequence of nonattainment.

It may seem improper to describe a person as being fearful of failure simply because some punishment has been made contingent on his not attaining the prescribed standard. But the point we are making is that fears in an achievement situation are directed towards the *consequences* of nonattainment, and that punishment in one form or another is one of the consequences.

The magnitude of this form of failure is obviously a function of the magnitude of the punishment. Whereas with the self-estimate, the importance of the attribute affects the magnitude of the failure experience, the importance of the attribute in this case is irrelevant. In fact, as the importance of the attribute is reduced, FF² increases in significance in the overall achievement picture.

The FF² will be a function not only of the magnitude of the punishment but also of the degree to which the individual believes the punishment will actually be applied. One factor affecting the belief that punishment will be administered is the same as in the fear regarding the self-estimate: the expectation of nonattainment. If the individual believes he will meet the performance requirements, then he also believes he will not experience the punishment. The fear of failure will increase as the probability of nonattainment increases. There is some question whether the relationship is linear. Unlike the fear of self-estimate reduction, acceptance of the standard as appropriate is not relevant to the fear of punishment. Regardless of what we are asked to accomplish, if a punishment is made contingent on nonattainment, the fear will increase with the size of the punishment. Thus when the probability of attainment approaches zero, we expect the fear to be very high. However, when the individual knows with certainty that he cannot attain the standard and that there is no question but that the punishment will be administered, his reaction may lose the character of fear and be converted into a resigned attitude often described as apathy.

Another factor affecting the belief in the application of the punishment is the degree of obvious inevitability with which the punishment attaches itself to the nonattainment. There are some punishments which are *intrinsically tied* to nonattainment, while others have the character of being *accidental* or *arbitrary*. Thus not making a long enough jump across a moat will result immediately in an unpleasant fall into the water, and there is little room to insert a doubt about such a consequence. On the other hand, the threat that the child's next visit to the zoo will be canceled unless he brings home a better report card may or may not be carried out by the parents; every child worth his salt knows this.

Although the expenditures of effort need not be contingent on nonattainment, they are nevertheless intrinsic costs of an achievement performance and must be balanced by the rewards of attainment. Not receiving rewards because of nonattainment means that time and effort were wasted and the expenditures then become punishments that the individual must endure for nonattainment.

PROPOSITION 2   The magnitude of FF^2 increases as (*a*) the magnitude of the punishment increases, (*b*) the probability of attainment decreases, and (*c*) the probability of carrying out the threat increases.

Social Devaluation: FF^3

To the extent that a culture values people who have made their mark through achievement, it follows that nonattainment can generate fears about one's loss in social value. Evaluation by others, irrespective of its function as information for the individual's self-estimate, is a consequence of an achievement outcome. The evaluation by others need not be in agreement with the self-evaluation. Thus, a person can feel he has failed because he did not attain a self-prescribed standard and at the same time can be evaluated as a success by others. The acclaim of others is satisfying in itself. It has reward value. Derogation by others, on the other hand, is punishing. Needless to say, a person may fear the poor opinion of others more than he fears self-devaluation or some nonego punishment.

We like to give lip service to the *value* that a person's worth is independent of what he does. But the fact of the matter is that we esteem those whom we evaluate highly. Success pays off not only in power and money but in respect and esteem as well. It is not surprising then to find that people avoid telling others about their poor performances.

There are many dimensions along which a person is evaluated. Being modest, sincere, kind, generous, and loyal is just as much a matter of achievement as are intelligence, beauty, and various motor skills. Since a person's social value is a function of his evaluation along a number of dimensions, nonattainment in one category can be compensated by attainments in the others. If the individual has established a high social value because of a consistently high evaluation on many attributes, the fear of nonattainment in a particular area will be small. In a way the individual has developed a sense of "social certitude," and a given nonattainment will have lost its ability to generate fear.

In any given community certain attributes are more important for social value than others. Thus the ability to shoot a rifle and follow the spoor of an animal is less important in our society than the ability to read and write. It would follow that the fear of nonattainment would be greater the more important the skill is to the determination of social value.

Another factor affecting the magnitude of the fear is the magnitude of the social-value loss. This factor is similar to the one we discussed in regard to the self-estimate. The greater the possible loss in social value the greater the fear.

The loss in social value, however, regardless of its magnitude will have little effect upon the fears of a person if the loss takes place in the eyes of others for whom the individual has no high regard. Although we desire to be highly valued by all people, not all people are equally important for judging our social value. People we love, esteem, and respect are more important referents for social value than those whom we dislike or consider our inferiors.

The factor of the probability of nonattainment which was discusesd in regard to the failures 1 and 2 is also a factor in the fear of social-value loss. We would expect that as the probability of nonattainment increases, the fear of social loss also increases. Since the standard is socially determined rather than established by the individual himself, rejection of the standard because the probability of attainment is zero will not exempt him from penalties. For this reason we expect that the relationship between the probability and the fear will be linear.

Since the loss of social value can take place only when others know about the nonattainment, it follows that the failure fear would be greater when others are watching the performance. Furthermore, since the magnitude of the loss is a function not only of the size of the loss but also of the extent to which it is public, the failure fear will be greater as the number of people who know about the non-attainment increases.

PROPOSITION 3 The magnitude of FF[3] increases as (*a*) the probability of nonattainment increases, (*b*) the importance of the attribute increases, (*c*) the reduction in social value increases, (*d*) the importance of those for whom there has been a loss in social value increases, and (*e*) the number of people who know about the nonattainment increases.

BEHAVIORS AFFECTED BY FEAR OF FAILURE

We shall have little to say about what follows upon a failure experience, since our primary interest is in what happens when a person anticipates failure. Whether the fear is a relatively stable personality trait or one that is created by the conditions of the achievement situation, it is a reaction to cues that signal future failure. Since the failure has not yet occurred, the individual has the opportunity to engage in avoidance behavior. As the fear increases in magnitude, we would expect a greater tendency to behave in a defensive manner. Which particular defensive maneuver will serve the function of reducing the fear, will depend in part on the type of failure fear, although some avoidance behavior will serve all three kinds of fears—i.e., fear of (1) reduction in self-estimate, (2) a nonego punishment, and (3) loss in social value.

THE DEFENSE AGAINST THE LOSS IN SELF-ESTIMATE: FF¹

Ignorance and space prevent us from considering all of the many defensive behaviors that can be engaged in to avoid self-devaluation. The ones we have chosen to discuss we believe are the most prominent and lead to interesting predictions.

Increasing the Probability of Attaining the Standard

The most obvious way of avoiding a loss in the self-estimate is to insure the attainment of the standard. One increases the probability of attainment by improving skill through practice and by putting out maximum effort when confronted with the standard. This very constructive behavior would, of course, serve each of the three forms of fear. There is one hitch to this strategy: there is no guarantee that the skill will be improved and that attainment will become more probable. Furthermore, practice and effort carry certain perils when the primary fear involves the loss of self-evaluation. For if nonattainment follows after the person has practiced and tried very hard, it becomes that much more difficult to avoid the implications about the underlying skill. It is doubtful whether a fear of self-devaluation ever produces increased effort or practice. If the fearful individual goes off to improve his skill and struggles with the achievement standard, the chances are it is because of one of the other forms of fear and in spite of the fear of self-estimate loss. However, if the individual has been trapped into accepting full responsibility for his performance and realizes that he has burned all his escape bridges, then we might expect him to run scared into practice and effort. One example that comes easily to mind is the student who has difficulty accepting any grade below an A. He is conscientious and works like a dog, whipped along by fears rather than being gently tugged by the rewards of knowledge. It may be that he fears a lowered self-estimate, but the chances are that his fears of low grades have been established through association with punishments and loss in social value.

We do not want to deny the FF¹ person the strategy of improving his skill and trying very hard at the task, but we believe this can happen only when such action is clearly buffered by the opportunity of discounting responsibility for the performance when it does not attain the standard. In general, it is doubtful whether practice and effort are popular strategies for someone who is fearful of having his self-estimate reduced.

A seemingly shrewd alternative way of improving the chances of attaining the standard would be by reducing the achievement standard. It must have been some such idea as this that persuaded workers in the area of level of aspiration to interpret low LA's as a way of increasing chances of attainment. But reducing an achievement standard, although increasing the probability of attaining that standard, does very little for the self-estimate. Lowering the achievement standard is essentially an admission of a lower self-estimate and is hardly a defense against it. It is doubtful whether low LA's scores are strategies to avoid or reduce the fear of lowering the self-estimate. We believe that LA statements do serve an achievement function, and we will discuss this behavior in a later section.

Avoiding a Precise Self-Estimate

As long as the self-estimate is kept vague, it remains unclear whether a performance confirms it or disconfirms it. We would therefore expect a person who is fearful of a self-estimate loss to avoid situations which promise to increase the precision of the self-estimate. It is true that one decreases the chances of success as well as of failure, but a person who is particularly fearful of a loss in self-estimate may prefer to forego the opportunity of raising his self-estimate in order to insure that there be no loss.

According to Festinger (*Hum. Rel.,* 1954), when an ability is important to the individual, there are pressures to find out how good he is. The more important the ability, the greater the pressure. But there are counterpressures as well that increase with the importance factor.

There is a strong need to find out how good we are, but an opposing desire not to find how poor we are. The opposing force stems from the possibility of finding out something we don't want to know. We have all been warned that curiosity killed the cat, and if we ask too many questions we might get hurt. When one's self-esteem is at stake, when a life is hanging by a shred of hope, ignorance may not be bliss but knowledge may be devastating. Uncertainty may be a state of mind that motivates the organism to search, but if it appears that the search will not uncover a satisfactory answer, the individual may prefer to remain ignorant. In nonachievement situations we can accept the hypothesis that uncertainty leads to searching and that not knowing is an unsatisfactory state of mind. But when there is a likelihood of being devalued, the motivational force arising out of uncertainty is opposed by the force of a fear of failure.

Preference for Noncomparable Groups

Festinger, in his theory of Social Comparison Processes (1954) argued that a comparison with others who are similar in ability produces the greatest amount of information regarding the ability. Other people who are considerably dissimilar as to level of ability are noncomparable, and a comparison of one's performance with the performances of such people leaves the individual relatively unenlightened in regard to his own level of ability. Some support for this thesis was offered in a study by Dreyer (*Hum. Rel.,* 1954) when he found that *S*s who scored far above or far below the average of the group did not experience a clear sense of failure or success. If Festinger is correct, we would expect that those who prefer to avoid information about their ability would be more inclined to compete with those who are noncomparable than those who are similar in ability.

Preference for Easy and Difficult Tasks. When one is much better or much worse than the others with whom one is competing, the outcome of the contest is highly predictable and there is little information to be gained from the performance. In the same way, tasks that are so easy that everyone can do them, and tasks that are so difficult that no one can do them, carry little information about the underlying skill. We would therefore expect that persons who are fearful of having their self-estimate lowered would prefer the very difficult and the very easy tasks over the moderately difficult tasks. This is the argument that Atkinson (1957) makes when he claims that fear-of-failure people prefer difficult or easy tasks. But since we maintain that the lack of information is the critical factor rather than the level of difficulty per se, a person fearful of a lowered self-estimate could just as well choose to engage in a moderately difficult task so long as the informational feedback is minimal.

Preference for Privacy. We have been considering situations in which the information about the ability level comes from fairly objective sources. But even when there is an objective measure that can be used to determine the ability level, the force of others' opinions can be considerable. The studies by Asch (1956) have dramatically shown that what appears obvious to the senses can be undermined by facing disagreement. More often than not there is no objective test available and the opinions of others become the sole determinants of what is correct. This is particularly true in matters of ability or worth of the individual. If the person wanted to avoid information about his ability level, we would expect him to avoid a public display of his ability.

Preference for Imprecise and Unreliable Performance Measures. An obvious situation in which the precision of the self-estimate is increased is one in which the measures of performance are held to be precise and reliable. Whenever we permit an objectively measured performance to be used as an indicator of the underlying skill we are taking the risk of discovering that we are less able than we thought we were. In areas where the measure of performance is ambiguous, the individual is able to maintain a satisfying self-evaluation. It is interesting to observe reactions among instructors to the teacher-rating schedules that are circulated from time to time at universities. Many of the rejections of the schedule bear all the earmarks of "I don't want to know." One might guess that the fear of a poor evaluation was enough to chase the curious away. We would therefore expect that the FF[1] would avoid achievement situations where tape measures, stop watches, and questionnaires abound.

Rejecting the Performance of a Measure of the Skill. Perhaps the most common and shrewdest way of avoiding a loss in self-estimate is to prevent the performance from being used to determine the self-estimate. Even when the measures of the performance are precise and reliable, it is always possible to argue that the performance is an inadequate indicator of the underlying skill.

Preferring Vague Achievement Standards. It is too simple an assumption that the world of achievement fits a neat Aristotelian logic, and in it a person either succeeds or fails. Rather, the individual seems to choose a level of difficulty that sets the baseline for failure—i.e., a line below which performance will generate a loss in self-evaluation—and a higher level of difficulty that sets the baseline for success—i.e., a line above performance which will generate an increase in self-evaluation. Between the two levels the performance is reacted to with indifference. The levels are not static nor are they equidistant from some specific performance score the person expects to attain.

It is to be expected that people will differ in the width of the confirming interval (CI). Most of the differences can be accounted for by the differences in practice and experience with the task. But even with experience held constant, we find differences in the interval width.

If a person has a wide interval, he can experience very low and very high scores relative to his expectation level without being disconfirmed in his self-evaluation. Although the wide-interval individual has a smaller chance of experiencing success, he also reduces the chances of failure. Such a person forgoes the pleasures of success disconfirmation so as to avoid the unpleasantness of failure disconfirmation, and he is willing to do this because he finds failure more unpleasant than success pleasant. We would therefore expect the FF[1] person to try to maintain a wide CI. Wide CI width might explain the rigid level-of-aspiration patterns of some people (Rotter, 1954). It seems that no matter how they perform, the aspirational pattern remains the same. We would argue that they are answering the aspirational question by stating a score within a CI so wide that low and high scores, i.e., performance scores much below and much above the score stated, will remain within the interval, producing no disconfirmation and, therefore, no change in the aspirational statement.

We have suggested that performance scores that were outside the CI, either below or above, would indicate that the individual was wrong in his expectations with the implication that he ought to change his self-estimate. But not every score outside the CI will act as a disconfirmation. From time to time, a person produces a performance that is so exceedingly bad or good that he does not know what to make of it. Such scores are so far removed from his expectation that he rejects them as flukes. Apparently there are limits beyond which a performance has little or no implication for the self-estimate. Put another way, such performances have little information value regarding the relevant ability. If such an event happens in a psychological experiment, the *S* becomes suspicious.

This is the experience of incongruity that Osgood and Tannenbaum (1955) discuss in their theory of balance.

Preference for "Practice" and "Games." Not only do the watchful eyes of others put pressure on us to accept the performance as a measure of the ability, but a public performance is irretrievable. If we were by ourselves, we could always convince ourselves that we were "merely practicing," or it is "only a game." The difference between practice and the real thing raises some curious definitional problems. But there is no question about the difference in impact on the sense of failure. There is a gentlemen's agreement that we do not evaluate the person if he claims he is practicing. Thus the critic waits till the producer decides the show is ready for evaluation, and that evening's performance is called the first night even though there have been a dozen earlier performances called previews.

It has always been a curious fact that when participants wage money on a contest, the tension of the play is increased far out of proportion to the amount of money bet. It is our guess that when money is put on the line, there is an unstated agreement that the performances are the real thing. Each contestant has committed himself to the performance and can no longer excuse his actions as practice.

Rejecting Responsibility. One way of reducing the significance of a performance as an indicator of an underlying skill is to reject responsibility for the performance. Some well-worn techniques that we seem to recognize only when other people use them are the claims that fatigue, bad luck, distraction, and not-trying were the primary causes of the nonattainment. There is little one can do about bad luck and fatigue except to try to convince oneself and others that they were operative. But not-trying is within the control of the individual, and we would expect a person who is particularly fearful of experiencing self-devaluation not to put out a maximum effort when involved in an achievement task.

There are some tasks for which it is difficult to claim that any factor other than the underlying skill was affecting the performance. Intelligence tests, steadiness tests, chess, and balancing a stick on one's nose are tasks for which it is difficult to deny responsibility for performance. Hitting a golf ball off a tee is another task in which responsibility for the performance rests completely on the individual; but how far the ball goes down the fairway may be affected by factors outside the control of the person. At disappointing moments like this, all good sportsmen are on the lookout for extenuating circumstances.

Toward the other end of the responsibility scale we have such tasks as course examinations and poker in which losers claim foul play and bad luck, while winners claim skill. Further down the road we come to games like roulette and horse racing and finally the lotteries. But even in games of this nature we find disagreements regarding the degree of skill involved.

It is tempting to suggest that people who are FF[1] prefer situations for which the outcome is outside their control. But it may well be that preference for such situations is rather a function of whether the person believes fate is kind or unkind to him than a desire to dismiss responsibility. All that we will say is that the FF[1] person would avoid situations in which it is difficult to reject responsibilty for the performance. If he believed the uncontrolled factor to be benign, he might prefer the pure gambling task. But our suspicion is that the FF person tends to see the unnamed factors as being somewhat hostile. If this is so, we would expect him to seek out tasks in which skill is a factor but a number of escapes from responsibility are available.

Reducing the Importance of the Attribute. If it is true that success breeds interest, as Allport's (1937) functional autonomy of motives suggests, then one might expect failure to breed indifference. If someone expected to fail in a certain area of achievement, we would expect him to lose interest in the relevant skill and turn to matters for which probabilities of attainment are higher. Losing interest in a skill is simply another way of saying that the individual has reduced the importance of the matter.

Reducing the importance of a skill as one discovers one's own incompetence is an ideal way of reducing the fear of failure. If one doesn't care, one can try with all one's might, thus giving oneself the outside chance of attainment, and yet remain a good loser when the performance does not reach the standard. This strategy is popular, as can be judged by the fact that it is one of the first things we recommend when we observe a child struggling and then weeping over his nonattainment.

Not Trying. One problem with reducing importance is that it cannot be done by the mere saying. If a person is going to convince himself that the skill is not important, he must do it through action rather than words. One way of demonstrating to oneself that the skill is unimportant is by not trying on the relevant task. By bringing about objective failure and suffering its consequences, the individual is proving that the whole matter is unimportant. If the whole matter is unimportant, then the skill is also unimportant and the experience of nonattainment does not produce the experience of failure.

Not trying apparently serves two functions in regard to failure fears: (1) it reduces the significance of the actual performance as an indicator of the underlying skill, thereby avoiding any implications for a lowering of the self-estimate and (2) it argues that the task and the relevant skill are really not important, and thus the loss of self-estimate is of little concern. The young girl who refuses to "pretty herself" is a classic example of someone who is so afraid of not being attractive that she makes it clear she is not interested in attracting. To make an effort would mean she is placing her attractiveness on the line to be evaluated and that she considers attracting the male an important achievement. That is a lot to ask of someone who is frightened of failure, especially when there is no guarantee of attainment.

Not trying is also affected by the probability of attainment. Thus if a person believes he has a very small chance of attaining the standard, he may reduce the cost of effort and time by not trying. The problem with this strategy is that the individual reduces his chances of attaining the standard. To be sure, he has avoided having to lower his self-estimate, but by not attaining the prescribed standard he does not receive any rewards and takes the chance of losing social value and of being exposed to nonego punishment. Whether he tries or not will depend on which kind of failure he fears most.

Seeking Social Support. We seek out and prefer people whose values are similar to our own. On the other hand, the values we hold are also established in interpersonal relations. In other words, we become convinced by the norms of the groups in which we participate. If a person wants to change a value, we would expect him to seek out people who hold alternative values. If a person wants to reduce the importance of a certain skill we would expect him to seek out those who do not consider the skill important.

It is not surprising to find nonathletes forming cohesive groups so that they can support one another in derogating athletic skills.

The minority group member who has been rejected by the majority can find solace in returning to his group, where the attributes, disparaged by the larger cultural group, are supported. Subcultural groupings are constantly being formed by people whose skills and characteristics are not being rewarded by the majority culture.

Misjudging Performance

Misperceiving the quality of the performance is perhaps the least efficient of all the defense strategies. It not only exposes the individual to criticism and rejection but it can end in a more disastrous loss in the self-estimate than a realistic performance judgment. When there are no witnesses, however, the strategy can serve as a momentary support and probably does little harm in small doses. The problem arises when the person becomes an addict; small distortions grow into big ones, and the individual loses an adequate sense of self.

So long as the performance is not measured precisely, it can be judged to be better than it actually is. Distortions of this kind are not uncommon when the evaluation tends to be subjective. We have yet to meet a painter who doesn't believe he deserves more recognition than he has received for his brilliant canvases. Parents who insist that their children perform for the guest's enjoyment seem to have lost all contact with reality in at least that area. The fish that got away grows in size each time the story is told, and the accomplishments of youth grow in stature as time goes by. The half-mile swim stretches to a mile, and the C— report cards are converted to scholastic honors. Exaggerating past performances is a common deceit that permits us all to maintain a decent self-concept. When an individual has a chronic fear of a loss in self-estimate, we expect that he will be more prone to seize an opportunity to distort. Furthermore, when he is comparing his performance with the performances of others, he will tend to judge theirs as being worse than they actually are.

Distortion of Probabilities

When fear of failure takes on ungovernable proportions (perhaps because of the importance of the attribute), panic can develop and spill over into dramatic misperceptions. One form such distortion can take is the exaggeration of the subjective probability of attainment. Studies by Marks (1951) and Irwin (1953) have shown that as the value of winning increases, the belief in the possibility of winning also increases.

The suggestion that an FF[1] would tend to distort his probabilities of attainment upward apparently goes contrary to Atkinson's assumption that the positive distorters are the hope-of-success people. The only data we possess in regard to this issue are somewhat equivocal. It has been suggested that Ss who have a disproportionately high level of aspiration are fearful of failure. If high LA's can be correlated with positive probability distortion, then there is some support for the assumption that fear of failure will distort probabilities upward. Our argument that the FF[1] will distort upwards is based on the assumption that such misperception can serve to prevent a loss in the self-estimate.

Forgetting Nonattainments

The strategy of forgetting past nonattainments is akin to forgetting uncompleted tasks when incompletions are perceived as due to a lack of ability. In the original study of Zeigarnik (1927) subjects tended to remember uncompleted tasks almost twice as frequently as completed tasks. However, the interruption of the task activity was informal and did not imply any inadequacy on the part of the subject. Rosenzweig (1943) in an attempt to test Freud's theory of repression repeated Zeigarnik's study with the modification of making the interruption a sign of failure. This study showed that the completed tasks were remembered more frequently than the uncompleted tasks. He interpreted his results as being consistent with the thesis that people tend to repress thoughts about failure. Exaggeration of the tendency to repress failure would be expected of people who are particularly fearful of failure. Some weak support for this thesis is suggested by the results of Atkinson's study (1953). He found that subjects who scored low on a measure of achievement motivation remembered fewer uncompleted tasks than those who scored high. Atkinson's assumption is that low n-achievers are more fear-of-failure than high n-achievers.

Sensitivity of Potential

Performance in any task when repeated over a number of trials will vary. Some darts will go into the target center; others will miss at varying distances. Some days we are on the top of our game; on others nothing seems to go right. It would seem proper for the individual to accept as the best estimate of his ability some typical performance. But in fact this is not what people tend to do. There is apparently a strong inclination to see ourselves in the light of our better (or even best) performances. Since such a tendency serves to bolster the self-estimate, we would expect the FF[1] to have an exaggerated tendency to see himself in terms of his best performances.

THE DEFENSE AGAINST PUNISHMENT: FF[2]

If the attainment of an achievement standard has no bearing on the person's self-estimate but the nonattainment would result in some punishment, restraining forces will be required to keep him in the achievement situation. Leaving the situation would have to promise more unpleasantness than the nonattainment. For a person who is particularly fearful of the punishment made contingent on nonattainment, the achievement situation is essentially a constrained one.

We are disinclined to suggest that people can be differentiated on the strength of fear about nonego punishment. But we do know, although the data is primarily anecdotal, that some people give in more quickly than others to threats of physical punishment. Some research by Applezweig, Moeller, and Burdick (1956) indicates that some people fear physical disablement more than they fear what others may think of them. Questionnaire data about the behavior of prisoners of war during the Korean conflict indicate that some soldiers conceded to the demands of their captors under threats of solitary confinement and deprivation, while others suffered the punishments without breaking.

Whether the fear is chronic or situational, it cancome into play in an achievement situation and will affect the nature of the achievement activity. If the individual *cannot escape,* either because of high prison walls or the presence of an experimenter or a threat of a truant officers, the question must be answered as to what he will do when faced with an achievement task.

If there is no issue about evaluating the underlying skill, the most direct way of avoiding the punishment is through increasing the chances of attainment through practice and effort. There are few achievement situations in which evaluation is not involved, and thus the individual has to decide whether devaluation is more or less important to him than the threatened punishment. If the threatened punishment is more fear-provoking, we would expect the person to expend his full effort and take his chances of devaluation. But for this to happen, he must be able to see his chances of attainment as reasonable. If the task is so difficult that the chances of attainment are nil, we expect he will resign himself to the punishment and save the energy of trying. As the magnitude of the punishment increases, the point of resignation will move closer to probability zero.

DEFENSE AGAINST A LOSS IN SOCIAL VALUE: FF[3]

We have argued that one outcome of an achievement experience is the knowledge obtained about an ability level. Such knowledge is useful in that it permits the individual to make intelligent decisions as to where and when he should compete and strive for rewards. Since low and high self-estimates, so long as they are precise, are equally informative, it should make little difference to the individual whether or not he discovers that he is competent. But, of course, we do care about the level of our ability and we all prefer to be better than worse. Competence reaps rewards, and attainment of standards gathers social value. A high self-estimate promises glory, while a low self-estimate bodes deprivation. In a sense, competence is instrumental, and its value is to serve as a means toward gaining more primary rewards. Social value is an important reward, for in an achieving society achievers are acclaimed and losers are ignored.

Informing Others of Attainment

It is difficult to imagine a person who has bowled a score of 280 not telling his bowling associates and friends about his exceptional feat. If all he wanted to know was how well he bowled, the performance itself was quite clear. As far as the self-estimate is concerned the matter is closed. But apparently self-knowledge is not enough, and the individual predictably goes on to inform others of his accomplishment. Of course, if the performance indicated a lack of ability we would expect the person to be quiet about what happened. The demand that others recognize our accomplishments and be ignorant of our defeats emanates from a desire for social value. The individual who is particularly concerned with his social value will exaggerate these tendencies to be informative or uninformative.

Informing others only when there has been an achievement is like a one-sided argument for one's worth. The fearful person cannot afford to point out his nonattainments because of the ever-present possibility of social-value loss. Not only would we expect the FF[3] not to tell others of his failures; we would also expect him to avoid performing before others unless he is totally confident of the outcome. There is no better way of informing others than by having them watch.

Making Excuses

A person who is fearful of losing social value will tend to avoid uncertain achievement situations whenever others can observe his performance. But such a person will also have difficulty avoiding the achievement situation when it is expected that he will participate. He is essentially caught in an avoidance-avoidance conflict where he can lose value if he does not participate, and might lose value if he does. Under such conditions a popular method of avoiding possible loss is the use of excuses. In order to prepare others for the nonattainment, the individual may point out that he is out of condition, unpracticed, or fatigued or is not trying because the skill is not important to him. These defensive behaviors are used to protect the self-estimate, but then the person himself has to believe them. When the primary function of the excuses is to prevent a loss in social value, the problem is to persuade the audience to believe them. We would expect the FF[3] to be more sensitive to and to exaggerate any sign of an extenuating factor that could excuse the nonattainment.

Level-of-Aspiration Statements

There are ways other than through achievement that a person can maintain his social value. We cannot all have the desired skills, but we can all be modest. The highly valued person is one who is both accomplished and modest. If one cannot be a good winner, one is appreciated for being a good loser. A good loser is someone who does not insist that he deserved to win. He can hope and wish all he wants, but he remains modest in his claims and does so through low expectancy announcements.

A basic assumption in level-of-aspiration studies is that the LA statements mirror the internal aspirational state, and that attainment of the level described by the person produces success and nonattainment generates failure. If one stops to think about it, it seems most odd to believe that a person becomes a success merely when he attains or overattains what he said he would. If this were true, then everyone would maintain a low expectancy, thereby insuring success and avoiding failure. But the fact is that only some do this, and it is doubtful whether it is done to reduce a fear of nonattainment. When a bowler, faced with a split, announces that he "won't make it," and then doesn't, he is given credit for not overestimating his ability. That he was commendably humble, however, does not disprove the fact that he failed to make the split. In regard to his ability to make the split he has demonstrated an incompetence. What he has accomplished by stating a low aspirational level was to avoid being accused of bragging and thereby losing social value. Seen in tihs light, LA statements become strategies to avoid a loss in social value rather than a way to reduce fears of nonattainment. They do not mirror private aspirational states but are essentially interpersonal behaviors.

What happens to our hypothetical bowler when he *does* make the split? Even though he is applauded and is probably experiencing a sense of accomplishment, by stating a low level of expectancy he has implied that the performance included a significant element of chance. He cannot be given full credit for the accomplishment; "he really isn't as good a bowler as his performance suggests." An achievement that has been predicted has a different meaning and significance from one that has not been predicted. To predict that you will do a certain thing and then do it means that chance has not entered into the picture and that one's ability is commensurate with the performance. Anyone who has had such an experience will appreciate the difference between the feelings of success under such conditions and the feelings of success when the accomplishment was not predicted. There is no question but that a high-level performance coming after a correct prediction is more satisfying than the same level of performance coming after a low-level prediction. Certainly it is more dramatic. Perhaps one of the most well-remembered instances in baseball was the time that Babe Ruth pointed to the outfield fence and then hit a home run.

The person who predicts a high-level performance still leaves himself open to social criticism. There are, therefore, pressures on the individual to keep his predictions within realistic bounds. Wanting to be given full credit for a good performance, he will tend to make a high performance prediction. Wanting to avoid being criticized as an "overestimator," he will keep his predictions realistic by anchoring them to his previous performance. By so doing he will minimize the shame of doing less well than his predictions, but will lose the opportunity of taking full credit for exceptionally good performances. If there are differences in the levels of expectations set by different people, they are probably due to differences in the concern with *social criticism* as compared with a concern with taking full credit for exceptionally good performance.

Accordingly, people who are afraid of losing social value should have smaller goal-discrepancy scores than those who are less concerned about such a loss. It would also follow that people who are more concerned about maintaining their self-estimate would attempt to take credit for exceptional performances by stating a high level of aspiration.

We have argued that an aspirational statement is essentially an interpersonal act. When it is inappropriately low it is an attempt to be modest. When it is inappropriately high it is an attempt to persuade others that actual ability is greater than the performance indicates. In both instances the person is trying to maintain his social value.

There are other reasons for setting low or high aspirational levels which do not involve the opinions of others. One function of a private goal setting is to convince oneself. If saying becomes believing (Janis and King, 1954), then an announcement to oneself of nonattainment might serve to reduce actual expectations and thereby reduce the sense of disappointment when nonattainment becomes a reality. On the other hand, high goal setting may be used by a person to convince himself that he could succeed "if only he tried." This old trick has been used by football coaches down through the fall seasons.

There is another reason why people set their expectations below what they "should" be. The reason has roots in prehistoric concerns with forces normally outside the control of man. So long as the performance is uncertain, "one can never trust what jealous gods might decide." Calling a manchild by a girl's name to fool the gods is really not much different from declaring a ridiculously low aspirational level. Perhaps we are not as aware of gods watching as we once were, but a sense of the appropriateness of modesty is still with us as we face uncontrolled forces. In brief, a low aspiration level may well be an act of simple superstition.

Summary

We have made a distinction between three kinds of fear of failure. This is not to deny that in any given situation all three fears may be operating simultaneously. By doing poorly in an achievement situation the individual is faced with the possibility of self-devaluation; he may also be informed that he will be punished; and generally present is the "watcher" who is evaluating the performance and possibly derogating the performer. Nevertheless, it is our contention that people differ in the degree to which they fear these three possible consequences of an achievement outcome. Thus, for some people the primary fear is directed at the lowering of their self-estimate, while for others the primary fear is the lowering of their worth in the eyes of others. Still others might be primarily fearful of the loss of rewards that often accompanies a nonattainment.

We have described the various strategies employed by each of the three types of FF. In many instances the strategies overlap so that each of the types would be doing the same thing. Thus the avoidance of the achievement situation would be characteristic behaviors of the FF^1 and the FF^2 and of the FF^3 as well, when there are others watching. But there are enough important differences in what each of the three will do when faced with an achievement standard to suggest that fear of failure should not be conceived as a unified construct. The inconsistencies of previous claims regarding the behavior of the fear-of-failure S have already hinted at the possibility of more than one dimension. We have taken the hint and tried to show what those dimensions are.

CHAPTER 11

Future Research

HOW CAN WE INTEGRATE THE FINDINGS OF THE LITERATURE ON fear of failure? To do this we must review the underlying assumptions of the motive measures. The self-report anxiety measures assume that Ss who suffer from anxiety in achievement situations both notice this fact and are willing to report it. According to our theory, the anxiety could be produced by any or all of the three sources of failure threat discussed in Chapter 10. The projective scoring systems which score for direct expression of Fear of Failure assume that pictures of achievement situations will cue off Fear of Failure in Ss whose basic response is avoidance in nature. Our HP system, which scores contents not directly related to the achievement cues in pictures, assumes that achievement cues produce generalized avoidance responses. Actually, we now know that experimental arousal of Fear of Failure using the forced-failure technique will produce increases in both types of story contents. However, Anderson (1962) and De Charms and Davé (1965), who did arousal studies, both used young children of elementary-school age, fourth through sixth grades. Suppose we approach the problem from a developmental point of view.

We have already suggested some of our thinking about the early reinforcement patterns which produce fear of failure. Now let us consider the pattern of reinforcement brought to bear on the expressions that the young child makes in achievement situations. Here, too, some major differences can occur. In the beginning we assume the child announces his fear and wish to avoid. How does the parent respond? He could encourage the child to express fear, or at least be neutral and not apply negative reinforcement. In such

226

a case, even if he is positively reinforcing approach tendencies, including statements, we would expect that the child's imagery will develop with Fear of Failure as a possible response. On the other hand, it may be that the parent will negatively reinforce direct Fear of Failure statements and expressions. He suggests to the child that such thoughts are to be avoided because they interfere with approach tendencies. Under these circumstances we might find that less direct expression of Fear of Failure appears in place of the direct statement. If we assume that young children in both German and American cultures tend initially to express their fears directly, we are left with the possibility that somehow in the socialization process the American youth learn to "think positive," while the Germans go on expressing Fear of Failure quite directly. Conceivably in the American case we are saying the authority figure discourages talk of fear while in the German case it is permitted or encouraged. Only more research will answer these questions, but for now it is clear that we do not have a necessary contradiction in the data.

Given the independence of fear of failure measures found in Table 8.3, p. 166, we have found it instructive to take a careful look at the actual content of the responses the S must make in order to receive an FF score. In our judgment the TAQ contains many items which permit considerable ambiguity of interpretation. Thus the S testifies that he worries, perspires, has an increased heartbeat, lacks confidence, and feels uneasy about taking intelligence tests or final examinations. What worries us is that affirmative answers to such suggestions may also reflect a more general arousal or excitement which is not necessarily a sign that the S fears the consequences of the testing outcome. In fact, it is possible to imagine someone saying yes to such questions, and then volunteering the information that he enjoys taking such tests!

The Haber-Alper measure is not as vulnerable to the above criticism, and our review shows that it has far fewer established relationships in the literature than the TAQ. Despite the failure of either measure to show relationships to the projective measures, we feel that the AAT is the more defensible device for those wishing to use reported anxiety.

The different TAT measures of FF also reflect strikingly different types of imagery. De Charms and Davé (1965) score for negative outcome to achievement themas, Anderson (1962) and Moulton

(1958) use negative categories of n Ach, Heckhausen (1963) uses clear statements of fear of achievement loss, usually at the hands of a social superior, and the HP system emphasizes victimization of the central figure in the story.

That TAT systems seem to reflect the system of negative incentives just used in our theorizing. That is, fear of nonego-involving consequences may parallel the De Charmes-Davé system; fear of self-devaluation, feelings of failure, and fear of social devaluation may imply a hostile environment. Certainly we are faced with the empirical fact that all of these measures can generate relationships to behavior and experience in achievement situations, and the outlines of a program of comparative research for these different measures are clear.

Another possibility also suggests itself which is more traditional but difficult to demonstrate experimentally. That is that our differences in measures reflect strength of Fear of Failure motivation. This argument would run that self-reported anxiety of the Haber-Alpert type reflects the level of anxiety about achievement which the S can stand to express. With the forced-failure studies we move to the stage where these fears are expressed projectively, and as the projective expression shifts from overt imagery to covert imagery, we move to the most repressed level of Fear of Failure. This hypothesis suggests that the order of magnitude of Fear of Failure is from children to German youth to American youth. This hypothesis also suggests that there should be some order of behavioral display of these fear effects such that Americans are most affected by their Fear of Failure. Obviously such scaling of responses is difficult to do. At the moment there is no way to choose among the various types of avoidance, whether it be bizarre LA or inefficiency in mastering new tasks, to assert that some behavior reflects greater fear than others.

Assuming that we can integrate the now disparate findings for projective scoring systems, what are we to make of the self-report measures and their data? First of all, we would hope that such scores would be subjected to some of the experimentation given projective scores, i.e., used as dependent variables in an effort to learn more about them. Carney et al. (1966) have recently reported success in getting an increase in n Ach scores taken from a self-reported Achievement Orientation measure.

Bearing in mind Mandler's (1952) work on emotion, which emphasizes the role that suggestion plays in interpreting excitement, it might be valuable to try to develop an approach measure for achievement situations, a Test Enjoyment Questionnaire, to learn more about the term "anxiety." Conceivably the *S* who reports various physical symptoms of anxiety would also testify that he enjoys the challenge of the achievement situation. This would not guarantee efficient performance, but it might shed some light on the motivation which lies behind or accompanies the anxiety.

The research programs we must continue to pursue are reasonably well defined. We describe them in the next section.

Researching Measures of Fear of Failure

Our proposals presented in Chapter 9 for the revision of current theories of fear of failure also dictate the new directions our research must take. According to the distinctions offered regarding the three major sources of threat in achievement situations, most of the experimental settings we have used have confounded these sources. This, in turn, may explain the success of three varieties of fear-of-failure measures. Since the threat of nonego consequences is essentially the study of punishment, we should leave it to the learning theorists. What we must now learn much more about is the distinction between the threat of self-devaluation and the threat of social devaluation. In particular, we must test for the effects of these respective threats on fantasy. In other words, more shift studies are indicated. It has been pointed out (Klinger, 1966) that various arousal techniques seemed to produce differences in thematic imagery but the source of these differences is not understood. What we now suggest is that the key variable in such differences may not be the instructions per se so much as the sense of the *S* regarding the evaluation being made of his performance. Obviously, it may be that most achievement situations are a compound of the two sources of threat, indeed, of the three (see Heckhausen, 1966, p. 36). But this merely makes it more important that we learn how to assess important achievement situations for the relative degrees of threat they contain, so that we can better anticipate the kinds of avoidance behavior they will elicit.

The second line of progress that now must be made is to learn more about the similar and dissimilar avoidance patterns the threats produce. Our work has led us to the conclusion that it is an error to assume that approach responses are efficient, rational, and adaptive, and avoidance responses necessarily inefficient, irrational, and maladaptive. The requirements of the task or situation have something to say about such judgments. So, too, it would be premature to anticipate that threat of self-devaluation produces more adaptive behavior than threat of social devaluation. What is now needed is to treat the achievement situation itself as an operator variable, and to test for the effects of fear of failure and hope of success across situations. We have been able to state propositions for the effect of the two sources of threat on behavior, and these must now be verified.

A third line of research which may be pursued is to place the Atkinson model for approach-avoidance motivation in a broader context so that the particular conditions under which it holds may be specified. Here we need to learn more about the role that is played by the TAQ measure, as well as the conditions which determine the relationship to be postulated for Expectancy and Incentive. In effect this means expanding the model in the interest of generality. We have seen that the use of the HP scoring system as the estimate of avoidance motivation will generate some of the same behavioral relationships as those found using the TAQ. With a more general model we will be able to contrast different measures of fear of failure for the relationships they generate. Most important, we must explore the full range of possible Incentive-Probability relationships.

Finally, we must pursue the study of the experience of the achievement situation as reported by the S. It now appears that such study must focus on the self-esteem that one carries into the achievement situation and on his understanding of the evaluation being made by others. With some dismay we have watched the concept of Self emerge in our understanding of our data. No one who has read Ruth Wylie's (1961) review of the difficulties encountered in empirical researches of the Self can welcome an opportunity to try his hand at it.

But the fact seems to be that achievement motivation, whether approach or avoidant, is learned under conditions which simultaneously teach the sense of Self. Atkinson has recently suggested that anxiety is a reaction to the knowledge that a particular path of behavior is leading to negative consequences. We are suggesting that the negative content of those consequences is devaluation of the Self, either by oneself, or by others. If this is true, it means that the need for achievement and fear of failure both serve a more cardinal motive, to use Allport's term, that of self-respect. In other words, it is self-preservation that provides the fundamental reinforcement for behavior patterns which may generate opposite reinforcements from the external world. But unless we research the content and meaning of this self-concept that must be preserved, we stand in danger of having invoked still another homunculus who "really" runs things. Stated in terms of relationships to be established, we wish to learn whether such measures of self-esteem as we can devise will display the relationships to behavior in achievement situations that our theorizing implies. This may mean moving outside the laboratory to obtain groups of Ss who objectively differ in competence and self-identity along a particular attribute necessary for success, e.g., athletes.

A fourth path for new research focuses on female psychology. Following the lead of the n Ach research program, we began our work with male Ss, built our measure on male responses, and have made no systematic attempt to determine its use with female Ss. In some studies we have done, we have gathered data on both sexes. In some of our technical reports we have published the data on both sexes. In all cases, however, the main attempt has been to work with and theorize about the male of the species.

In three of our technical reports, Teevan and Hartsough (1964a), (1964b), and Smith and Teevan (1964) we have found that the female results are often in the opposite direction to the male results and quite often these differences are significant. We do not have enough data, nor have we spent enough time thinking about the data we have, to know what these results mean. It has been suggested in the past (see Veroff, Wilcox, and Atkinson, 1953) that achievement means something different to the female in this culture than it means to the male. Some feel that achievement is aroused in the female only through some kind of affiliative motive. One of our colleagues in this research (Joan Barlow) has suggested that the aspirations of a female may be more "individual-personally-relevant" than socially related. This would suggest that the aspirations and goals of the female are internal and related to herself as a "person" rather than related to anything or anyone on the outside. These seem very opposing views of what is going on: both may be right or both wrong. At present we can only say

that the problem is there, it is important, it is not solved. We hope
to come closer to some kind of an answer in the near future.

From time to time the authors, and perhaps readers too, are
startled by the resemblance between some circumstance described
in this book and circumstances they encounter in teaching and in
life. It is natural at such times to pursue speculation for a while and
ask how the theories developed here might apply to this or that
social problem. Let us accordingly bring our book to a close with
some thoughts about possible applications.

We look first for working situations in which we would expect
fear of failure to be a serious problem. Yet where is it not a
problem? Our research shows that standards of evaluation, by self
or other, bulk large at all levels in the range of social strata, and
that fear of failure has a range correspondingly wide. Wherever
the subject can recognize his situation as one in which evaluation
is appropriate, either FF^1 or FF^3 is likely. This likelihood should
grow as social standards become more discriminating and refined
and as the hierarchy of rankings for excellence shows ever greater
complexity in our society. Both FF^1 and FF^3 should be strong in
the upper classes, where achievement situations involve great social
responsibility and where there are so many ways to judge oneself
(or be judged) to deserve devaluation. In the lower middle classes,
on the other hand, where work situations involve few operations
and where habits of reliability are more congenial, we might expect
fear of failure to be less usual.

Is there any sort of work situation that does not stimulate fear
of failure in some subjects? The place to look might be in the very
lowest of the social strata, by the following reasoning. Fear of
failure arises only after standards of task excellence are established
against which self-evaluation or social evaluation may be made.
Such standards are unlikely to develop in people who have as their
main worry where their next meal is coming from. Again, if the
poor and rejected work under authorities that they do not trust, we
doubt whether they often internalize the authorities' standards. For
such workers, we suspect, the standards of performance are missing
on which self-evaluation depends, and little occurs to make them
concerned with task excellence. Perhaps the task behaviors of such
people will turn out to be determined by straightforward schedules
of reinforcement on ego consequence.

If the physical and social environment of people in the very lowest economic strata is as hostile as we are told, we would expect HP levels to be high (though we have done no TAT studies here to ascertain the facts). Among people of the lowest social strata, even high HP levels may have little of the predictive value for behavior in achievement situations that they have for people of middle and upper strata. Those in the lowest strata learn their imagery, we surmise, in circumstances that do not involve achievement. If so, children and adolescents in the lowest strata may not be very appropriate subjects of research if we are looking for subjects whose achievement behaviors are depressed by fear of failure. Among people who live at a subsistence level it may not be easy to find a good definition of the achievement situation in the first place.

Suppose that fear of failure as discussed in this book has truly deleterious effects. What can be done to relieve them? After all, negative task outcomes can be controlled only up to a point. Failure is the outcome in some achievement situations for even the most promising forms of behavior. Following the lead of McClelland (1965) we might try to set up separate schedules of reinforcement for subjective reactions to failure. That is, when subjects fail they are asked to comment on their failure and are then taught to react in task-adaptive ways. We might couple this with McClelland's procedure for teaching n Ach fantasy in hopes of producing competitive hope-of-success patterns of fantasy and reaction—patterns that would include striving in achievement situations. Let the authority evaluate performances by style of approach, not by achievement. The subject's trust in authority, thus strengthened, would favor a lessening of FF [3] as personal standards appear. But if fear of failure is to be reduced, some other approach motive must replace it—say, n Achievement. We doubt whether fear reaction can be expected to lapse and disappear through extinction alone.

A proper course might be suggested for dealing with the very young child, no matter what his social stratum. To avoid fear-of-failure reactions, make a neutral response when the child voices his fears, and offer a suggestion of a way to react hopefully. Then when he adopts the suggestion, reinforce it. This atmosphere should produce an approach motivation in achievement situations, especially if the tasks demanded of the child are paced in a way that favors achievement and lets him experience its rewards.

As the child grows older he can be helped to internalize standards of achievement if his tasks are made relevant to long-range goals. If a child does not internalize standards of achievement, it is not hard to foresee that nonachievement reactions to work situations may displace his early training. Such reactions may well prove the greatest threat to the early-training projects now being sponsored by the Poverty Program.

In fear of failure we have a measurable and testable aspect of human behavior and experience: such is our conviction. As understanding grows in this field, it may well favor the development of more humane and rational programs for work and study, and it is not too early to begin research on such applications now. Perhaps this book will stimulate efforts in this direction, as a worthy by-product of what is for all of us in all our studies the main goal: a better understanding of human motivation.

References

Allport, G. *The nature of prejudice.* Garden City, New York: Double-day & Co., Inc., 1958.

Allport, G. W. *Personality.* New York: Holt, 1937.

Alper, Thelma, G. Predicting the direction of selective recall: its relation to ego strength and n Achievement. *J. abnorm. soc. Psychol.,* 1957, *55,* 149-165.

Anderson, R. C. Failure imagery in the fantasy of induced arousal. *J. educ. Psychol.,* 1962, *53,* 293-298.

Applesweig, M. H., Moeller, G., & Burdick, H. Multimotive prediction of academic success. *Psychol. Rpts.,* 1956, *2,* 489-496.

Argyle, M. & Robinson, P. Two origins of achievement motivation. *Brit. J. soc. clin. Psychol.,* 1962, *1,* 107-120.

Aronson, L. Self-distortion and the distortion of others. *Dissert. Abstr.,* 1957, *17,* 1570-1951. Abstract.

Asch, S. E. Studies of independence and conformity: I. A minority of one against a unanimous majority. *Psychol. Monogr.,* 1956, 70 (9), No. 416.

Atkinson, J. W. The achievement motive and recall of interrupted and completed tasks. *J. exp. Psychol.,* 1953, *46,* 381-390.

Atkinson, J. W. Explorations using imaginative thought to assess the strength of human motives. In M. R. Jones (Ed.), *Nebraska symposium on motivation.* Lincoln: University of Nebraska Press, 1954, pp. 56-112.

Atkinson, J. W. Motivational determinants of risk-taking behavior. *Psychol. Rev.,* 1957, *64,* 359-372. (Also in Atkinson, 1958.)

Atkinson, J. W. (Ed.) *Motives in fantasy, action, and society.* Princeton, N. J.: Van Nostrand, 1958.

Atkinson, J. W. *An introduction to motivation.* Princeton, N.J.: Van Nostrand, 1964.

Atkinson, J. W., & Feather, N. T. (Eds.). *A theory of achievement motivation.* New York: Wiley, 1966.

Atkinson, J. W., & Litwin, G. H. Achievement motive and test anxiety conceived as motive to approach success and motive to avoid failure. *J. abnorm. soc. Psychol.,* 1960, *60,* 52-63.

Atkinson, J. W., Bastian, J. R., Earl, R. W, & Litwin, G H. The achievement motive, goal-setting, and probability preferences. *J. abnorm. soc. Psychol.,* 1960, *60,* 27-36.

Bartmann, T. Der Einfluss von Zeitdruk auf die Leistung and das Denkverhalten bei Volkssch ü lern. *Psychol. Forsch.*, 1963, *27*, 1-61.

Bartmann, T. *Denkerziehung im programmierten Unterricht.* Munich: Manz, 1965.

Berkun, M. M., & Burdick, H. A. Effect of knowledge of test results on subsequent test performance as a joint function of need achievement and test anxiety. Unpublished paper presented at APA, August 1963.

Birney, R. C. Thematic content and the cue characteristics of pictures. In J. W. Atkinson (Ed.), *Motives in fantasy, action, and society.* Princeton, N.J.: Van Nostrand, 1958. Pp. 630-643.

Birney, R. C. Research on the achievement motive. In E. F Borgatta & W. F. Lambert (Eds.), *Handbook of personality theory and research.* Chicago: Rand McNally. In preparation.

Birney, R. C., & Rolf, E. The effects of fear of failure on risk taking and performance. Technical Report.

Birney, R. C., & Stillings, N. A. The effect of hostile press on choice of strategy in prisoner's dilemma. Technical Report No. 22, Office of Naval Research, 1967.

Brody, N. n Achievement, test anxiety and subjective probability of success in risk taking behavior. *J. abnorm. soc. Psychol.*, 1963, *66*, 413-418.

Brown, R. W. A determinant of the relationship between rigidity and authoritarianism. *J. abnorm. soc. Psychol.*, 1953, *48:* 469-476.

Brown, R. Models of attitude change. In R. Brown et al., *New Directions in Pychology.* New York: Holt, Rinehart and Winston, 1962. Pp. 1-85.

Brownfain, J. J. Stability of the self-concept as a dimension of personality. *J. abnorm. soc. Psychol.*, 1952, *47*, 597-606.

Burdick, H. A. The relationship of attraction, need achievement and certainty to conformity under conditions of a simulated group atmosphere. Unpublished doctoral desertation, University of Michigan, 1955.

Burdick, H. A. The effect of value of success upon the expectation of success. Technical Report No. 14, Office of Naval Research, 1965.

Burnstein, E. Fear of failure, achievement motivation, and aspiring to prestigeful occupations. *J. abnorm. soc. Psychol.*, 1963, *67*, 189-193.

Butler, J., & Haigh, G. Changes in the relation between self-concepts and ideal concepts consequent upon client-centered counseling. In C. R. Rogers and Rosalind Diamond (Eds.), *Psychotherapy and personality change.* Chicago: University of Chicago Press, 1954.

Carney, R. E., Mann, P. A., & McCormick, R. P. Validation of an objective measure of achievement motivation. *Psychol. Rpts.*, August 1966. Pp. 243-248.

Caron, A. J. Curiosity, achievement, and avoidant motivation as determinants of epistemic behavior. *J. abnorm. soc. Psychol.*, 1963, *67*, 535-549.

Clark, R. A., Teevan, R., & Ricciuti, H. N. Hope of success and fear of failure as aspects of need for achievement. *J. abnorm. soc. Psychol.,* 1956, *53,* 182-186. Also in J. W. Atkinson, 1958.

Cohen, A., Hovland, C. I., & Janis, I. L. (Eds.). *Personality and persuasibility.* New Haven: Yale University Press, 1959. Pp. 102-120.

Costello, C. G. Ego-involvement, success and failure: a review of the literature. In H. J. Eysenck (Ed.), *Experiments in motivation.* New York: Macmillan, 1964. Pp. 161-208.

Crutchfield, R. C. Conformity and character. *Amer. Psychologist,* 1955, *10,* 191-198.

De Charms, R., & Davé, Prafulachandra N. Hope of success, fear of failure, subjective probability, and risk-taking behavior. *J. person. soc. Psychol.,* 1965, *1,* 558-568.

De Charms, R., Morrison, W., Reitman, W., & McClelland, D. C. Behavioral correlates of directly and indirectly measured achievement motivation. In D. C. McClelland (Ed.), *Studies in motivation,* New York: Appleton, 1955. Pp. 414-423.

Dembo, Tamara. Arger als dynamisches Problem. *Psychol. Forsch.,* 1931, *15,* 1-114.

Deutsch, M. Trust, worthiness, and the F scale. *J. abnorm. soc. Psychol.,* 1960, *61,* 138-140.

Dittes, T. E. Effect of changes in self-esteem upon impulsiveness and deliberation in making judgments. *J. abnorm. soc. Psychol.,* 1959, *58,* 348-356.

Doris, T. Test-anxiety and blame assignment in grade school children. *J. abnorm. soc. Psychol.,* 1959, *58,* 181-190.

Dreyer, A. S. Aspiration behavior as influenced by expectation and group comparison. *Hum. Relat.,* 1954, *7,* 175-190.

Dymond, R. An adjustment score for Q sorts. *J. Consult. Psychol.,* 1953, *17,* 339-342.

Edwards, A. L. *Edwards Personal Preference Schedule.* New York: Psychol. Corp., 1954.

Epstein, S., & Fenz, W. D. Theory and experiment on the measurement of approach-avoidance conflict. *J. abnorm. soc. Psychol.,* 1962, *64,* 97-112.

Ertel, S. Die emotionale Natur des "semantischen Raumes." *Psychol. Forsch.,* 1964, *28,* 1-32.

Evans, G. W., & Crumbaugh, C. M. Effects of Prisoner's Dilemma format on cooperative behavior. *J. person. soc. Psychol.,* 1966, *4,* 486-488.

Eysenck, H. J., & Himmelweit, H. T. An experimental study of the reactions of neurotics to experiences of success and failure. *J. gen. Psychol.,* 1946, *35,* 59-75.

Feather, N. T. Success probability and choice behavior. *J. exp. Psychol.,* 1959, *58,* 257-266. (a)

Feather, N. T. Subjective probability and decision under uncertainty. *Psychol. Rev.,* 1959, *66,* 150-164. (b)

Feather, N. T. The relationship of persistence at a task to expectation of success and achievement-related motives. *J. abnorm. soc. Psychol.*, 1961, *63*, 552-561.

Feather, N. T. The relationship of expectation of success to reported probability, task structure, and achievement related motivation. *J. abnorm. soc. Psychol.*, 1963, *66*, 231-283. (a)

Feather, N. T. Persistence at a difficult task with alternative task of intermediate difficulty. *J. abnorm. soc. Psychol.*, 1963, *66*, 604-609. (b)

Feather, N. T. The effect of differential failure on expectation of success, reported anxiety, and response uncertainty. *J. Person.*, 1963, *31*, 289-312. (c)

Feather, N. T. The relationship of expectation of success to need achievement and test anxiety. *J. Person. soc. Psychol.*, 1965, *1*, 118-126. (a)

Feather, N. T. Performance at a difficult task in relation to initial expectancies of sucess, text anxiety, and need achievement. *J. Person.*, 1965, *33*, 200-217. (b)

Feather, N. T. Effects of prior success and failure on expectations of success and subsequent performance. *J. person. soc. Psychol.*, 1966, *3*, 287-298.

Festinger, L. A theoretical interpretation of shifts in level of aspiration. *Psychol. Rev.*, 1942, *49*, 325-250. (a)

Festinger, L. Wish, expectation, and group standards as factors influencing level of aspiration. *J. abnorm, soc. Psychol.*, 1962, *37*, 184-200. (b)

Festinger, L. A. theory of social comparison processes. *Hum. Relat.*, 1954, *7*, 117-140.

Festinger, L. *Theory of cognitive dissonance.* Stanford, Cal.: Stanford University Press, 1957.

Festinger, L. *Conflict, decision and dissonance.* Stanford, Cal.: Stanford University Press, 1964.

Frank, J. D. Some psychological determinants of the level of aspiration. *Amer. J. Psychol.*, 1935, *47*, 285-293.

Frank, J. D. Level of aspiration test. In H. A. Murray et al., *Explorations in personality.* New York: Oxford University Press, 1938. Pp. 461-471.

Gardner, J. W. The relation of certain personality variables to level of aspiration. *J. Psychol.*, 1940, *9*, 191-206.

Gardner, R. W., Holzmann, P. S., Klein, C. S., Linton, Harriet, and Spence, D. P. Cognitive control; A study of individual consistencies in cognitive behavior. *Psychol. Issues,* 1959, *1*, No. 4.

Gotzl, H. Beziehungen zwischen Leistungsmotivation, Zeitperspektive und Zeigarnik-Effekt. Unpublished manuscript, Phychol. Inst. Univer. Münster, 160.

Gould, R. An experimental analysis of "level of aspiration." *Genet. Psychol. Monogr.*, 1939, *21*, 3-115.

Hancock, J. The relationship between fear of failure and grades. Unpublished paper. Cortland University, 1964.

Hancock, J. G., & Teevan, R. C. Fear of failure and risk-taking behavior. *J. Person.,* 1964, *32,* 200-209.

Hausmann, M. F. A test to evaluate some personality traits. *J. genet. Psychol.,* 1933, *9,* 179-189.

Heckhausen, H. Anfänge und Entwicklung der Leistungsmotivation: I. In Wetteifer des Kleinkindes. *Psychol. Forsch.,* 1962, *26*(5). heim Glan: Hain, 1963.

Heckhausen, H. *Hoffnung und Furcht in der Leistungsmotivation.* Meisenheim Glan: Hain, 1963.

Heckhausen, H. *The anatomy of achievement motivation.* Translated by K. F. Butler, R. C. Birney, and D. C. McClelland. Academic Press, New York, 1966.

Himmelweit, H. T. A Comparative study of the level of aspiration of normal and neurotic persons. *Brit. J. Psychol.,* 1947, *37,* 41-59.

Hoppe, E. Erfolg und Misserfolg. *Psychol. Forsch.,* 1930, *14,* 1-62.

Hovland, C. I., & Janis, I. L. (Eds.). *Personality and persuasability.* New Haven, 1958.

Hoyos, C. Graf. Motivationspsychologische Utersuchungen von Kraftfahrern mit dem TAT n ach McClelland. *Arch. ges. Psychol.,* 1965, Supplem. Vol. 7.

Innocentia, Sister Mary. TAT prediction of success in teaching. Paper read at APA meetings of 1959.

Irwin, F. W. Stated expectations as a function of probability and desirability of outcome. *J. Person.,* 1953, *21,* 329-334.

Isaacson, R. L. Relation between n achievement, test anxiety, and curricular choices. *J. abnorm. soc. Psychol.,* 1964, *68,* 447-452.

James, W. H. External and internal control of reinforcement as a basic variable in learning theory. Unpublished doctoral dissertation. Ohio State University, 1957.

Janis, I. L., & King, B. T. The influence of role playing on opinion change. *J. abnorm. soc. Psychol.,* 1954, *49,* 211-218.

Kassarjian, H. H. Success, failure, and personality. *Psychol. Rep.,* 1963, *13,* 567-574.

Klinger, E. Fantasy need achievement as a motivational construct. *Psychol. Bull,* 1966, *66,* 291-308.

Kogan, N. & Wallach, M. *Risk taking: a study in cognition and personality.* New York: Holt, Rinehart & Winston, 1964.

Lewin, K., Dembo, T., Festinger, L., & Sears, P. S. Level of aspiration. In McV. Hunt (Ed.), *Personality and the behavior disorders.* New York: The Ronald Press Co., 1944, pp. 333-378.

Littig, L. W. The effect of motivation on probability preference and subjective personality. Unpublished doctoral dissertation. University of Michigan, 1959.

Loomis, D. L. A comparison of the need achievement test anxiety and hostile press measures of fear of failure. Unpublished master's thesis, Bucknell University, 1963.

Lowell, E. L. The effect of need for achievement on learning and speed performance. *J. Psychol.,* 1952, *33,* 31-40.

Lundwall, L., & Teevan, R. C. Fear of failure and cognitive controls. Technical Report No. 17, 1966.

McClelland, D. C. Measuring motivation in phantasy: the achievement motive. In H. Getzkow (Ed.), *Groups, leadership, and men,* Pittsburgh: Carnegie Press, 1951. Pp. 191-205.

McClelland, D. C. Methods of measuring human motivation. In J. W. Atkinson, (Ed.), *Motives in fantasy, action, and society,* Princeton: Van Nostrand, 1958.

McClelland, D. C. *The achieving society.* Princeton, N.J.: Van Nostrand Co. Inc. 1961.

McClelland, D. C. Toward a theory of motive acquisition. *Amer. Psychologist,* 1965, *20,* 321-333.

McClelland, D. C., & Liberman, A. M. The effects of need for achievement on recogntion of need-related words. *J. Person.,* 1949, *18,* 236-251.

Mclelland, D., Atkinson, J., Clark, R., & Lowell, E. *The achievement motive.* New York: Appleton-Century-Crofts, 1953.

Mace, C. A. The influence of indirect incentives upon the accuracy of skilled movements. *Brit. J. Psychol. (Gen. Sect.),* 1931, *22,* 101-114.

McGhee, P., & Teevan, R. C. Conformity and need for affiliation. Technical Report No. 15, 1965.

Mahone, C. H. Fear of failure and unrealistic vocational aspiration. *J. abnorm. soc. Psychol.,* 1960, *60,* 253-261.

Mandler, G., & Sarason, S. B. A study of anxiety and learning. *J. abnorm. soc. Psychol.,* 1952, *47,* 166-173.

Marks, R. W. The effect of probability, desirability and "privilege" on the stated expectations of children. *J. Person.,* 1951, *19,* 332-351.

Martire, J. G. Relationship between the self concept and differences in the strength and generality of achievement motivation. *J. Person.,* 1956, *24,* 364-375.

Meyer, W. U., Heckhausen, H., & Kemmler, Lilly. Validierungskorrelate der inhaltsanalytisch erfassten Leistungsmotivation guter und schwacher Schüller des dritten Schuljahres. *Psychol. Forsch.,* 1965, *28,* 301-328.

Meyer, H. H., Walker, W. B., & Litwin, G. H. Motive patterns and risk preferences associated with entrepreneurship. *J. abnorm. soc. Psychol.,* 1961, *63,* 570-574.

Miller, N. E. Experimental studies of conflict. In McV. Hunt (Ed.), *Personality and the behavior disorders,* Vol. 1, New York: Ronald Press, 1944.

Miller, N. E. Comments on theoretical models illustrated by the development of a theory of conflict. *J. Person.,* 1951, *20,* 82-99.

Morris, J. L. Propensity of risk taking as a determinant of vocational choice: and extension of the Theory of Achievement Motivation. *J. person soc. Psychol.,* 1966, *3,* 328-335.

Moulton, R. W. Effects of success and failure on level of aspiration as related to achievement motives. *J. person. soc. Psychol.,* 1965, *1,* 399-406.

Moulton, R. W. Notes for a projective measure for fear of failure. In J. W. Atkinson, 1958c, Pp. 563-571.

Murray, H. A., et al. *Explorations in personality.* New York: Oxford University Press, 1938.

Osgood, G. E., & Tannenbaum, P. H. The principle of congruity in the prediction of attitude change. *Psychol. Rev.*, 1955, *62*, 42-55.

Postman, L. The experimental analysis of motivation factors in perception. In M. R. Jones (Ed.), *Current theory and research in motivation.* Lincoln: University of Nebraska Press, 1938.

Postman, L., & Brown, D. R. The perceptual consequences of success and failure. *J. abnorm. soc. Psychol.*, 1952, *47*, 213-221.

Pottharst, Barbara C. The achievement motive and level of aspiration after experimentally induced success and failure. Unpublished doctoral dissertation. University of Michigan, 1955. Cf. Atkinson, 1958c, p. 299.

Preston, M. G., & Bayton, J. A. Correlations between level of aspiration. *J. Psychol.*, 1942, *13*, 369-373.

Raphelson, A. C., & Moulton, R. W. The relationship between imaginative and direct verbal measures of test anxiety under two conditions of uncertainty. *J. Person.*, 1958, *26*, 556-567.

Rapoport, A., Chammah, A., Dwyer, J., & Gyr. J. Three-person non-zero-sum nonegotiable games. *Behav. Sci.*, 1962, *7*, 38-58.

Reitman, W. R. Need achievement, fear of failure, and selective recall. *J. abnorm. soc. Psychol.*, 1961, *62*, 142-144.

Ricciuti, H. N. *The prediction of academic grades with a projective measure test of achievement motivation:* I. *Initial validation studies.* Princeton, N.J.: Educational Testing Service, 1954.

Rogers, C. R. *Client-centered therapy.* Boston: Houghton Mifflin, 1951.

Rogers, C. R. A theory of therapy, personality and interpersonal relationships, as developed in the client-centered framework. In S. Koch (Ed.), *Psychology: a study of a science:* Vol. III. Formulations of the person and the social context. New York: McGraw-Hill, 1959.

Rosenzweig, S. Experimental study of repression with specific reference to need-persistive and ego-defensive reactions to frustration. *J. exp. Psychol.*, 1943, *32*, 64-74.

Rotter, J. B. *Social learning and clinical psychology.* New York: Prentice Hall, 1954.

Rotter, J. B. Generalized expectancies for internal versus external control of reinforcement. *Psychol. Monogr.*, 1966, *80*, (Whole No. 609).

Ryan, D. E., & Lakie, W. L. Competitive and noncompetitive performance in relation to achievement motive and manifest anxiety. *J. Person Soc. Psychol.*, 1965, *1*, 342-345.

Sansom, W. *A contest of ladies.* London: Hogarth Press, 1956.

Sarason, I. Empirical findings and theoretical problems in the use of anxiety scales. *Psychol. Bull.*, 1960, *67*, 403-415.

Sarason, I. G. The effects of anxiety and threat on the solution of a difficult task. *J. abnorm. soc. Psychol.*, 1961, *62*, 165-168.

Schachter, S. *The psychology of affiliation: experimental studies of the sources of gregariousness.* Stanford, Cal.: Stanford University Press, 1959.

Schroder, H. M., & Hunt, D. E. Failure-avoidance in situational interpretation and problem solving. *Psychol. Monogr.,* 1957, *72*(3), #432.

Sears, Pauline S. Levels of aspiration in academically successful and unsuccessful children. *J. abnorm. soc. Psychol.,* 1940, *35,* 498-536.

Sears, Pauline S. Level of aspiration in relation to some variables of personality. *J. soc. Psychol.,* 1941, *4,* 311-335.

Shipley, T. E., & Veroff, J. A projective measure of need for affiliation. *J. exp. Psychol.,* 1952, *43,* 349-356.

Silverman, J. Self-esteem and differential responsiveness to success and failure. *J. abnorm. soc. Psychol.,* 1964, *69,* 115-118.

Slovic, P. Convergent validation of risk-taking measures. *J. abnorm. soc. Psychol.,* 1962, *65,* 68-71.

Smith, B., & Teevan, R. C. Relationship of the hostile press measure of fear of failure to self-ideal congruence and adjustment. Technical Report, No. 11, 1964.

Spence, K. Anxiety (drive) level and performance in eyelid conditioning. *Psychol. Bull.* 1964, *61* (2), 129-139.

Stamps, L. & Teevan, R. C. Fear of failure and conformity in Asch and Crutchfield situations. Technical Report #18, 1966.

Sussman, L. *Freshmen morale at MIT.* Mass. Institute of Technology, 1960.

Taylor, Janet A. A personality scale of manifest anxiety, *J. abnorm. soc. Psychol.,* 1953, *48,* 285-290.

Teevan, R. C. High school grades and hostile press. Unpublished paper, Bucknell University, 1962.

Teevan, R. C. Hostile press and the volunteer. Unpublished paper, Bucknell University, 1963.

Teevan, R. C., & Custer, J. Hostile press and grades in elementary school. Unpublished paper, Bucknell University, 1965.

Teevan, R. C., & Fischer, R. Hostile press and internal vs. external standards of success and failure. Technical Report #19, 1966.

Teevan, R. C., & Fischer, R. I. Hostile press and childhood reinforcement patterns: a replication. Unpublished manuscript. Bucknell University, 1967.

Teevan, R. C., & Hartsough, R. Personality correlates of fear of failure vs. need achievement individuals—value scales. Technical Report No. 5, 1964a.

Teevan, R. C., & Hartsough, R. Personality correlates of the fear of failure and need achievement individual—a clinical picture. Technical Report No. 6, 1964b.

Teeven, R. C., & McGhee, G. The childhood development of fear of failure motivation. Technical Report No. 15, 1965.

Teevan, R. C., & Myers, S. S. The importance of abilities and the confirming interval. Unpublished paper, Bucknell University, 1964.

Teevan, R. C. & Pearson, L. Hostile press and the college student. Unpublished paper, Bucknell University, 1965.

Teevan, R. C., & Smith, B. College grades and the hostile press system. Unpublished paper, Bucknell University, 1964a.

Teevan, R. C., & Smith, B. The relationship of fear of failure to the confirming interval measure of goal-setting behavior. Technical Report No. 12, 1964.

Teevan, R. C., Smith, B., & Loomis, D. C. Dimensions of "Confirming Interval" as a measure of level of aspiration. Technical Report No. 8, 1964.

Teevan, R. C., & Stamps, L. Motivational correlates of Viet Nam protest group members. Technical Report No. 20, 1966a.

Teevan, R. C., & Stamps, L. Hostile press and anxiety. Unpublished paper, 1966b.

Thomas, C., & Teevan, R. C. Level of aspiration and motive patterns. Technical Report No. 2, 1964.

Veroff, J. Development and validation of a projective measure of power motivation. *J. abnorm. soc. Psychol.*, 1967, *54*, 1-8.

Veroff, J., Wilcox, S., & Atkinson, J. W. The achievement motive in high school and college age women. *J. abnorm. soc. Psychol.*, 1958, *48*, 108-119.

Vukovich, A., Heckhausen, H., & von Hatzfeld, Annette. Konstruktion eines Fragebogens sur Leistungsmotivation. 1964 (in preparation).

Wallach, M., & Kogan, N. Aspects of judgment and decision-making: Interrelationships and changes with age. *Behav. Sci.*, 1961, *6*, 23-26.

Weiner, B. Need achievement and the resumption of incompleted tasks. *J. Person.*, 1965, *1*, 165-168. (a)

Weiner, B. The effects of unsatisfied achievement motivation on persistence and subsequent performance. *J. Person.*, 1965, *33:* 428-442. (b)

Weiner, B., & Rosenbaum, R. M. Determinants of choice between achievement- and nonachievement-related activities. *J. exp. res. Pers.*, 1965, *1*, 114-121.

Winterbottom, Marian R. The relation of need for achievement to learning experiences in independence and mastery. 1958. In J. W. Atkinson, 1958c. Pp. 453-478.

Wylie, Ruth. *The self concept: a critical survey of the pertinent research literature.* Lincoln, Neb.: Univ. of Nebraska Press, 1961.

Young, Michael. *The rise of the Meritocracy, 1870-2033,* London: Thames & Hudson, 1958.

Zeigarnik, B. Über das Behalten von erledigten und unerledigten Handlungen. *Psychol. Forsch.*, 1927, *9*, 1-85.

Sample Stories Written to the Four Hostile Press Pictures

FATHER-SON

THE FOLLOWING ONE HUNDRED STORIES WERE WRITTEN IN A GROUP TAT situation under the standard neutral instructions from McClelland et al., (1953, p. 98). The blank protocol sheets were divided into four sections, each beginning with questions designed to insure complete coverage of a plot. The four sets of questions were:

(1) What is happening? Who are the persons?
(2) What has led up to this situation—that is, what has happened in the past?
(3) What is being thought—what is wanted? By whom?
(4) What will happen? What will be done?

The stories are divided into four blocks of 25 stories each. The first block of stories was written to picture A, the second block to picture B, etc. The pictures used were as follows:

A Father-Son (Card 7BM from Murray's Thematic Apperception Test)
B Boy in checked shirt (from McClelland et. al., 1953, p. 101 ff.)
C Man at mirror (Birney et al., 1964)
D Man in barren office (Birney et al., 1964)

The master scoring for these stories is found in Appendix II.

A-1

1. The older man is the father of the young man. The father's name is Hans. He is saying good-bye to his son, Jeremiah, who is being taken to a concentration camp.

2. The event follows the Nazi invasion. The mother of Jeremiah has been killed.
3. The father is thinking desperately, "Why our family?" Some miracle is wanted. The son feels completely defeated and lost, as if everyone has forsaken him.
4. Jeremiah will be taken to the camp. His father will flee to a free country. They will never meet again although at times they will hear news of each other.

A-2

1. These men appear to be two spys from some foreign country who are plotting a crime against their native land.
2. This is taking place during the second world war. These two men have been warped by past experience and feel no pangs of conscience at betraying their land.
3. These men think only of the satisfaction they will feel if their scheme materializes and they can bring a weakening of the regime in power.
4. These men will make an attempt to give away some of their countries valued war secrets.

A-3

1. Mr. Thomson, Sr., and his son are looking upon the tomb of the wife and the younger's mother.
2. Mrs. Thomson had been driving in a car through a busy intersection in New York when a plane flew overhead. Suddenly, she panicked and thought it was the Russians attacking. In her panic, she ran into a building on the side of the road.
3. The father is thinking what a loving wife and wonderful mother she was. The son, on the other hand, thinks what a fool she was to think such a silly thing was happening.
4. Tomorrow the funeral will be held and she will be buried. At this time, Mr. Thomson, Jr., will go beserk and kill himself.

A-4

1. People, a mother and a father are waiting to hear news of their son who was in auto accident.
2. The boy was driving home from an away basketball game and slid off the road into an inbankment on a snowy night.
3. The parents are praying for their son's recovery. He is in the operating room of a local hospital.
4. The boy will live but he will have a bad leg for the rest of his life. His leg was smashed by the steering wheel. The boy although handicapped, will go on to complete school and become a surgeon.

A-5

1. A father and son are having their last meeting before he leaves for the army. The father is rather old, the son is in his early twenties.
2. He has led a sheltered life because his mother died when he was very young. Consequently, the father has protected him excessively and he has never been away from home for any length of time.
3. The son, although anxious to leave and "try his wings' is hesitant to leave his shelter and protection. The father, although he realizes what is best for his son, hesitates to suffer a second loss.
4. The son is a failure in the army. He is not physically or mentally prepared. Thus, he suffers nervous breakdown, returns home.

A-6

1. A sad event has just occurred. A doctor and his patient. The doctor has had to tell his patient that he, or a member of his family has an incurable disease.
2. A check-up by the person which came too late. The person had contacted a disease in the past.
3. Wonder, bewilderment is being thought. To know the answers for what will happen to the patient is wanted by both doctor and patient.
4. The patient will continue in his state of bewilderment and waiting. He will continue living until he dies. The doctor will observe and learn, then pass his knowledge and also die.

A-7

1. The older man is about to tell his son the good news. He has just "made good" in the stock market.
2. They has lived a good life up until now, but cash has been somewhat lacking.
3. The older man feels a strong need to divulge this information to his son. His son is mildly surious as to what he intends to say.
4. The man will tell his son the news. They will both celebrate gaily.

A-8

1. The oldest is the father of the other one. The father is talking to his son and the son is upset.
2. The son has wrecked his father's car. The father is preaching to him on the idea of safe driving.
3. The father is not really angry, but wants to make sure that the son does not wreck again. The son doesn't want to hear his father's preaching.
4. The son will not be allowed to drive for a while.

A-9

1. It is a picture of a father and a son. The father is listening sympathetically to his son who is telling him a personal problem.
2. The son has gotten in trouble in school with a girl. Not only did he have relation with the girl, but also, because of the relationship, he has failed out of school.
3. The son is remorseful, and ashamed of what he has done. He is sorry he has disappointed his father, a judge who wanted his son to follow in his footsteps.
4. The father, being a sympathetic, kind individual, understands and has faith in his son. The son and the girl will be married, and he will enter another school.

A-10

1. A father is talking to his son. The son has committed a crime, and the father is asking him why he did it.
2. A few hours earlier, the son was caught stealing in a drug store. His motivation was money for drugs. He is on drugs.
3. The father is thinking, "where have I gone wrong?" The boy is thinking, "leave me alone!" The father wants an answer but the boy is set in his mind.
4. The boy will go to court, be sentenced and go to jail. In jail, he will change his ideas about narcotics and emerge a free and worthwhile young man.

A-11

1. The older man is the father of the younger man. The younger man has been a complete failure and he is discussing it with his father.
2. The younger man's life was a failure in ever aspect. His work, schooling and marriage.
3. The father is trying to soothe his son in a kind gentle manner. The son is thinking of the past failures and hopes to make an new start.
4. The young man will make a new start on life and he will hopefully succeed.

A-12

1. A young scientist has just made what he deems to be a great discovery. While it is brilliant in part it is based on not entirely scientific supposition.
2. The older man realizes that the young man has potential, but is as is the case with most men rash.
3. The young man has led a rather gay life, and is aware of his ability and confident in it. He is seeking recognition for his brilliance.
4. The old man recognizes that the young man is intelligent but must

be cured of his rashness and self esteem, so he will probably disprove certain things.

A-13

1. At a secret meeting place in a lower flat in the North Side of Washington D.C. Agent X9 and B21 both Russian.
2. The F.B.I. has been tracking down these two Russian agent for the allegded murder of the Senator in charge of U.S. defiance committees·
3. Agent X9 (left) is devising plans of escape while Agent B21 is refusing his proposal because it his more political complications.
4. They will escape only after destroy an U.S. Battle-ship by the aid of an sub—This will be the start of an conventional war between the U.S. & USSR.

A-14

1. A *Father* is talking with his *Son*. The father is explaining an argument between himself and his wife.
2. The son has heard his father and mother fighting and has felt for some time that the family was deteriorating.
3. Son is thinking father is a beast, a brute for beating mother. Father is hoping for understanding or forgiveness. He is trying to make light for the situation.
4. Son will storm out of the meeting. Father will feel badly, feel that he has failed his family but will not.

A-15

1. The old family doctor has just broken the news of the death of the man's wife. She had been sick since childhood with an incurable blood disease.
2. The man has put himself into large debt by trying to cure his wife. Many people said it was a hopeless case but he kept faith.
3. The man is on the point of dispair. He has no children because they thought the disease might be passed on. He needs a sheltering, guiding influence.
4. Someone, probably a new friend, will restore this man's faith in God and the world and he will once again become a useful, purposeful being.

A-16

1. A trial scene just after the verdict has been past. The elderly man on the left is the defense attorney, on the right the defendant.
2. Three years ago, in a controversial argument, a young boy was slain. Guilt was blamed on the young man previously scene.

3. The verdict has been decided as guilty. The elder reassures the younger of an appeal. This brings little comfort to the man.
4. The young man in complete despair will hang himself in his cell rather than die in the electric chair. Days after the appeal would have been granted.

A-17

1. Father is talking to his son in a heart-to-heart talk in the study of their home.
2. His son has just failed at school and has flunked out.
3. The boy is thinking that what has happened to him is not justified. His father realizes that it is and that he must comfort him and make him get another start.
4. The boy will re-enter another school but with bitterness. He will succeed here, but not with any great success.

A-18

1. The persons are a man and his son. The son is telling his father that he has just committed a terrible crime and is afraid to face the penalty.
2. The father's love for the son has been overbearing in the past. The son has done this to break away from his father.
3. The father is thinking—how can he report his son's actions. The son wants to be forgiven and is a coward.
4. The father will report his son even though his love for him is great.

A-19

1. The man on the left is a lawyer, while the one on the right is the defendent. The lawyer is telling his client that there is not much of a chance left, that they must appeal to a higher court.
2. The defendent has been accused of manslaughter on a New York subway car. The man he killed was 75, and was brutally stabbed and beaten.
3. The lawyer is thinking it might be wise to appeal the case. The defendent is not sure. He has suffered a long time under his false accusation, and his life has been ruined.
4. Most likely, the defendent will be convicted as guilty. There is too much evidence against him.

A-20

1. The father and his son are contemplating the sons marriage and whether it should continue. The son is thinking of divorce.
2. The wife has been dating another man and is actually falling in

love with him. She now wants a divorce but the husband isn't
sure what it might do to him.
3. Both parties are thinking of being separated but only one really
wants to be divorced. The husband actually loves his wife.
4. The lives of these two people are going to change and the man will
be lost while the wife can start another life.

A-21

1. The persons are father and son. The son has done something wrong
and is being chastised by his father. The father is an understanding
man.
2. The son has been wayward and in need of more parental guidance
and sympathy.
3. The son is thinking that he has been poor in the past as far as living
up to his fathers name. The father is thinking that he has been a
failure as a parent.
4. From now on there will be a closer unity between the two. And they
will live in better understanding of each other.

A-22

1. A father is discussing a critical decision with his son.
2. The son has been in an automobile accident; that is, he was the
driver in an accident in which two of his friends were killed.
3. The son has considered no longer driving a car and his father wants
him to think out very carefully whether such action is really necessary for his son to punish himself.
4. The son will finally decide to continue driving, thinking that this
will make him a better driver.

A-23

1. A father is consoling his son in a time of crisis. The father is trying
to remain calm while the son sits almost in a state of shock.
2. This situation was caused by some tragic event such as the death of
the son's wife.
3. The father is trying to get his son to come out of his sorrow and
build a new life.
4. The son will remain single and live in sorrow because of his very
sensitive make-up.

A-24

1. A father and his son are consoling each other.
2. The young man's wife has died.
3. The young man cannot understand why *his* wife has died. He, of
course, wants her back, saying he cannot live without her.

4. The young man will eventually get over his feeling about his wife to an extent that he can live normally again.

A-25

1. Prof. Barnett, an advisor to pre-med students at a noted Hospital is trying to break the news to a once hopeful med student.
2. Prof. B and student F have been long acquainted to each other and instead of sending a slip of paper he wants to tell his young friend.
3. Student F knows what the Prof. is trying to tell him, he is just waiting to hear the bad words ———
4. Student F will sulk for a while, but Dr. B will advise him to do a yr. of graduate work and then reapply to Med. school. Dr. B dies in a car accident the way home from work.

BOY IN CHECKED SHIRT

B-1

1. Young boy in elementary school—first contact with a question which contradicts the ideas given him by his parents.
2. In past he was limited to simple knowledge of arithmetic, reading, etc. and thus had had no contact with anything he could not conceive.
3. His mind is puzzled. He wants to believe his parents about his idea, perhaps it concerns God, and yet the teacher symbolizes knowledge and right to him.
4. The teacher will probably win out in the end. However, it may be years before this happens. But constant contact with education tends to change even family set ideas.

B-2

1. A little boy is in analytic geometry class. He is trying to understand a theorum, the teacher is talking about.
2. In the past he has learned facts to lead up to this theorum, but there was a gap between the last fact he learned and the facts he should know for the basis of this theorum.
3. (1) He is wondering how to do the problem. Probably day-dreaming a little.
   (2) The boy wants to know how to do the problem.
4. He will not understand how to do the problem. Will stay after school for help. He will then be taught privately about the problem, it will be explained in detail to him, and he will understand it.

B-3

1. Mike is sitting in a classroom day-dreaming about his first girl friend, Melinda.

2. During a game during recess, Melinda, who has pigtails with blue ribbons on them, told Mike she loved him, then kicked him in the shins. He's sure it's the "real thing".
3. He wants to see Melinda after school and ride his bike home beside her. He wishes he could kiss her.
4. The next day Mike will realize that there is another cute girl in the spelling class or that he'd rather play baseball. Melinda will be forgotten.

B-4

1. This is a young adolescent boy who is suffering from the fears and confusion of this new time in his life. He has just been reprimanded by someone for doing something.
2. The boy has been severely reprimanded for a situation that he can't fully grasp. He can not understand why the world seems to be against him.
3. He is pondering the complexities and confusions of the new adult world to which he is being introduced. He wants understanding.
4. If this boy gets the proper love and understanding, he will make the transition to adulthood with a minimum of suffering and confusion.

B-5

1. Oscar Smith is in a daze and is trying to stop the pain in his head by holding his head.
2. Oscar had been playing baseball, when a ball came at him and hit him square in the head.
3. He isn't really thinking anything except that his head really hurts. No one is paying any attention to him, thinking he is all right.
   the hospital, and he will be treated for a concussion: Because of
4. Finally, when he doesn't come out of the daze, he will be taken to people's unconcern, Oscar will never fully recover.

B-6

1. The young boy is at a church meeting and everyone is gathered around in a circle. Right now the boy is day dreaming about his girl friend who is in the hospital.
2. The boy went to this meeting because his parents made him. Actually he wanted to visit his girl at the hospital, but the meeting will end to late.
3. The boy is worrying about his girl. He is afraid that she is really seriously ill. Also he's thinking about the good times they've had together.
4. The boy will have the meeting and race to the hospital but won't be let in because it's too late.

B-7

1. The boy is a Bucknell freshmen, sitting in the cafeteria.
2. The boy is desconsulate because he fears that he won't get into the fraternity he wants. In the past, the members of his House have been friendly to him, but now, with rush week approaching, they leave him alone.
3. He is thinking about why they don't like him. He wants to join. Isn't he good enough?
4. He probably won't get in, which dooms him to a terrible fate: lack of association with a crowd where he can lose is meagre identity.

B-8

1. A boy is grief stricken about his house being burnt down and his parents killed.
2. He was very dependent on his family and loved them very much. However, he disobeyed them often and now regrets it.
3. He is thinking how wrong he was in his behavior and how he regrets it so much now. All he wants is his family forgive him.
4. He will live a life of regret and grief but someday will find happiness.

B-9

1. The boy is taking an important civil service test and he knows he can cheat. He has come to a part of the test where he is stuck and now its his decision whether to use the answers he has written on the inside of his shirt or to fail the test.
2. The boy is an immigrant slum work and has tried for many years to get a job in his bigotted society but now is his only chance. He has had a hard life and a miserable existence and now is his chance to succeed.
3. He can not decide whether or not to cheat. He must make the decision quickly or the time for the test will be over.
4. He will decide to cheat and be caught by the instructor. They will then lead him away from his country into exile and in three years he will be shot by the instructor who gave the test.

B-10

1. A boy has stolen a very volnable watch and is sitting in a class worrying about the consequences of his deed. The watch belonged to his best friend.
2. He was extremely jealous of his friend, and knowing that the friend loved the watch, he took it. The jealousy stemmed from a lack of self confidence on his part.
3. He now realizes that it was stupid to steal a watch over such a thin gas jealousy. He is scared and would like desperately to return the watch under cover.

4. The boy will get a "break". He manages to return the watch without having anyone discover his theft and he comes out respecting his friend for some reason.

B-11

1. Joe, a school boy, is being drawn away from his studies by many illusions.
2. Joe's dislike of his studies has obviously stemmed from a poor parental encouragement, i.e., his background has been such that it did not encourage his development.
3. Joe is thinking about how nice it would be not to be in school.
4. Obviously, Joe will not do well in school. Perhaps he will even flunk out.

B-12

1. The boy is a student who has just been caught cheating on an exam.
2. The boy had forgotten about the exam, having overslept that morning. Therefore, desperate for a much-needed passing grade, he copied his neighbor's answers.
3. The boy is in a state of panic. He asks why he has done it. He is sorry; he is scared. And, naturally, he wants understanding from the teachers. He wishes he were back in bed.
4. The boy will be failed in the exam, perhaps even the course, depending upon the whims of the teacher. He will probably not cheat again, unless he has to.

B-13

1. There is a boy, or young man, in class. He is just sitting, and thinking about something. Actually he's taking a test but his mind is elsewhere.
2. Last night the boy stayed out late and didn't study. Therefore he can't do the test very well, so he lets his mind wonder.
3. He is thinking about his mother. She is sick in the hospital and he's worrying. He wants to be able to see her and he wants her to get better.
4. He will flunk the test. The teacher will wonder why. She'll question him, find out about his mother, and then offer him sympathy.

B-14

1. Sam is a college student during the time when his country is at war. He is trying to decide whether he should stay in school or enlist in the service.
2. Sam received a draft notice, but through Congressional aid he found a way of getting away from his obligation.

3. Sam is considering leaving his studies to join his country's army.
4. Sam will leave school and become a combat hero, but will eventually die in action.

B-15

1. In a lonely class-room—Mike Fruse a junior trys to comprehend a portion of physics then the class bell rings:
2. Mike knows that Physics use to be easy until he met a girl with long blonde hair name Donna. Everywhere Mike goes he is haunted by her face.
3. Mike is thinking about how wonderful he love could be—he wanted to take Dona to a party be he knows she will not go because of Bill.
4. Mike and Bill meet in an alley and have a knife fight Mike is killed.

B-16

1. George Martin is taking his first hour exam at Bucknell Univ. The class is calculus and he is stuck on a difficult derivation.
2. Last night he was up till 4:30 A.M. getting to know some of the TKE brothers down a Tacks. When he got back to the dorm he studied till dawn.
3. He wishes he had stayed home last night and is trying desperately to see Gloria's paper. She sits next to him and is very smart.
4. He will be caught trying to copy the answer and will thrown out of school.

B-17

1. The young boy in math class has just learned that an unsatisfactory progress report has been sent to his parents and that it should arrive in the mail today.
2. The lad has been working ardiously but just does not have the mental capacity to keep up with the more intelligent members of his class.
3. He now feels despair. He sees no use for continuing because he simply cannot do the work. He looks for an easy way out.
4. After his parents receive a note, they will find a special instructor for their child possibly, with more individual instruction he will understand better.

B-18

1. The teacher in the room has just announced a spot quiz to the class. The boy in the picture is one of the students.
2. The class has of late been unruley and has not been keeping up with assignments and the teacher is teaching them a lesson for their misbehavior.

3. The boy is thinking that he is in real straights now. He wants nothing but to get the whole thing over with.
4. The boy will flunk the quiz and as a result he will pay more proper attention in the future.

B-19

1. The boy is a school boy who is completely bored with what is happening. He lack interest in his subjects and wishes he was outside playing.
2. In the past as now he has never done very well in his school work and he doesn't understand what is happening.
3. He is thinking how much he would like to be outside playing.
4. He will be caught day dreaming by the teacher who will make him stay after school.

B-20

1. A young man (a student in a classroom) is staring across the room at a girl instead of doing his studying.
2. He has a "crush" on the particular female who "doesn't know he's alive."
3. He longs for them to get together, and his serious contemplating asking the girl for a date.
4. Soon, he will discover she already has a boy friend and will be sad, but will also find out she's not quite the girl he thought she was.

B-21

1. Here is a college freshmen taking his final exam in Calculus.
2. The student is dumbfounded for he realizes that he can't do the work because he didn't study.
3. He wants an angel to come and wisper the answers in his ear.
4. He realizes that no divine aid will help him and only by constant hard work will he be able to pass his subjects.

B-22

1. The central figure in this story is a High School Sr. who made all A's, but is now faced with taking a final for which he didn't bother to study.
2. Student A, call him Dave, was very bright in H.S., and had a way with teachers. Being in a Southern High School, he never knew what it was like to study.
3. Dave wants to get the hell out of High School. The work is too easy for him and he sees nothing in high school to keep his interest.
4. He will overcome his temporary frustrations and make a C on the

exam. But it didn't teach him to study, cause he was the same way for the other final.

B-23

1. The boy is taking a test in trignometry which he is totally unprepared for.
2. Instead of studying, the boy played football all afternoon the previous day with his neighborhood team, and he didn't do so well either.
3. He is probably day dreaming, trying to figure out why he played such a poor game, not even thinking about the test.
4. He will, of course, get the highest grade in class since he is a child wonder, except at football.

B-24

1. The boy is a student puzzling over a difficult math problem which he does not understand.
2. He finds himself in this situation because he failed to complete his out of class assignment. Finding it difficult he decided to let it ride not expecting a quiz in class.
3. He is now feeling that he should have tried harder on the homework and regretting his laziness in not doing it.
4. He will most likely flunk the quiz and in the future will probably be more diligent about his assigned work.

B-25

1. The boy is a student who is very befuddled by his classwork. He is perhaps a sophmore in high school.
2. He has had a very good time in the past, taking in lots of parties having lots of dates and now he finds he is too far behind to catch up.
3. He is thinking that he doesn't deserve all of this punishment. He has been a basically good boy and can't see why he has to take a ridiculous course like math.
4. The boy will fall farther and farther behind because he never has time to see the teacher for help, since he has to work after school every day.

MAN AT MIRROR

C-1

1. Man is looking in the mirror before he goes out to a social function and wonders if he has brushed his teeth, also if he looks all right— but in the back of his mind he is wondering about a psychological

problem of his wife's sickness, or of how he will do on a business deal.

3. His wife has gotten sick, or something has gone wrong in his business.
3. Do I look all right? Will she be all right? Will the deal come through?
4. He will continue living, doing the mechanical things of everyday life. Trying to make a good impression and straighten out his life.

C-2

1. A man getting ready for work in the morning is looking back on the past events of the last year.
2. The man has been going out with a fellow worker from the office. However, this man is divorced from a girl who also works in the same office.
3. The man now believes that he loves the new girl but he doesn't want to rush into things to hastily. He knows that if he should ask this girl to marry him, there will be new rumor spread about him and the girl.
4. The man will ask the new girl to marry him. He will be transferred to a different branch of the same company but in a different city. Their engagement will last over two years during which time the man can make absolutely sure of himself.

C-3

1. Mr. Jones is just receiving the feared news from his doctor he is dying from some uncurable disease.
2. Mr. Jones has expected a diagnosis such as this because of the symptoms he has had in the last months.
3. Mr. Jones is thinking of the short time he has left and all he wants to see and do before he dies. Mainly he is thinking of his family, how he will tell them, and how they will manage.
4. Mr. Jones will die but because he knew in advance his family will be prepared as much as possible in a situation like this and they will be able to get along.

C-4

1. A man is straightening his tie in the mirror. He is on his way to a date.
2. He has finally gotten a date with this beautiful girl who he has been crazy about for months.
3. He thinks he looks lousy. He wants to commit suicide.
4. He commits suicide.

C-5

1. He hears a sound coming from the other room. He is a salesman in a hotel in a far-away city.
2. He was fixing up to go to meet a client. He doesn't know that a man from his past, whom he once kept out of a big job, has finally found him after all these years.
3. "Could it be Jack (the man from the past)—will he try to kill me? I've got to get help."
4. He'll realize its only the maid who wants to make the bed.

C-6

1. The man is a traveling salesman who is straightening his tie. He has just been asleep and forgot to take his tie off.
2. He had a long day on the road, and when he walked into his motel room, he found it already make up so he collapsed into bed.
3. He is thinking what a "handsome devil" he is, and wants to go out on the town with some chick, since he's away from home and his wife.
4. He will go out and bring his date back to the motel and have fun, till her husband walks in and unstraightens his head.

C-7

1. A man—Madison Avenue advertising type is dressed in front of a mirror one morning—fixing his tie. Married.
2. This is just like any other day to him as what he did the night before has no effect on him—he is a stone-hearted guy. He probably had relations with his secretary the previous night.
3. Nothing—no conscience on this guy. He will grab it all himself if he could.
4. He will get richer and have more fun and then the boom will be lowered as he gets in trouble—big trouble. Then his dream world collapses.

C-8

1. The two men are doctors. They are going out for a break having just successfully completed a very critical operation.
2. The patient was brought in to emergency and these men were the only two doctors available. They had to work fast to save a life.
3. Each man is thinking that the other is a very fine doctor and each wishes he could be as talented as the other. They are also wondering who is going to pick up the tab for lunch.
4. The men will go to lunch and compliment each other on the hasty operation. Then they will get into a fight each saying the other is a better doctor.

C-9

1. The man is dressing for an important business meeting with his boss and client.
2. The client has been disatisfied with the work put out by this man, and, being the major stockholder of the company, is trying to decide whether he should be replaced.
3. The man is thinking how he can convince the client that his work has been as good as possible, considering the death of his son a month ago.
4. The client will understand the situation and suggest a month's vacation with pay.

C-10

1. Mr. Jones is repremanding his employee Mr. Smith for failing to collect an insurance premium, thus lapsing the policy.
2. Mr. Smith has been negligent before in the past, so, Mr. Jones is all the more angry.
3. Mr. Jones is thinking that Smith is no very interested in his job, while Smith wants Jones to leave him alone and let him do what he wants.
4. The incident will reoccur & Jones will fire Smith, and consequently Smith will turn to stealing & end up in prison.

C-11

1. This person is in a very tight situation. He has just completed a horrifying mission (he shot DeGaulle he's an undercover agent for the U.S.) and now as he stands in front of his mirror in his hotel suite a beautiful girl has entered his room with a gun she is going to kill him.
2. He shot De Gualle to aid his country. The girl loved De Gualle and now she wants to kill him. He has been a good spy and the girl knows that but she hates him. He once killed her brother—Pres. Kennedy.
3. She will kill him. He stares into the mirror and can see her standing behind him. She does not know this and is just about to shot. He must decide what to do.
4. He pulls a derringer from his shirt stay in his collar and swivels and shots the girl. However, he just knocks the gun out of her hand with the bullet and in the end she stab him to death with her fingernail.

C-12

1. The man is tying his tie, in preparation to going to breakfast, where he intends to tell his wife of his affair with another woman.

2. This man, a salesman, while at a convention, had an affair with an unmarried woman, who is pregnant as a result.
3. He is wondering how he can tell her this, and still impress it upon his wife that he loves her. He hopes she will forgive him, for he is deeply in love with her, but he doubts that she will.
4. The wife will forgive him, or at least she will say this, for she will never fully trust him again.

C-13

1. This Joseph James and he is a very typical, average upper middle class commuting, suburban husband with a wife, 3 small kids, and a nice house.
2. He is beginning to feel the pressures of his existence. His wife has been charging a fortune in new clothes, the kids are enrolled in activities like ballet, etc. etc. and he doesn't feel he can put up with the burden.
3. He has been contemplating running off; he & his wife are incompatible, the kids are nagging brats, and the neighbors are a busy, nosey lot.
4. However, this course of action would cause a scandal; he'll stay on, be miserable, and get ulcers like most of his fellow husbands.

C-14

1. A man is looking in the mirror and thinking. A big decision weighs heavily on his mind.
2. He is a country doctor. It is snowing hard and he has just gotten two calls. One is from a neighbor who is almost dead. The other is from a woman about to give birth.
3. He's thinking about which he should go to. The neighbor was not a very good friend of his, while the woman is having her first child. Which should he help first?
4. He will go to the neighbor first and administer help. He'll next go to the woman, but she'll have her child before he gets there. Mother and child will do fine.

C-15

1. The man is a important executive who nevertheless does not enjoy his job. He is gazing at himself attempting to answer the question who is he?
2. A feeling of frustration and disillusionment engendered by the lack of morality in his job.
3. The executive wishes to find himself; he wonders if through another profession he can discover himself.
4. The executive will keep his position and finish his life frustrated and unhappy.

C-16

1. The man has just been working out at the club's gym. He has been running, swimming, and playing handball.
2. He severe argument with his wife has caused him to be very disturbed and he knows that exercise will relax him.
3. After cooling off, the man realizes his error in arguing with his wife and is ready to make apologies so that a peaceful solution may soon be found.
4. He will go back home and make up with his wife although it will be quite a while before they are able to work out an agreeable solution to the problem.

C-17

1. Two brothers are discussing the problem of the failure of their young brother. They themselves are successful.
2. The younger brother was born with a physical defect. In has normal intelligence, but lack confidence because of his affirmity.
3. One chance for a decent job is wanted. An employer who will hire their brother for his talent, not his appearance.
4. He will find a job. Evidently he will start a business of his own to employ the handicapped.

C-18

1. As Melvin Band, secret agent 700 (a little backwards) adjusted his tie, he thought of the coming evening with the mysterious oriental seductress. Wanna Lai.
2. When M & M, Band's boss, gave him this assignment, to track down a ruthless gang of radio active yo-yo makers (thereby destroying our youth in their play) Band thought it was a joke. After 2 attempts on his life, he knew better.
3. Band thought of the coming date, and wondered if he could really convince M & M that Wanna was a contact for him, instead of just actually being a date for the evening at the Secret Service's expense. I think we know what Band wants.
4. It turns out that Wanna is really M & M in disquise, and Band gets fired on the ground of homosexuality.

C-19

1. The man is fixing his tie in the mirror, and is tidying himself up.
2. Joe has just had a fight with his wife. She had been riding him all night. Joe knew she was drunk, but he could take it no longer. He hit her. She clawed furiously at his shirt and tie, and then collapsed in drunken exhaustion.
3. Joe wants a divorce. Martha began drinking 2 years after they were

married, when their only baby was born dead. That was 5 years ago.
4. Since Martha is almost a complete alcoholic, Joe will have some grounds for a divorce, and very well might get it.

C-20

1. These two different men are preparing to go onto T.V. casting program which is a direct art on a T.V. program where almost identical people are played by the same people.
2. These men were cheat actors in the past, but because of their similar looks, they have been offered $200,000.53 to do this T.V. series.
3. The men are thinking how they will spend their money and what stupid people the T.V. audience must be to watch them and R. C. hairdressing.
4. The T.V. show will go good for a season, but then the opposite network will put in a better show and the similar looking men will retire wealthy.

C-21

1. In a doctor's office, the doctor has just told his patient he has lung cancer.
2. Constant smoking and high blood pressure were probably the cause.
3. The patient wonders if he will die, how will he tell his wife and family, & who will take care of them if he must die.
4. His understanding family will try all methods of save their father. Unfortunately it will be to no avail.

C-22

1. The man is an insurance salesman. His conscience is being bothered.
2. The man recently was the driver in a hit and run accident and now he can't stop thinking about it.
3. He is suffering guilt feelings and is undecided as whether to turn himself in or not.
4. Eventually the man goes out of his mind.

C-23

1. The man is a young executive preparing for work in the morning.
2. Well, he has gotten out of bed after a good night sleep with his lovely wife, and he is moderately cheerful.
3. He is thinking about the work and/or sales he has to make this day. He wants and expects to do well.
4. When he goes out a dog will bite him, he'll lose his keys to his car, he'll be late for an appointment so he'll rush—and get a speeding ticket—But in the end he'll land a big client & take his wife out to dinner to celebrate.

C-24

1. This is Mr. James Lawson, a prominent lead of the local community who has been lately charged with embezzlement of company funds.
2. Jim is in love with his wife but she plays cards & loses a great deal of money & this has led him to embezzle the funds.
3. He is wondering about what will happen to he & his wife if he is convicted.
4. He will be convicted & his wife falls in love with the president of her husband's company.

C-25

1. A man is worried about his relationship with his wife.
2. They have not slept together for several weeks and he is afraid that she no longer loves him. She has always said she loves him when they were making love.
3. He has no confidence in himself and wants to over come this by approaching her first without fear of rejection. She knows nothing of his fears and herself has wondered why there was a lag in their relations.
4. They will get divorced. He never gets up the guts to approach her. They will fight alot and she, out of anxiety and frustration, finally sues for divorce.

MAN IN BARREN OFFICE

D-1

1. Man is feeling anxiety and tiredness over his office work. He is a business man but not necessarily a top executive.
2. The pressures of work and possible home life have been building up slowly. They make it hard for him to concentrate and think properly.
3. He is thinking about his failures (imminent and past) and is afraid of losing his position at business.
4. Worrying like this rather than acting to alleviate his burdens will lead to his downfall. He is just about "dead." He will not succeed.

D-2

1. A man is thinking very deeply in thoughts. A business problem has come up that he is thinking about.
2. Something went wrong with the machinery of his company. It broke down. The job cannot be continued.
3. He is trying to find a solution to the problem. He hopes that the damage can be fixed.
4. The machinery will be fixed, everything will be fine, the job will be completed, everybody will be happy.

D-3

1. This business executive has been at his office for an hour is worried about a problem that could change his entire future.
2. He was approach—this morning by the president of a corporation who offered him double his present salary to take a new job.
3. He is wondering whether he can leave his present job after so many years of service without causing real resentment, and will this job be actually what he wants.
4. He will take the new job. He will move into a higher social standing. The resentment of his former employer will be almost forgotten.

D-4

1. The man is sitting at his desk in a barren office. His business has just failed. It is early in the morning. The warehouse downstairs is quiet.
2. As a result of bad advice and pressure from close friends he has made speculative investments which have tumbled. Last evening he had a one-sided argument with his wife.
3. He is thinking about where he should go from here. He wants to leave his wife & daughter, neither of whom understand him.
4. He will leave his wife & drift. She will remarry successfully & complete her empty life. He will see the vanity of his previous attempts and become a satisfied, if not happy, clerk.

D-5

1. The man is suffering from an unsolved problem. The bare room shows that he is unsuccessful in business. He does not understand how he failed, how to approach his wife? Hard times loom ahead.
2. He started off in business with a company. He worked his way up the ladder and was fairly competent and successful. However when he quit his job and went in on his own he failed. His hopes were smashed.
3. How can he solve the situation. I am as good as the next person. What can be done for my family and my future. Should I commit suicide—no, I have too many dependents.
4. He will try to face reality. Approach his old position possibly attain a position getting paid less money. He will finally live fairly successfully.

D-6

1. A businessman seems to be deeply worried as to his business success. He has lost heavily financially.
2. Business has been going down for some time and he didn't prepare for such a complete failure.

3. He doesn't see any way out of his calamity and wonders what he'll do. He wishes he had never been involved in the situation.
4. The man will eventually drop his present business and look for other employment to make up for his losses.

D-7

1. The man is thinking of committing suicide in his office. He is an important man in a big business.
2. He has been embezzling money from his company and has just been found out. His nagging wife has forced him to do so.
3. He is thinking of committing suicide. He is beyond forgiveness.
4. He will kill himself and his disgrace will fall on his family.

D-8

1. Empty room. Young businessman learned that his new company has no chances of success. Stock market falling. He had a fight with his wife this morning.
2. Attended top-rate college, decided to begin his own business. It is only a year-old at this time. Has made no progress, no demand for products.
3. He wants to think "I'm a failure", but there's still hope in him. "I attended the best college, I had a good idea, I can't loose now."
4. Business will fail, man commit suicide when he realizes that he who could do no wrong, has not succeeded.

D-9

1. Gregory's wife has just called and told him that she's suing him for divorce. He is sitting in his office wondering what to do about it.
2. Gregory has had several affairs with other women, but up 'til now his wife has never objected. She, too, has entertained other men.
3. "My wife's leaving me. What have I done to deserve this. Sure, I've enjoyed the company of other women, but so has she. Why can't we just remain as we were? How can I keep her money; who cares about her?"
4. Finally, Gregory kills his wife but makes it look like a suicide so that he can get her money. He then runs away to Europe, before the truth is discovered.

D-10

1. This is one of the men who invested very heavily in stocks in the "Roaring 20's." He has just heard of the stock market crash and has now lost everything.

2. The man invested very heavily in stocks. For a long while he was very prosperous like many others but now he has lost everything.
3. The man is wondering how he will support his family and how anyone will even get started again since this has affected so many.
4. The people will suffer through the depression. Slowly but surely they will get back on their feet and eventually things will be back to normal and a state of stability and prosperity will once again exist.

D-11

1. A young business executive sitting in his small office. He is shielding his eyes from the bright sunlight.
2. His boss has refused to give him window shades.
3. He is cursing out his boss. He wants to be the boss and wants the boss to be under him.
4. He will go to the boss and complain. He will be reprimanded and he will finally quit.

D-12

1. The man is leaning on the desk thinking.
2. His business has just gone bankrupt and he has to sell everything.
3. He is worried about the future of himself and his family. He doesn't know how he will support them now.
4. He will have to find a job somewhere else and eventually hope to be able to go into business for himself again.

D-13

1. Sam is pondering what happened to his business. He had been successful in his penthouse office for many years.
2. Things (business) have begun to deteriorate lately. Nothing has worked. He's had to sell one asset after another to pay his bills.
3. He's trying to think of a way to save himself, a way to get back on his financial feet.
4. He'll be bankrupt, his wife will leave him, and he'll commit suicide.

D-14

1. The man is contemplating the fact that his business has just gone bankrupt.
2. He has made several unintelligent investments.
3. He is thinking of what might possibly be in the future for himself and his family.
4. Things will get worse and worse until our character commits suicide.

D-15

1. This Man is Confused. He has just been admonished By his Boss for something he did not do but knows who did—his co-worker, and a rival. He will not come forward with the information.
2. He has been trying to become a Vice Pres. and so has one of his co-workers. The co-worker forgot to fill in order for a big company and our boy was blamed.
3. John (our boy) wonders why he cannot just tell his boss the whole story but he cannot squeal on the other one even though it is the truth an the co made a mistake.
4. The boss will fire the co. John will become Vice President and eventually President the Boss admired his integrety.

D-16

1. This is a picture of Jim at his office. He is obviously suffering from the worries of his work and his insecurity. The barren room doesn't help.
2. Jim has joined the company because it offered a decent living and a fair amount of security. He has found that he is trapped.
3. He feels trapped on a senseless marri-go-round and wants to get away from it all. He desires to get into some field of endeavor which will allow him to express his individuality.
4. Jim wil stay in his present rat race. He has a family to support and can't risk unemployment. He will just cont———

D-17

1. A man sitting in his office has stopped work. He is in business for himself. He is an insurance agent.
2. The man's office is in a small town and therefore he doesn't have much business. He had a tiresome night before trying to talk some people into purchasing some insurance.
3. The man is half awake and half asleep. He is playing with the idea of moving his agency to a bigger town and more customers.
4. The man will not move. He has been raised in this town and has too many ties. He will become a small town farmer, there fulfilling his ambition. He has always wanted to farm but his father wanted him to go to a higher way of life.

D-18

1. The man has just suffered a great loss. His son died.
2. All his life he has been telling himself that his main purpose in life was to raise his kid and make something out of him. This was his driving force for making money & the source of his greatest pleasure.

3. Now the grip of death has snatched his teen-age son from him, and his life seems empty & purposeless.
4. He eventually recovers from his shock & turns his attention toward his wife.

D-19

1. The man is a psychology professor, contemplating suicide over the reaction of his students in a test. He feels he has failed them, and doesn't belong in the world.
2. His despair has been brought on by the fact that 90% of his classes failed the final.
3. He is wondering where he went wrong, and how he can correct his past mistakes. If no solution is found, drastic measures may be taken.
4. The man, being himself a student of psychology, will recognize his problem, and those of the students, and will take measures to correct them. He will be a better man and teacher as a result. He will not fail them again.

D-20

1. Jeff Parker has been fired by the company at which he had been employed for twenty-years.
2. Jeff was fired because of excessive drinking which resulted in a steady decline of his work efficiency.
3. Jeff is thinking about the horrible position in which he has placed himself and he is hoping for another chance at his job.
4. Jeff will get his job back after a month away from work and he never again drank in excess.

D-21

1. Dim light shines on the salesman's account books as he crys; realizing he financially in the red.
2. The salesman knows.
3. Salesman in this little dim and dusty office feel self-pity as he pleads his case (situation) with his God. "Help me", please help me, he crys.
4. There is and old World War II pistol in the top left draw of his desk—5 minutes later the salesman shot himself.

D-22

1. An accountant who has been fixing the books in contemplating the disgrace will accompany the discovery of his actions.
2. He has been running around with women.

3. He is wondering what he can do to correct the mistakes he has made.
4. He will flee to Brazil where he will killed in an automobile accident while driving in his flashy sports car.

D-23

1. Arnold Ratt, president of the 1st national bank is sitting in his office at 3 A.M. in deep thought.
2. Recently he has embezzled $100,000.
3. The books are to be checked tomorrow and he knows he will be caught.
4. He will take the "easy" way out and jump from the 12th story window pictured at the left.

D-24

1. Ted Levitt is waiting for his lawyer to come in.
2. It seems that Ted's Secretary has stolen all the furniture out of the office & left town. Ted wants the lawyer to press charges.
3. "Of all things, she even took the water cooler." Ted wants his water cooler more than anything in the world because the gurgling sound makes him feel content.
4. Ted's Sec. will sell the water cooler & spend the money to help her brother Jack buy a wig.

D-25

1. The man has just committed one of the worst crimes. He has killed his wife and has tried to escape undetected.
2. He has a feeling of remorse and he really doesn't know why he killed her. He thinks it might be his own feeling that he was inferior and his wife was too good for him.
3. He is thinking about whether he should turn himself in or run. He knows that either way he will be caught, tried, and probably convicted.
4. He does not get caught after he runs away and now the police are giving up the hunt even though there are still agents on the job.

Master Scoring for
the Four Hostile Press Pictures

THE ABBREVIATIONS IN THE RIGHT-HAND COLUMN DENOTE CATEGORIES AND specific cases of imagery which are scored in the Hostile Press scoring system. The standard abreviations follow:

None	Unrelated, not scorable
Rep.	Reprimand for personal actions
JRet.	Legal or judicial retaliation for action or alleged action
Dep.	Deprivation of affiliative relationships
HVEF	Hostile, vague environmental forces
VoP	Violation of privacy
ItC	Inducement to crime
DoB	Destruction of beliefs
MAslt.	Major assault on well-being
Fired	Character is fired from a job
Flunk	He is thrown out of or flunks out of school
F.S.A.	Failure with strong affect
Suicide	Suicide (G- is always inferred in this case)
PwAff.	Pain with affect
Div.	Divorce

PICTURE A. FATHER-SON

Story No.	HP Im		N	Ir		Ga			G		Pth	Source of Imagery
	Im	UPI		+	−	+	?	−	+	−		
A–1	x		x						x		x	Dep.
A–2		x										None
A–3	x			x					x		x	Dep.
A–4	x											MAslt.
A–5	x										x	MAslt.
A–6	x		x								x	MAslt.
A–7		x										None
A–8	x		x								x	Rep.
A–9	x				x				x		x	Flunk
A–10	x				x				x		x	MAslt.
A–11		x										None
A–12		x										None
A–13		x										None
A–14		x										None
A–15	x				x				x		x	MAslt.
A–16	x			x					x		x	JRet.
A–17	x			x					x		x	Flunk
A–18	x		x								x	JRet.
A–19	x						x		x		x	JRet.
A–20	x										x	Div.
A–21	x										x	Rep.
A–22	x										x	Dep.
A–23	x								x		x	Dep.
A–24	x		x						x		x	Dep.
A–25	x											MAslt.

Picture B. Boy in Checked Shirt

Story No.	HP Im		N	Ir		Ga			G		Pth	Source of Imagery
	Im	UPI		+	−	+	?	−	+	−		
B–1	x		x								x	DoB
B–2		x										None
B–3		x										None
B–4	x		x								x	Rep.
B–5	x				x						x	MAslt.
B–6		x										None
B–7	x		x					x	x		x	Dep.
B–8	x								x		x	Dep.
B–9	x										x	MAslt.
B–10		x										None
B–11		x										None
B–12	x		x						x		x	Rep.
B–13		x										MAslt.
B–14	x										x	MAslt.
B–15	x										x	Dep.
B–16	x										x	Flunk
B–17	x							x	x		x	F.S.A.
B–18		x										None
B–19	x										x	Rep.
B–20	x											None
B–21		x										None
B–22		x										None
B–23		x										None
B–24		x										None
B–25		x										None

PICTURE C. MAN BEFORE MIRROR

Story No.	HP Im		N	Ir		Ga			G		Pth	Source of
	Im	UPI		+	−	+	?	−	+	−		Imagery
C−1		x										None
C−2	x										x	Dep.
C−3	x						x				x	MAslt.
C−4	x								x		x	Suicide
C−5		x										None
C−6	x										x	MAslt.
C−7		x										None
C−8		x										None
C−9	x										x	Dep.
C−10	x		x								x	Rep.
C−11	x										x	Dep.
C−12		x										None
C−13	x				x				x		x	HVEF
C−14	x										x	MAslt.
C−15		x										None
C−16		x										None
C−17		x										None
C−18	x										x	Fired
C−19	x										x	MAslt.
C−20		x										None
C−21	x				x	x					x	MAslt.
C−22	x										x	MAslt.
C−23		x										None
C−24	x						x				x	JRet.
C−25	x										x	Dep.

PICTURE D. MAN IN BARREN OFFICE

Story No.	HP Im		N	Ir		Ga			G		Pth	Source of Imagery
	Im	UPI		+	−	+	?	−	+	−		
D−1	x						x		x		x	HVEF
D−2		x										None
D−3		x										None
D−4	x			x							x	Dep.
D−5	x			x					x		x	F.S.A.
D−6	x		x					x	x		x	F.S.A.
D−7	x			x					x		x	ITC.
D−8	x								x		x	Suicide
D−9	x										x	MAslt.
D−10		x										None
D−11	x			x							x	Rep.
D−12		x										None
D−13	x								x		x	Suicide
D−14	x								x		x	Suicide
D−15	x											Rep.
D−16	x		x						x		x	HVEF
D−17		x										None
D−18	x								x		x	Dep.
D−19	x			x					x		x	F.S.A.
D−20	x										x	Fired
D−21	x								x		x	Suicide
D−22	x										x	MAslt.
D−23	x								x		x	Suicide
D−24		x										None
D−25	x										x	MAslt.

Index

135, 140, 143, 145, 174, 199,
231
Test Anxiety Questionnaire, 7, 149–
154, 227
Thomas, 101, 112
Thorndike-Lorge, 120

Veroff, 69, 93, 231

Walker, 25

Wallach, 26, 151, 165
Wilcox, 231
Winterbottom, 141
Wylie, 230

Young, 1

Zeigarnik, 219
Zeigarnik task, 26